P9-DMH-046

DATE DUE

APR 1 9 1994	APR 2 0 1998
NOV 1 4 1994	APR 2 8 1998
APR 0 4 1995	NOV 2 5 1998
MAY 1 7 1995	MAY 0 4 2000
JUN 2 6 1995	DEC 0 7 2000
JUL 0 6 1995	NOV 0 5 2001
NOV 2 1 1995	DEC 0 1 2003
APR 0 1 1996	JUN 2 2 2004
APR 3 0 1996	OCT 2 6 2005
OCT 1 5 1996	
NOV 0 6 1996	
MAR 3 1 1997	
APR 0 8 1997	
DEC 1 8 1997	

Demco, Inc. 38-293

Renner Learning Resource Center
Elgin Community College
Elgin, IL 60123

LETTING GO

Also by Melvin I. Urofsky

Big Steel and the Wilson Administration (1969)

A Mind of One Piece: Brandeis and American Reform (1970)

American Zionism from Herzl to the Holocaust (1975)

We Are One! American Jewry and Israel (1978)

Louis D. Brandeis and the Progressive Tradition (1980)

A Voice That Spoke for Justice: The Life and Times of Stephen S. Wise (1981)

Two Hundred Years of Mr. Jefferson's Idea: Religious Liberty in America (1986)

A March of Liberty: A Constitutional History of the United States (1987)

The Continuity of Change: The Supreme Court and Individual Liberties (1990)

Felix Frankfurter: Judicial Restraint and Individual Liberties (1991)

A Conflict of Rights: The Supreme Court and Affirmative Action (1991)

Edited by Melvin I. Urofsky

Why Teachers Strike: Teachers' Rights and Community Control (1970)

Perspectives on Urban America (1973)

Letters of Louis D. Brandeis (5 vols., 1971–1978) (with David W. Levy)

Essays on American Zionism (1979)

Turn to the South: Essays on Southern Jewish History (1979) (with Nathan Kaganoff)

The Supreme Court, the Bill of Rights, and the Law (1986)

The Douglas Papers (1987) (with Philip E. Urofsky)

From Confederation to Constitution: Documents on the Constitution and Ratification (1988)

Documents of American Constitutional and Legal History (1989)

"Half-Son, Half-Brother": Letters of Louis D. Brandeis to Felix Frankfurter (1990) (with David W. Levy)

LETTING GO

Death, Dying, and the Law

Melvin I. Urofsky

Charles Scribner's Sons
New York

Maxwell Macmillan Canada
Toronto

Maxwell Macmillan International
New York   Oxford   Singapore   Sydney

RENNER LEARNING RESOURCE CENTER
ELGIN COMMUNITY COLLEGE
ELGIN, ILLINOIS 60123

Copyright © 1993 by Melvin I. Urofsky

All rights reserved. No part of this book may be reproduced or transmitted in any form or by any means, electronic or mechanical, including photocopying, recording, or by any information storage and retrieval system, without permission in writing from the Publisher.

Charles Scribner's Sons
Macmillan Publishing Company
866 Third Avenue
New York, NY 10022

Maxwell Macmillan Canada, Inc.
1200 Eglinton Avenue East
Suite 200
Don Mills, Ontario M3C 3N1

Macmillan Publishing Company is part of the Maxwell Communication Group of Companies.

Library of Congress Cataloging-in-Publication Data
Urofsky, Melvin I.
    Letting go : death, dying, and the law / Melvin I. Urofsky.
        p.   cm.
    Includes index.
    ISBN 0-684-19344-2
    1. Right to die—Law and legislation—United States.   2. Terminally ill—Legal status, laws, etc.—United States.   I. Title.
    KF3827.E87U76   1993
    344.73'04197—dc20
    [347.3044197]   92-39405   CIP

Macmillan Books are available at special discounts for bulk purchases for sales promotions, premiums, fund-raising, or educational use. For details: contact:

        Special Sales Director
        Macmillan Publishing Company
        866 Third Avenue
        New York, NY 10022

10 9 8 7 6 5 4 3 2 1

Printed in the United States of America

099791

6.4.93 22.50

For
Ken and Sheila Handel
and
Fred and Susan Weiss

Contents

Preface — ix

Prelude: Two Scenes from a Hospital — 1

1. Karen Ann: The Debate Begins — 11

2. Is there a "Right" to Die? — 31

3. Suicide — 55

4. On Death Row — 76

5. Baby Doe — 97

6. Mercy Killings — 118

7. Advance Directives — 130

8. Who Decides? — 151

Coda: Theresa Ann — 175

Notes — 179

Index — 197

Preface

My son and I walked into the house, and both of us immediately sensed something not right, something missing. Then Philip said "Where's Cuz?"

Cuz was our dog, a fourteen-year-old hybrid of collie, shep, lab, and Lord knows what else. He had grown up with my two sons, slept in their rooms, frequently on their beds, accompanied them to school, and, at times, tried to go into school with them. Often we lumped the three of them together, Philip, Robert, and Cuz, and both boys considered that as it should be. When they and Cuz got caught roughhousing indoors, we scolded them equally, and Susan and I easily fell into the habit of assuming that when we spoke to Cuz, he understood what we said. After all, we never had any proof that he didn't.

Although now too old to come bounding and jumping on us when we came home, he would still walk up to us, stiff-legged but proud, his tail wagging at half speed, and wait for us to scratch him behind the ears and acknowledge our sin for having left him alone.

But this time Cuz did not come to greet us, and since neither my wife's car nor that of our other son was outside, we knew that neither of them had gotten home earlier and taken Cuz for a walk. The place seemed eerily silent, and we did fidgety things until we finally heard Susan drive up. The minute she came through the door, we had only to look at her face to know something was terribly wrong.

Philip and I had been out of town overnight, and when Susan

had come home the previous evening, Cuz had been unable to move; worse, he had seemed totally disoriented and did not respond to anything she said or did. We had realized that he was getting old, and that like most dogs with shepherd strain, he suffered from a degenerative hip disease. In the last two visits to the vet, we could see that the doctor, who had treated Cuz since he was a pup and had sewn him up on more than one occasion, was clearly worried.

"He's getting old, and the dysplasia is getting worse. You need to think what you want to do. You don't want him to suffer."

We certainly didn't, but as long as Cuz could get around, as long as he could get out of the house for brief walks, as long as he still showed enthusiasm for chocolate chip cookies or ice cream, we ignored the problem, pushing it to the back of our minds.

Now we could no longer ignore it. Two of the neighbors had helped Susan put Cuz in the back of her car, and she had taken him to the vet. He had said it was time, but she told him to wait until Philip and I came back the next day. She knew we would want to say goodbye, and the vet, bless him, understood we needed to do that. So now we were home, and what we had dreaded could no longer be put off.

People without pets may not understand; those who have kept animals know exactly how we felt. This was not some dumb animal; this was a member of our family. When I had dedicated one of my earlier books to them, they all insisted that Cuz should be included, and by name. Though we knew, intellectually, that he was a dog and not a person made no difference; we were going to say goodbye to someone we loved.

As we left the house to go to the veterinary clinic, I put a chocolate chip cookie in my pocket. At the clinic, the vet brought Cuz in on a gurney, and then tenderly lifted him off and placed him on a towel on the floor. Philip sat down next to him and cradled his head, and we all took time to pet him, to say things, and above all, to try to get some reaction from him. I took the cookie from my pocket and put it up to his nose so he could sniff it, but there was no response.

In some ways, that made it easier. The Cuz we had loved, the personality who had been such an integral part of our family for fourteen years, that personality was gone; this was merely a body, an empty shell, and in a few minutes the doctor would put an end to its pain. As Philip held him, the vet gently gave him a needle, and in a moment it was over. A small convulsion, and peace. We were all crying but, as Susan said, it was as if we had released him; the memories we would have would be of the Cuz we had loved. And she was right.

Cuz died on December 24, 1986, and the next day I went, at the request of some friends, to serve as a volunteer at Beth Shalom, the Jewish home for the aged and infirm in Richmond. My friends had been part of Switch Days at the home for several years now. On Christmas and Easter, Jewish volunteers worked the various shifts so that Christian staff members could spend the holidays with their families. We did some maintenance work, delivered meals, checked out rooms to make sure that light switches and other appliances worked, and visited with the patients. It was one of the worst days of my life.

Some of the residents of Beth Shalom had merely grown old in their bodies, and they had moved into the home because it provided the care they now needed. But their minds remained sharp; they could converse and tell jokes, they read the papers and watched television, and they still led active lives outside of the home. To them, Beth Shalom meant no more than a new address, and they continued to enjoy life, to see children and grandchildren, to go to movies and theaters and shopping. The home gave them the additional support that made it possible for them to enjoy their retirement.

But there were others there, people who were barely holding on to life, who no longer knew who or where they were, who did not recognize their children or grandchildren when they came to visit. Many of them suffered not only from Alzheimer's, but from other diseases as well, and there was more than one person there whose eyes were as vacant as Cuz's had been the day before. Beth Shalom's residents get the best care that is possible. But some of them, people who are terribly sick but still retain some measure of their former selves, know that the only thing that remains for them is death, which will free them from their prison.

I came home late that afternoon shaking and told Susan and the boys about what I had seen. Putting Cuz to sleep had been the right thing to do, the merciful and decent thing to do, and if I ever got to be like that, I said, I hoped it would be possible to do the humane thing for me as well.

Two years later I first heard of the Nancy Cruzan case, and began to follow its progress through the courts. It did not take much prompting after the Supreme Court had handed down its decision in that case to get me to undertake this book. The reader needs to understand both what this book is and what it is not.

It is not, for example, a debate on the moral issues involved in euthanasia or suicide; nor is it an examination of the medical technology that has so radically changed how we must look at death; nor is it a manual explaining methods of committing suicide.

Rather, I am interested in the way the law has responded to what is, in my mind, a central issue of our day, namely, how each one of us, as an individual, may or may not control a critical phase in our lives. It is not a new question, but it has taken on whole new dimensions because of scientific and technological breakthroughs.

A few years ago, at the twenty-fifth reunion of my college class, one program focused on changes that had occurred in our professions since we had graduated. One of the panel members, a physician, said that the medicine he now practiced had not even existed when he graduated from medical school. He now used tools that had not then been invented, drugs that did wonders, and surgical procedures that could only be considered miraculous in saving lives and repairing the injuries of disease and trauma. To take just two examples, in the early 1960s neither the knowledge of the human body nor the tools had existed to do either laser surgery on the eyes or arthroscopic surgery on the joints. Moreover, he said, the rate of discovery was not slowing down, and the half-life of new techniques and medicines might be no more than five or six years.

Many of us have benefited from these new medicines and techniques, but there has been a troubling side to it as well. People who would have died from injuries or diseases or just the ravages of age thirty years ago can now be kept alive. They are not functional or independent, but life-support systems can keep their bodies going even if they are not conscious or have lost all mental powers. Even if their brains cease to function, the machines can keep them breathing and their hearts pumping blood to inert limbs. At the other end of the spectrum, seriously deformed infants who normally would have died within hours or days of birth can now be "saved," kept alive, although little can be done to repair their physical defects or remedy their mental retardation.

To some people, life—*any* life—is so precious that if it can be saved or prolonged then it should be—indeed it *must* be. Others talk about the "quality" of life, and believe that if this quality deteriorates, death may be preferable. Between these two views yawns a wide and at times seemingly unbreachable gulf, with the two sides divided by a myriad of moral and philosophical views. Religion also plays a role, with some people claiming that since only God can give life, only God can or should determine when to take it away.

My interest is in one particular aspect of this debate—what does the law say regarding death and dying? Not too many years ago a writer interested in this subject might, at best, have found the material for one or maybe two articles. When people grew old and sick, when they had been critically injured in accidents, when they had been born with serious handicaps, medical arts could do little, and the sick and the injured and the disabled died. No recourse to the law took place, because no legal problems existed. But since we live in a society governed by laws, as medical technology has changed the course of death, it has also raised new legal issues.

At the heart of the legal question is the matter of personal autonomy, which is not a new concept. English common law recognized the right of the individual to refuse unwanted medical care, even if such refusal might lead to serious harm or even death. An "unwanted touching" by a doctor, even if it proved beneficial to the patient, could be the basis of a suit in tort. More recently, American courts have become concerned with the right of individual autonomy, which is, in a different way, at the heart of the debate over abortion. In the Cruzan case the United States Supreme Court held that there is a constitutionally protected "right to die."

But the Court also held that the state has an interest in promoting and protecting life, so that the "right to die" is not absolute; rather, a balancing must take place between the state's interest in preserving life and the individual's wish to end it. It is this balance that is at the heart of most court cases on the subject, and there is, I suggest, no more difficult area of the law in which judges have to make decisions.

Moreover, few of these cases involve a situation of "I want to die; just leave me alone so I can do it." The law has long held that a competent person can refuse treatment, even life-saving treatment. But what if the person is in a coma? What if someone wants another person to help him or her commit suicide? What are the rights of family members, either in keeping someone alive or letting that person die? To what extent should the moral views of third parties be allowed to control individual decisions? Should the law allow death to be obtained as easily as one can secure medical care? Are the views of a competent individual, even if expressed in a clear and convincing manner, always to govern?

These are some of the issues explored in the chapters that follow. The legal principles involved are not difficult to understand, and I have tried to elucidate them in terms that nonlawyers can understand. This is also a study in public policy, because many of these questions involve decisions by government agencies, decisions that may enlarge or limit the scope of personal autonomy.

One cannot explore such a subject in a totally neutral manner; the effects of debilitating illness or devastating accidents can alter anyone's life and affect that of their families and friends as well. While I have tried to portray differing legal and moral attitudes fairly, my research has reinforced my beliefs in the importance in this area of personal autonomy. I would like to think that I value life as much as the next person, but there is such a thing as quality of life, and what that means is very much an individual judgment. There are some people who live fruitful lives and make important contributions to society despite severe disabilities; others would choose death rather than to endure what strikes them not as life but as mere existence.

These are extremely personal judgments and involve one's deepest religious and philosophical beliefs. The decisions a person makes must reflect those beliefs. Any society which claims to value individual liberty must grant to the individual the right to decide if and when life is no longer worth living. The state does have certain interests that cannot and should not be ignored, but in the hard cases, the law ought, insofar as it is able, to value personal autonomy as the most important consideration.

This book has not been an easy one to write, but a number of friends and colleagues made the task immeasurably lighter. Jerome Eckstein, David W. Levy, Jack D. Spiro, and Philippa Strum all read at least one version of the manuscript, and their comments, especially where they disagreed with me, made me rethink some of my assumptions. While they are in no way responsible for the final results, their contributions have made this a far better book, and I am extremely grateful for their efforts. Fred Weiss took the time to sit and talk with me about the medical and emotional problems he confronts in his practice with seriously ill patients.

My agent, Audrey Wolf, suggested that I turn my interest in the Cruzan case into a book, and my editor at Scribners, Ned Chase, came to support that idea with his usual enthusiasm. Ned's comments on the manuscript also helped me to clarify a number of ideas. A manuscript, however, does not magically turn into a book, although the production crew at Scribners often make it seem that way. My thanks go to Patricia McEldon and Barbara Campo for copyediting, designer Erich Hobbing, Erika Goldman who oversaw production, and Charles Flowers, who as Ned's assistant did all sorts of things to ease the book along.

My family, and especially Susan, tolerated my aberrant behavior while writing, and contributed clippings and more than an occasional word of encouragement.

The book is dedicated to old friends. Ken Handel and Fred

Weiss were my roommates at Columbia more than three decades ago, and we have stayed friends ever since. Moreover, their wives, Sheila and Susan, like my own Susan, give a whole new meaning to the term "better half." This book is a token of my esteem and love for them all.

Richmond, Virginia
January 1993

LETTING GO

Two Scenes from a Hospital

Two things a person does alone, the ancient maxim held, are come into the world and leave it. It is true that for most of human existence, people died by themselves, the victims of predators, war, disease, or aging. As civilization tamed humanity, people died at home, in their own beds, surrounded by loving family who might ease the final pains but could do nothing to delay death. Only in the recent past have people gone to hospitals to die, and only within the last decade or so has medicine developed drugs, procedures, and technology to hold off death.

These developments raise a host of questions, but in the end they all come down to what does the individual want, and if the individual is incapable of deciding, what does the family want. But there are others who now demand a voice in the decision— doctors, nurses, hospital administrators, insurance companies, and, very often, agents of the state. In most instances, the person dies without interference, since there is still little that medicine can do when age or disease have taken their ultimate toll. But in other situations, instead of death coming peacefully and with dignity, there is conflict and suffering, rage and public controversy.

In these cases, the key issue is who will decide whether or not care should be provided or withheld, whether enormous energy and resources should be expended to delay death, or whether nothing should be done, so that death may have its way. Who decides, and what role, if any, should the law play in this process? These are not easy questions, as can be seen in the following stories.

Rocco Musolino was a big man, one who enjoyed good food and drink and people, a gregarious man who had run a liquor store in College Park, Maryland, until his retirement. He also hated hospitals, and never wanted to end his days in one.[1]

To avoid that possibility, Musolino wrote a living will in 1989 in which he specifically declared that if he were terminally ill, he did not want to be kept alive by machine. Aware that if he were really sick he might not be able to make decisions on his own, he also signed a durable power of attorney giving his wife of fifty years, Edith, the authority to make decisions about his care. Repeatedly he told his family he did not want to be hooked up to any "damn machine" or "kept alive as a vegetable."

Rocco Musolino had drawn up his living will shortly after he had suffered a major heart attack in 1988. While he was in the hospital at that time doctors had performed a catheterization procedure that revealed that he had severe blockages in the coronary arteries and that one-fourth of his heart muscle was already dead. The damage was so extensive that doctors ruled out coronary bypass surgery.

Musolino had no illusions as to the prognosis of the disease, nor the fact that his diabetes seriously compounded the problem. In the two years following his heart attack, his condition deteriorated to the point that he had difficulty moving around his house. "If he made it to the bathroom, that was a big deal," his daughter Edith Scott said. "He couldn't shave. He would get all out of breath."

On October 24, 1990, following a night of chest pains and difficulty in breathing, he told his wife he couldn't stand the pain anymore. She called an ambulance to take him to Georgetown University Medical Center. There his regular cardiologist, Dr. Richard Rubin, examined Musolino, and then called in a surgeon, Dr. Nevin Katz, who told the family that Rocco's only hope lay in bypass surgery, the same procedure that had been ruled out two years earlier.

"He'll die without an operation," Katz told Edith Musolino. "He's got a 50-50 chance with it." The family agreed reluctantly, since it appeared that potential kidney failure would also require dialysis, the type of machine treatment that Musolino had always feared. Musolino stayed in the hospital to undergo tests and build up his strength, and the medical staff scheduled him for bypass surgery on November 12. The night before the operation, Dr. Rubin went in to visit his patient, and later said that Rocco expressed a strong desire to live, even if it meant he might have to go onto dialysis for the rest of his life.

Later that night, Musolino suffered two cardiac arrests but survived, and Rubin and Katz decided to go ahead with the surgery. Rubin called to get Edith Musolino's consent and then wrote in the patient's record: "He is awake and wishes to proceed. He is aware of the risk. I have reviewed the high risk of death (40 percent), high risk of renal failure (long term about 50 percent) with wife and daughter." His daughter later said she could not recall any such discussion.

The operation appeared successful, at least in relieving strain on the heart, but Musolino's kidneys failed, and he required dialysis several times a week. Since he could not breathe without a respirator, his wife reluctantly agreed to a tracheotomy, in which doctors inserted a breathing tube into his neck. In addition to causing constant pain, the breathing tube left Rocco unable to talk.

Musolino remained conscious and aware of what was happening, but his family claims he was never fully alert, and his medical records seemed to bear this out. Doctors' notes show that he slept a lot, and often responded to questions only with a grimace. A neurologist who examined him noted that his fluctuating state of consciousness resulted from severe medical problems; if he overcame them, he would probably regain full mental clarity.

But Rocco Musolino did not improve, and as the weeks went on his family concluded he would never recover. In late November they asked the doctors to put a "Do Not Resuscitate" order on his chart, so that he would not be treated if he suffered another cardiac arrest. Dr. Katz refused. When the family requested that he stop some of the medication, he angrily told them: "I stay awake at night trying to keep your father alive, and you want me to kill him. What is wrong with you people?" Only after his patient's condition deteriorated further did Katz agree to a "DNR" order.

Edith Musolino watched her husband's condition worsen. "Everything that could be wrong with him was wrong with him. I knew he was dying. I knew his body couldn't take any more." She made up her mind in December to ask the hospital to stop the dialysis sessions and to let her husband die in peace.

On December 21, 1990, the hospital's ethics committee met to consider the request, and recommended a psychiatric examination to determine whether Musolino was mentally competent. Under District of Columbia law, if he were declared incompetent, then the durable power of attorney would become operative, and his wife would have the authority to make the medical decisions.

The hospital named Dr. Steven A. Epstein to do the evaluation, and he visited Musolino twice at times when the patient seemed to rally a bit. Epstein's initial report, dated December 27, was inconclusive, and the family pushed for a second evaluation. This time the doctor reported the patient "lethargic and barely responding to voice. Today he clearly cannot make health care decisions on his own." Musolino, he told the family, was not mentally competent.

On New Year's Day 1991, Edith Musolino filed a note in her husband's medical record withdrawing her consent for dialysis. According to her, doctors, hospital administrators, and the hospital's lawyers agreed that she had the authority; they ordered dialysis stopped and removed the tube used to connect Musolino to the machine. Advised that without the treatment he would probably die within a few days, she and her children went to a funeral home to make the necessary arrangements.

They returned to the hospital to learn that Katz had changed his mind, and wanted to restart dialysis. He wrote on January 2, "I cannot in good conscience carry out their request," and he asked the hospital's lawyers and the chairman of the ethics committee to reopen the case.

The family now tried to find another physician or to have Musolino transferred to another hospital that would honor their requests. Katz agreed to turn over the case if the family could find a heart specialist with intensive-care experience. As Scott Musolino reported, "I called so many doctors. No one was willing to touch my father."

The next day Georgetown Hospital's lawyers wrote to the family's attorney informing him that the hospital would seek "emergency temporary guardianship" unless the family agreed to resume dialysis. Edith Musolino felt she had no choice but to agree.

Ten days later, her husband's condition deteriorating, her frustration and anger at the indignities that had been heaped upon him in spite of his express wishes finally erupted in a confrontation with Katz at Rocco's bedside. With her husband's legs and arms twitching, his face grimacing, she demanded of Katz: "What are you trying to prove here? You have made him suffer so much."

Katz asked her what she wanted. She said she wanted another doctor, Taveira Da Silva, the head of the hospital's intensive-care unit, who had earlier agreed to take the case on condition that dialysis be continued. Katz agreed, and the next morning nurses wheeled Rocco to the ICU, where the staff gradually began treating him as a dying patient. While Da Silva described Musolino as "terminal," he nonetheless continued dialysis, even though by this point the patient had become totally disoriented and his arms had to be tied down during the procedure.

His family had reached the end of their patience as well and had agreed that the only way to save Rocco from further indignity was to take him home. At a meeting on January 24, Dr. Da Silva agreed to stop the dialysis if they wanted to do that. A few days later, however, Da Silva finally came to the conclusion the family had reached much earlier—Rocco Musolino had "virtually a fatal, irreversible disease," that no medical care could help, and that the living will, which the hospital and doctors had ignored for three months, should be enforced. He told Edith that he would stop the dialysis and let her husband die in the hospital.

Instead of relief that her husband's long ordeal would soon be over, Edith Musolino felt only anger. "You know, Doctor," she said, "I was beginning not to know who to pray to anymore. Do I pray to you, or do I pray to God?"

On February 2, 1991, Rocco Musolino died, after a stay of 102 days in Georgetown University Medical Center, a place he had never wanted to be and where he and his family had lost all power to decide his fate.

While Rocco Musolino's wife fought to get hospital authorities to stop treating him, halfway across the continent hospital officials were trying to get a patient's family to consent to cessation of treatment.

On December 14, 1989, Helga Wanglie, an eighty-six-year-old retired schoolteacher, tripped on a scatter rug in her home in Minneapolis and fractured her hip. After surgery in a small private hospital, she developed breathing problems and was transferred to Hennepin County Medical Center. There, although on a respirator, she remained fully conscious and alert, writing notes to her husband, since the breathing tube prevented her from talking.

After five months, the hospital weaned her from the respirator in May 1990, and she entered Bethesda Lutheran Hospital across the river in St. Paul, a facility specializing in the care of respiratory ailments. A few days later, her heart stopped suddenly, and by the time doctors and nurses could resuscitate her, she had suffered severe brain damage. An ambulance brought her back to Hennepin Medical in a comatose state, her breathing sustained by a ventilator. When it became clear that doctors could do nothing for Mrs. Wanglie, they spoke with her husband of fifty-three years, Oliver, a retired attorney, about turning off the ventilator.

Although her husband and sons recognized that Helga had no cognition and might never regain consciousness, they would not hear of turning off the machine. His wife had strong religious convictions, Oliver told reporters, and they had talked about the possibility that if anything happened to her, she wanted "everything" done to keep her alive. "She told me, 'Only He who gave life has the right to take life.' . . . It seems to me [the hospital officials] are trying to play God. Who are they to determine who's to die and who's to live? I take the position that as long as her heart is beating there's life there."

Eight months after readmitting Helga Wanglie and trying to

convince her family to stop treatment, Hennepin Medical Center officials announced they would go to court seeking the appointment of a guardian to determine Helga Wanglie's medical treatment. The hospital did not request that the court authorize discontinuing treatment. To the best of my knowledge, no hospital has ever made such a request, nor has there been any case law on it. Rather, the hospital sought the appointment of a "stranger" conservator, that is, one independent of both family and hospital, to make decisions based on the best interests of the patient. The hospital believed that a neutral party would agree with its position.

While in most right-to-die cases it is the patient or the family that wants the hospital to stop treatment, the Wanglie case is the rarely seen other side of the coin. Dr. Michael B. Belzer, the hospital's medical director, said he sympathized with the Wanglie family, but a heartbeat no longer signified life, since machines could artificially do the heart's work. The real question, he believed, was whether the hospital had an obligation to provide "inappropriate medical treatment."

Mrs. Wanglie's medical bills were paid in full by her insurance company, so money was not an issue in the hospital's decision. "This is a pure ethics case," said Dr. Arthur Caplan, director of the Center for Biomedical Ethics at the University of Minnesota. For years, he explained, we've used the "smokescreen of 'Can we afford to do this?' There's been a harder question buried under that layer of blather about money, namely: 'What's the point of medical care?' "

Dr. Belzer noted that Hennepin had the facilities and "the technology to keep fifty Helga Wanglies alive for an indefinite period of time. That would be the easy thing to do. The harder thing is to say just because we can do it, do we have to do it?"

Hennepin Medical Center is a public hospital, one of the best in the upper midwest, and before it could petition a court to appoint a conservator or guardian for Mrs. Wanglie (in order to have consent for turning off the life support), it needed the approval of the county's Board of Commissioners. The board members gave the hospital permission by a 4–3 vote, with the tiebreaker cast by a member who had known the Wanglie family for more than thirty years. It took him a month to make up his mind.

The commissioner, Randy Jackson, said that he finally voted to let the hospital go to the courts because "I don't think this is a decision to be made by a board of elected commissioners who happen to be trustees of the hospital. These are issues that we're going to be confronted with more and more often as medical machinery becomes more and more able to keep people alive."[2]

Hospital attorneys presented their case to county judge Patricia Belois on May 28, 1991, asking her to appoint a conservator to decide Mrs. Wanglie's fate. They did not question her husband's sincerity, but argued instead that her condition was hopeless, and respirators had never been intended to prolong life in such cases.

On July 1, Judge Belois ruled against the hospital and left power to decide questions on Helga's medical treatment in her husband's hands. "He is in the best position to investigate and act upon Helga Wanglie's conscientious, religious, and moral beliefs." After the decision Oliver Wanglie said "I think she'd be proud of me. She knew where I stood. I have a high regard for the sanctity of human life."[3]

A little while after this decision, Helga Wanglie died.

These two episodes highlight many of the questions examined in this book, but the key issue is that of who decides what is best for a terminally ill person and what role the law and the courts have in that process. In an ideal world, perhaps, the interests of patients, families, doctors, hospitals, and courts would all coincide. But aside from the fact that this is an imperfect world, the interests of these groups are not necessarily congruent.

For centuries doctors have sworn to uphold life, and now for the first time they are being asked, openly and at times defiantly, what gives them the right to decide other people's fate? Hospitals, caught in a crunch between escalating expenses and new technology, must weigh costs that never before mattered. Moreover, in a society as litigious as ours, doctors and hospitals walk in constant fear that a "wrong" judgment will lead to a ruinous lawsuit. While elective bodies are responsible for broad policy decisions, it is difficult if not impossible to frame legislation in such a way as to cover all contingencies, and so courts must step in to interpret not only what the laws say and mean, but also what the limits of self-autonomy are under both the common law and constitutional protection.

Two things a person does alone, the ancient maxim held: come into the world and leave it. But at the end of the twentieth century, before one can leave this world, he or she may find it necessary to traverse a bewildering legal, moral, and medical maze.

CHAPTER ONE

Karen Ann:
The Debate Begins

The insistent ringing finally woke Julia Quinlan. Groping for the telephone she looked at the clock. Two in the morning. She picked up the receiver and heard a woman say, "Is this Mrs. Quinlan?"

"Yes."

"I'm sorry to tell you, but your daughter is in the hospital. She's in serious condition, unconscious . . . Karen is being treated right now in Intensive Care."

Earlier in the evening of April 15, 1975, Karen Ann Quinlan, a vivacious, attractive twenty-one year old, had been rushed to Newton Memorial Hospital in suburban New Jersey, about fifty miles west of New York. When Joseph and Julia Quinlan arrived at the hospital, they found some of her daughter's friends there who told them that Karen had eaten very little the previous four days, and then had taken some drugs along with alcohol at a birthday party. Then she had started "to act kind of strange," and her friends, thinking she was drunk, drove her home and put her to bed. When they checked on her later, they discovered that she was not breathing. They tried mouth-to-mouth resuscitation and called a rescue squad. A policeman with the squad managed to revive the girl's breathing, but she remained comatose as they rushed her to the hospital.

Doctors never determined just why Karen Ann Quinlan stopped breathing for several minutes, but during that time she

suffered anoxia, a condition in which the brain gets an insuffi-
cient amount of oxygen. To assist her breathing, Dr. Paul McGee,
in charge of Intensive Care that evening, placed Karen Ann on a
respirator. Then all he and the family could do was wait to see if
she would awaken from the coma. She never did.

Although Karen Ann had suffered some brain damage from the
anoxia, she did not have a flat electroencephalogram (EEG), which
meant that, technically at least, she was not brain-dead. (An
electroencephalogram measures and charts the electrical activity
of the brain and displays it either on a television screen or on
continuous graph paper. A normal EEG shows jagged lines of
peaks and valleys indicating brain activity; a flat EEG, a straight
horizontal line, indicates that the brain is not functioning and
that the person is brain-dead.) Moreover, Karen exhibited involuntary muscle activity, and reflexively responded to certain stimuli, including light, sound, smell, and pain.

Three months after she had been rushed to the hospital, Karen
Ann Quinlan remained in a coma, and her father, as next of kin,
signed a release to permit her doctors to take her off the respirator
and let her die. The Quinlans had prayed constantly for Karen's
recovery, but with no signs of change, Joe Quinlan said, "I'm
convinced it is our Lord's will that Karen be allowed to die."

But the doctors, even though they held out no hope of recovery,
refused to remove the respirator, fearing that if they did they
might be held liable for murder. Joe Quinlan then went to court
to have himself appointed Karen's guardian and to secure authority to discontinue all extraordinary measures. What had been a
private and personal nightmare for the Quinlans suddenly triggered a national debate.[1]

At the trial, a number of expert witnesses testified in support
of the Quinlans' request, and newspapers carried daily stories
about how doctors normally allowed terminally ill patients to
die. Dr. Julius Korein, a neurologist, explained what he called
"judicious neglect," in which the doctor would say: "Don't treat
this patient anymore. . . . It does not serve either the patient, the
family, or society in any meaningful way to continue treatment
with this patient."[2]

The public also learned about the initials DNR, which Dr. Korein explained stood for the instructions "Do Not Resuscitate," on a terminally ill patient's chart. "No physician that I know personally," he testified, "is going to try and resuscitate a man riddled with cancer and in agony and he stops breathing. They are not going to put him on a respirator. . . . I think that would be the height of misuse of technology."[3]

The trial court refused to approve termination of the respirator, since Karen did not meet the standard for brain death, namely, a flat EEG. "There is a duty to continue the life-assisting apparatus," Judge Robert Muir declared. "There is no constitutional right to die that can be asserted by a parent for his incompetent adult child."[4] The Supreme Court of New Jersey, though, reversed the trial judge and ordered that the respirator could be removed, without any legal or civil liability attached to the hospital or the medical staff.[5] The doctors removed the respirator.

The nuns in charge of Karen's care at the Catholic hospital, however, anticipating the court's decision, had begun to wean Karen from the machine, hoping that she would thus remain alive after the respirator had been disconnected.[6] She did, and much to the anguish of her family, Karen Quinlan remained in a persistent vegetative state, * emaciated and with deformed limbs, until she finally died in July 1985, ten years after her parents had entered court to release her from a "living death."

Although the problems raised in the Quinlan case were not new either to the medical profession or to the many families that had faced the problem of a terminally ill person, the American public now discovered the issue. People suddenly realized that they faced a dilemma that could affect anyone regardless of race, sex, or age, rich or poor, urban or rural, in good health or not. Modern medical technology could keep alive people who would have died in the past, but were they really alive? If a person had lost

---

* A persistent, or chronic, vegetative state is one in which a person does register some brain activity, and so is not brain-dead. There is also some reflexive movement in response to stimuli, but there is no consciousness and no cognitive functioning.

consciousness, had no hope of regaining it, and depended on a machine for breathing and a tube for nourishment, did that person "live"? If someone seriously ill no longer wanted to live, but drugs could postpone death, did the patient have any voice in what would happen to his or her life?

While there had been a few cases dealing with what has since been termed "the right to die," the Karen Ann Quinlan case focused public attention on the legal problems of the terminally ill. It would be fifteen years from the time the ambulance rushed Karen Quinlan to Newton Memorial Hospital until the day the Supreme Court of the United States formally recognized a constitutionally protected right to die in the case of another young woman, Nancy Cruzan.[7]

During that decade and a half the law changed significantly, with many states adopting right-to-die laws and approving living wills, in which a person may direct whether or what sort of medical treatment he or she wishes to receive in case of an incapacitating illness or injury. But even as the law changed, new technologies and new problems arose. The stories that follow illustrate the legal issues surrounding particular types of death, and the need for citizens to understand the situation in order not to be victimized by it.

Before examining those cases, however, one must become familiar with certain terms and also to consider briefly the religious and ethical views that surround the debate.

One might think that the definition of *death* would be simple, and the common law in fact took a fairly straightforward approach; it viewed death as the stopping of breathing and blood circulation. Most religions also see the test of death as "mainly whether there is any breathing. When the breathing has finished and the pulse has ceased, the person is declared dead."[8]

Modern medical technology has rendered this definition all but obsolete, as machines have been devised that will breathe for a person and even keep his or her heart beating. In 1968 a committee at the Harvard Medical School recommended that *brain death*, the cessation of all brain functions, become the accepted medical definition of death.[9] The Harvard criterion is sometimes referred to as "whole brain death," the state in which all parts of the brain have ceased to function and which would appear on the EEG monitor as a flat line.

Some doctors and ethicists have suggested the "higher-brain activity" test, referring to that part of the brain that controls cognitive function. Death would be defined as the absence of any cognitive ability, that is, the cessation of higher brain activity. The Harvard criteria did not apply in the Quinlan case because even though she had lost all cognitive ability, associated with the higher brain, her brain stem, which controls involuntary activity such as breathing, continued to function. Although use of the higher-brain activity test would have ended the Quinlan family's suffering much earlier, both technical and symbolic obstacles stand in the way. One problem is that it is impossible to determine that the higher brain has ceased to function with the same certitude that one can have in determining that the whole brain has stopped. And so long as there is any pattern on an EEG monitor, it cannot be said with certainty that life has ended.[10]

The word *euthanasia* comes from two Greek words that mean "good death" or "happy death," and refers to any action that brings a painless death to a person suffering from injury, disease, or the ravages of age. Although judges are reluctant to use the term, this is what they usually mean when they talk about a right to die.

There is a distinction between *active euthanasia* and *passive euthanasia*. In the former, one takes a positive action that leads directly to the death of another person. A man may have put his sick and suffering spouse out of misery; he may even have acted on her wishes. Nonetheless, active euthanasia is considered murder in most legal and religious systems.

Passive euthanasia is the withdrawal of "heroic" or other measures that keep a moribund person alive. This may mean, as Joseph Quinlan hoped, that taking Karen off the respirator would allow her to die a natural death. Or it may mean failing to treat people in the final stages of their illness with medication or technology. The line between active and passive euthanasia is not always clear. Withdrawing artificial means of feeding and hydration, for example, has prompted a vigorous debate over whether this constitutes acceptable passive euthanasia or unac-

ceptable active euthanasia. One thing, however, should be kept
in mind. In both instances, a decision is made to take or cease
certain procedures in the expectation that death will result.

Part of the debate over euthanasia occurs because someone
other than the patient often makes the decision to withdraw
treatment. When one takes one's own life, we call it *suicide*, and
despite the fact that nearly all the major religions of the world
condemn suicide, it is a widespread phenomenon. But if a patient
suffering from a painful and debilitating disease decides to forgo
life-extending treatment, is this suicide? While the question has
definite ethical implications, in law the decision to terminate or
forgo medical treatment is *not* considered suicide.

A more difficult question in both ethics and law is the relationship of the health care professional or anyone else to the person
hastening his or her own death. No American state currently
makes suicide a crime, but there are a host of laws, involving
both civil liability and criminal penalty, that may apply to a
person assisting a suicide.

If we view forgoing treatment, at least when it involves a terminally ill person, as a form of euthanasia, then we run into some
other terms that inform the debate, namely questions of *voluntariness, competence,* and *consent.* When we talk about consent,
we mean that a person has agreed to a certain course of action.
For this consent to be meaningful, it must be given voluntarily, it
must be informed, and the decision must be made by a competent
person.

In the law, these words are precise terms, but their applications
may vary from situation to situation. Informed consent means
that a person has been given all the relevant facts pertaining to
his or her condition so that he or she may decide to undergo,
or refuse, or stop, particular treatments. Courts have held that
consent requires a doctor to inform a patient plainly, and in
nontechnical language, what is at stake.

As for voluntariness, much of that law has developed outside
the medical field. Lawyers dealing in contracts, torts (civil wrongs
committed by one person against another or against property), or
even criminal law usually can point to clearer precedents than

those trying to evaluate whether a person facing death from disease has acted "voluntarily."

Another element of consent is competence, which means that the person making the decision has the capacity or understanding to do so. A person in a coma lacks the competence to decide anything, but being conscious by itself does not necessarily prove that one understands what is happening.

For those who are incompetent, either because of mental or physical limitations, the court may appoint a *guardian ad litem*, a person who may or may not be a relative but whose sole legal responsibility is to act in the best interest of the disabled person. Joseph Quinlan went to court to secure his appointment as his daughter's guardian, with the express authority to terminate mechanical life support. The guardian will represent to the court what he or she believes the patient would do if competent and able to give informed, voluntary consent.

In nearly all jurisdictions, the courts will accept a *living will* as evidence of what a formerly competent person would have chosen regarding the continuance or termination of life support. While the exact provisions of such documents vary from state to state, essentially a person, while in a state of competence, indicates that he or she is making an informed, voluntary decision about future treatment. The will can also designate a third party to act for that person should he or she become disabled.

Although interest in living wills increased dramatically after both the Quinlan case in 1976 and the Cruzan case a decade and a half later, a majority of Americans still do not have a regular will, much less a living will.

Because death so often reflects religious and moral beliefs, and because these precepts often affect the debate over public policy, one must look briefly at how the major religions view questions of death and dying and how these views in turn influence their policies, if any, on euthansia and suicide. While it is possible to describe the general position of major religions on these questions, it is important to understand that even within hierarchical religions there may be divergences of opinion and strong debate

over particulars. For example, while the Roman Catholic Church
has an official statement on euthanasia, Catholic theologians
in Germany have engaged in an extensive discussion over the
difference between "help in dying" (*Sterbehilfe*) and "help to die"
(*Sternnachhilfe*).[11]

Many think wrongly that the Greeks and Romans uniformly
approved of euthanasia and suicide, when in fact disagreement
existed in both societies. Hippocrates, considered the father of
medicine, wrote an oath that is still recited by new doctors today,
in which they pledge that "if any shall ask of me a drug to produce
death I will not give it, nor will I suggest such counsel."

The Epicureans, who highly valued the pleasures of the mind,
contended that it would be better to die than to endure a life of
pain. The Stoic philosopher Seneca wrote without apology that
"we destroy monstrous births and drown our children if they are
born weakly and unnaturally formed." Since the Stoics regarded
self-control as the highest good, they believed that one might kill
oneself if suffering would lead to a loss of self-control or to ignoble
acts. Again, quoting Seneca: "If I know that I must suffer without
hope of relief I will depart not through fear of the pain itself but
because it prevents all for which I would live."[12]

The monotheistic religions, beginning with Judaism, rejected
these views and saw life as a gift from God, a gift that only God
could take back. Their views on suicide and euthanasia developed
over the millennia and grew out of the conditions of the times.
When medicine could not alleviate pain, Catholic theologians
termed pain a means by which God purified man of sin. Before
modern technology created devices and drugs to prolong life,
religious leaders viewed dying as a natural stage of life, with
which one should not interfere. There is a time for all things,
Ecclesiastes said, a time to live and a time to die.

Modern theological problems regarding euthanasia and suicide
grow out of the difficult effort to reconcile a law or tradition
grounded in premodern conditions with the new and often radically different situations of contemporary life and medicine. It is
not that one is better than the other, but this is a problem. The
following summaries of major religious views cannot begin to do
justice to the delicate and often painful efforts that theologians

have made to reconcile religious beliefs with the opportunities and dangers of modern medicine.

JUDAISM

On Yom Kippur, the Day of Atonement, Jews throughout the world read the words of Deuteronomy, in which God tells the children of Israel that He has given them a choice of life or death, of a blessing or a curse, and then commands them to "choose life." Traditional Jewish law forbids suicide, and although there is no specific biblical prohibition against it, the passage in Genesis 9:5, "surely your blood of your lives will I require," has been construed to mean that only God may take one's life. The Jewish Bible mentions only four suicides,[13] and while none of these is condemned either in the sacred text itself or in the various rabbinical commentaries, they are seen as the results of great stress. The Talmud, distinguishes between suicide by one of sound mind (*la-da'at*) and by one of unsound mind (*she-lo la-da'at*). Throughout the ages it appears that rabbis have sought even the slightest evidence of mental strain so as to place the suicide in the latter category and therefore not responsible.[14]

Should a tyrant command one to violate a Torah law or be killed, one should choose life and commit the violations—except for three biblical prohibitions, which must never be transgressed: idolatry, murder, and sexual abominations (e.g., incest). An oppressor's command to break the law or die, even if the law might be a minor one, must sometimes also be resisted to the death, if the purpose is to destroy Jewish religion. While Jews who died for *kiddush hashem*, for the "sanctification of God's name," that is, as martyrs, are praised in the liturgical literature, Jewish tradition objects to martyrdom on the grounds that is better to live, a view markedly at odds with the Christian attitude.

Giving one's life in defense of one's country is, of course, different from martyrdom. Yet one might well note the criticism that hailed down on Rabbi Shlomo Goren, who while the chief rabbi of the Israeli army, declared that a soldier taken prisoner had the right, even the obligation, to commit suicide if he feared that he would be unable to withstand torture, and by revealing military secrets, put his fellow soldiers at risk. In general, contemporary rabbinical authorities continue the view that suicide is not compatible with Jewish law and tradition.[15]

As one would expect from a religion that so values life, there is a specific prohibition against active euthanasia. Even when one is on the deathbed, tradition forbids doing anything to hasten death. The matter, according to the Talmud, "can be compared with a flickering flame; as soon as one touches it, the light is extinguished."[16] In the twelfth century the great Jewish physician and philosopher Maimonides prohibited doing anything that might hasten the death of a seriously ill patient. Four centuries later, Rabbi Joseph Karo reaffirmed this rule in his definitive code of Jewish law, the Shulchan Aruch.[17] Mercy killing, the deliberate act of putting a dying person out of his or her misery, is considered equivalent to murder, no matter how sick or near death the victim may be.

While there is general agreement on active euthanasia, the record is less clear on passive euthanasia. One medieval rabbinical commentary allowed the removal of anything hindering the soul's departure, "because there is no act involved in this at all but only the removal of the impediment."[18] This applies only to a *goses*, a terminally ill patient who is expected to die within three days; while it is not permitted to speed that person's death, nothing need be done to continue a life in that state. It is not altogether clear, though, just when a person can be considered in a state of *gesisah*. If the condition is reversible, there is an obligation to heal.[19]

A strict reading of Jewish law and tradition, at least as interpreted by some contemporary Orthodox scholars, suggests that one must not do anything to hasten death, and regardless of any other considerations, do everything possible to prolong life. The doctor who rigorously follows Jewish law may not even tell the patient the full seriousness of the illness, lest the news cause the patient to lose hope and thereby succumb more quickly to the disease.[20]

Reform Judaism takes a less severe attitude, and while it also reveres life, its interpreters put more weight on the idea that death may at times be welcome and fitting. Rabbi Solomon B.

Freehof, the leading Reform authority on modern ethical issues, cites approvingly the medieval axiom that while it is our duty to pray for a sick person that he may recover, there comes a time when we should pray for God's mercy that he may die.[21]

For Freehof, "Jewish law is quite clear. [The physician] is not in duty bound to force [a patient] to live a few more days or hours."[22] The physician may thus remove impediments to death, such as artificial feeding. "The physician is not really hastening the death; he has simply ceased his efforts to delay it . . . [and] no sin has been committed by him."[23]

This view was directly contradicted by the late Rabbi Moshe Feinstein, whom many considered the preeminent Orthodox authority on Jewish law of his time. Feinstein drew a sharp distinction between withholding medicine and withholding food. He excused a physician from administering a medicine that would, at best, briefly prolong the life of a person suffering pain. But he allowed no similar option for nutrition. For an incurably ill patient who has difficulty breathing, Feinstein wrote, "one must give him oxygen to relieve his suffering. It is also clear that such a patient who cannot eat normally must be fed intravenously . . . even if the patient is comatose. Food is not at all comparable to medication since food is a natural substance which all living creatures require to sustain life."[24]

The Karen Quinlan case occasioned a great deal of discussion among Jewish scholars. Rabbi Norman Lamm, the president of the Orthodox-sponsored Yeshiva University, noted that tradition did not require heroic measures to prolong the lives of the hopelessly sick, "but we are forbidden to terminate the use of such measures once they have begun. . . . Jewish law cannot sanction pulling the plug, which is tantamount to severing a vital organ of the patient, which is forbidden."[25]

Conservative and Reform rabbis took a different view. Seymour Siegel, of the Conservative Jewish Theological Seminary, believed it permissible to remove Karen Quinlan from the respirator and let nature take its course. Joseph Perman, rabbi of the Free Synagogue of Westchester, declared it would not be "ethically justifable to prolong the life of a person in a vegetative state for an indeterminate period of time." And he noted that aside from any tradition or law, no parent faced with a situation like that of the Quinlans "should ever have to beg that their child's life be taken."[26]

To sum up, the Jewish tradition reveres life, but recognizes that a time comes when death is not only inevitable but may be welcome. There is disagreement among authorities, however, over the responsibility of the doctor to try to prolong life. Some Orthodox scholars argue that a physician must do everything possible, while other Orthodox commentators, together with Conservative and Reform scholars, believe that so long as the doctor does not practice active euthanasia, he or she may remove artificial impediments to dying for a terminally ill patient.

CATHOLICISM

Early Christianity had two models from which to choose, that of contemporary Greco-Roman societies which practiced both active and passive euthanasia, and that of Judaism, its parent religion, which commanded its adherents to choose life. It is no surprise that Jesus, who proclaimed that he would not change one jot or tittle of the Law, followed his Jewish heritage. The gospels are full of accounts of Jesus as healer who urges his followers to help others, and the parable of the Good Samaritan (Luke 10:25–37) is interpreted to mean that one should help the sick and wounded. Instead of viewing the sick and the elderly as burdens that society could eliminate, the Church viewed illness as suffering that purifies the victims and enobles those who help them.[27]

Early Church leaders not only carried on this tradition, but gradually began to condemn any activity that destroyed life, such as abortion, infanticide, exposure, or suicide. Saint Augustine declared that God's command against killing others also prohibited self-destruction. One should not end one's own life because of great pain or suffering, or help others to end theirs, for Augustine saw suffering as a necessary purification before a person could enter the kingdom of heaven. "The tides of trouble will test, purify, and improve the good, but beat, crush, and wash away the wicked."[28] In 563 the Council of Braga denied funeral rites to all suicides, and in 693 the Council of Toledo announced that anyone who attempted suicide would be excommunicated.

Modern Catholic thinkers have been torn between absolute proscriptions against active and even passive euthanasia and the problems they see in the modern world.[29] Typical of the traditional attitude is the comment by J. P. Kenney that "there is a certain unnaturalness associated with the desire to terminate one's life deliberately. . . . Moreover, ecclesiastical penalties imposed by Canon Law upon those guilty of violating the Fifth Commandment by suicide or homicide are no less applicable to cases where a 'mercy' motive could be alleged."[30] Catholic doctrine considers suicide an "unlawful moral act," and the suicide is not given ecclesiastical burial unless he or she showed repentance before death. The only exception is the category of "indirect suicide," where a person is aware that certain actions may result in his or her death, but balances that by a greater good, for example, by deliberating steering one's car over a cliff in order to avoid a fatal crash with a school bus full of children.

Some Catholic thinkers, however, have adopted a form of situation ethics, in which individual choices have to be judged within the context of the situation. Thus Daniel Maguire has declared that "the morality of terminating life, innocent or not, is an open question although it is widely treated as a closed one."[31]

Opinions such as this led traditional Catholics to reaffirm their opposition to any form of mercy killing. In 1978, the *Linacre Quarterly*, the official journal of the National Federation of Catholic Physicians' Guilds, carried a widely quoted article by Dr. Russell L. McIntyre in which he declared that under no circumstances ought "euthanasia be considered as an alternative to care. We have no moral ground on which to stand, whatever, if we euthanize to avoid care." However, McIntyre went on to say that prolonging life after "the presence of God [is] being withdrawn" is also indefensible. Thus, in specific instances where a person is brain-dead, in an irreversible coma, or in a persistent vegetative state, the physician should do nothing to prolong life. Using Charles Curran's terminology, Dr. McIntyre noted that when the "process of dying" has overtaken the "process of living," the

physician should recognize this as God's will and not try to interfere.[32]

The debate within the Church in the 1970s, as well as the fact
that two of the major right-to-die cases in the United States
involved Catholic patients, Karen Quinlan and Brother Joseph
Fox, led to the issuance by the Sacred Congregation for the Doctrine of the Faith of a "Declaration on Euthanasia," approved by
Pope John Paul II on May 5, 1980. Even before the declaration,
John Paul and his predecessor, Pope Paul VI, had condemned
euthanasia as incompatible with Catholic teaching. Paul VI had
paired euthanasia with abortion, and denounced both as inimical
to the right to life. An even earlier document, *Gaudium et Spes*
(1965), had lumped euthanasia with murder, genocide, and abortion.

The Vatican declaration reaffirmed the historic Catholic view
regarding the value and sanctity of life as a gift from God. The
statement also repeated the church's traditional condemnation
of suicide, an act it equated with murder and denounced as "a
rejection of God's sovereignty and loving plan." While also de-
nouncing active euthanasia, the document acknowledged a right
to die, not by suicide or at another's hands, "but to die peacefully
with human and Christian dignity."

The Vatican, without using the term explicitly, went on to
permit passive euthanasia, and to absolve Catholic physicians
from an obligation to use heroic measures on terminally ill patients.

> When inevitable death is imminent in spite of the means used,
> it is permitted in conscience to take the decision to refuse
> forms of treatment that would only secure a precarious and
> burdensome prolongation of life, so long as the normal care due
> to the sick person in similar cases is not interrupted. In such
> circumstances the doctor has no reason to reproach himself
> with failing to help the person in danger.[33]

For Catholics then, suicide and active euthanasia are forbidden
by the Church's teaching, but passive euthanasia, or forgoing
extraordinary measures for those who are terminally ill, is permitted. The Vatican pronouncement also approves of the cessa-

tion of such treatments already in place "where the results fall short of expectation." The Pro-Life Committee of the U.S. Catholic Conference, in its statement, "The Rights of the Terminally Ill," expanded on this theme when it declared that "Laws dealing with medical treatment may have to take account of exceptional circumstances where even means of providing nourishment may be too ineffective or burdensome to be obligatory."[34]

However, Church leaders are quite disturbed by medical claims that artificial nutrition and hydration are no different in terms of treatment than a respirator. A 1987 *amicus curiae* brief filed by the New Jersey Catholic Conference asserted that Catholic tradition forbade the removal of artifical nutrition and hydration once begun. Nutrition and water should always be provided to a patient. "Not to do so would introduce a new attack upon human life."[35] In its most recent statement, the Committee for Pro-Life Activities of the National Conference of Catholic Bishops warned against withdrawing food and liquid from irreversibly comatose patients. However, the bishops acknowledged the widespread debate on the issue, and termed their statement "our first word, not our last word" on the subject.[36]

PROTESTANTISM

It would be impossible to detail the views of every Protestant faith, especially since many have no official doctrine on the subject, while those that emphasize congregational organization may leave the decision either to individual conscience or to local mores. Typical of the latter is the statement of John K. Martin of the Anglican Consultative Council. As far as he could tell, the Anglican Church had never adopted any statement on euthanasia, but a number of individual churches that belonged to the Anglican Communion had "expressed their mind on this matter, if not through their synods, then through research and the engagement of their Boards for Social Responsibility."[37]

Similarly, the Baptists are not only split into several associations, but each church is an independent unit. Probably most Baptists would subscribe to the statement of the General Associa-

RENNER LEARNING RESOURCE CENTER
ELGIN COMMUNITY COLLEGE
ELGIN, ILLINOIS 60123

tion of General Baptists: "We believe life and death belong in the hands of God. . . . We oppose euthanasia, sometimes referred to as mercy killing. . . . We affirm the right of every person to die with dignity. We reject efforts made to prolong terminal illnesses merely because the technology is available to do so."[38]

The first Protestant reformers, including Martin Luther and John Calvin, shared the Catholic view that God utilized mortal suffering as a means to cleanse the soul.[39] In the prayer he composed for the afflicted, Calvin wrote: "We commend to Thee those whom Thou art pleased to visit and chasten with any cross or tribulation, all persons oppressed with poverty, imprisonment, sickness, banishment, or any other distress of body or sorrow of mind, that it may please Thee to show them thy fatherly kindness, chastening them for their profit."[40] Naturally, holding the view that pain served God's purpose, the reformers could approve of neither suicide nor euthanasia as an escape from affliction.

As the Reformation spread to England, so too did the idea of pain as a necessary adjunct of religious salvation. John Owen, sometimes called the "Calvin of England," told his followers that "God may deliver you, first of all, by sending you an affliction to mortify your heart." The Puritans did not despise medical help in curing their illnesses. The great divine Cotton Mather told his congregation in New England that if afflicted, they should "go to physicians in obedience to God, who has commanded the use of means. But place thy dependence on God alone."[41]

Although it is assumed that Protestants, like the Catholics and Jews, proscribe suicide and active euthanasia, most Protestant denominations have no formal theological position. As a result, one finds prominent clerics and laypersons advocating suicide and even active euthanasia as within the traditions of their faiths. The Reverend Joseph Fletcher, for example, argued for legalized euthanasia on the grounds that suffering is purposeless, human personality is worth more than mere existence, and, perhaps most important, the phrase "Blessed are the merciful, for they shall obtain mercy," is as important as "Thou shalt not kill." The then Archbishop of Canterbury, in addressing the Royal Society of Medicine in 1976, denounced the idea that it is "Christian" to prolong life artificially in extreme cases, and he quoted approvingly the nineteenth-century poet Arthur Clough, that "Thou should not kill, but needst not strive officiously to keep alive."[42]

Paul D. Simmons of the Southern Baptist Seminary shocked many people when he argued that Christianity could approve of some types of suicide. Those who elect death by direct and voluntary means, he declared:

> may be seen as acting in the context of the Christian freedom to choose the terms under which they are to die. Suicide of this type is hardly to be regarded as a sin for which there is no forgiveness. On the contrary, such a decision may be based upon a commitment to the truth that "whether we live or whether we die, we are the Lord's" (Rom 14:8).[43]

In general, however, the various Protestant denominations do not offer any cohesive approach to euthanasia or suicide, leaving the decision to the individual. A few groups have issued doctrinal statements; the governing body of the United Church of Christ, for example, recently affirmed the right of terminally ill people to commit suicide and of their relatives to end their lives for them.[44] The recent rise in interest in the right to die has also led some social action committees to issue statements that, for the most part, oppose active euthanasia while affirming the right of each individual to die with dignity.

NON-WESTERN RELIGIONS

Some Western moralists and anthropologists have made the mistake of ignoring the serious manner in which Eastern religions view death. Margaret Pabst Battin exemplifies this attitude when she practically dismisses non-Christian attitudes as irrelevant to any serious discussion of suicide and its ethics.[45] It is possible however, to value the quality of one's life so highly that one welcomes death at an appropriate time. Some cultures deemed primitive by Western standards as a matter of course take positive actions to help the sick and the elderly or sick persons inform their families that they are ready to die, and the families, out of love, will either take them out and leave them on the "mother ice," or kill them outright. As Derek Humphrey observes, death in primitive societies "was treated more realistically than it is today. It was treated as a natural part of life. Aiding death was often done out of respect for an ill person."[46]

Islamic views are greatly misunderstood by Westerners, who have heard so much about *jihad*, or "holy war," in which a person dying for Allah's cause will immediately go to paradise. Western media, especially during the decade-long war between Iraq and Iran, carried countless stories of fanatical young men rushing off to seek death against the enemy. While it is true that religious demagogues can go to extremes, and often take their followers along with them, these situations are just that—extremes—and not at all representative of the faith held by millions of Allah's followers.

In normal life Islam opposes both suicide and euthanasia, and believes that God has provided a cure for all diseases. During the Middle Ages, when medical science stagnated in Europe, Arab physicians advanced the art of healing, and expanded upon the Hippocratic oath to enunciate an ethos of saving life. Curing the sick and relieving suffering is a duty not only of doctors but of all persons.

But when a person is old, very sick, and has lost sentience, the doctor should not extend life needlessly, since such symptoms are a sign that God has willed death. The terminally ill person is entitled to respect God's verdict and to die in dignity at home, surrounded by family. The physician may not interfere, nor may he expedite death; Islam forbids euthanasia as an insult to Allah.[47] As for suicide, it is strictly forbidden by the Koran, which declares that perpetrators will not be allowed entrance to Heaven, but will instead be punished in Hell. Under strict Islamic law, suicide and attempted suicide are felonies.

Where Jewish and Christian doctors may look to the Bible for guidance and the Islamic healer to the Koran, Hindu medical ethics derive from a series of writings known collectively as the Ayurveda, parts of which date back to the first millennium B.C.

Hindu thought reveres life in all forms and has a general proscription against killing and violence; it thus forbids mercy killing, even if the patient is in great suffering. All the family or doctor can do is not treat, and let death take its course.

The Ayurveda contains several oaths, one of which lists people whom the physician should not treat, and includes those "hated by the king or who are haters of the king," those who are "on the point of death," and those who are "extremely abnormal, wicked, and of miserable character." The doctrine of karma, or fate, and the idea of continuous rebirth, informs Hindu medical ethics and thus justifies giving certain persons medical assistance while withholding it from others. A "miserable" person in this life is paying for having been an evil person in a previous life, and is therefore less entitled to care than a "good" person, who is being rewarded for virtue in another existence. While this would appear to countenance at least passive euthansia, the Charaka Samhita, one of the sources of the larger Ayurveda, directs a doctor to withhold disturbing information from a dying patient. "Even knowing that the patient's span of life has come to its close, it shall not be mentioned by them, where if so done, it would cause shock to the patient and to others."[48]

Traditional Hindu thought also condemns suicide. A verse from the Isavaya Upanishad declares: "He who takes his self [life] reaches after death, sunless regions covered with darkness." Later writings, however, seemed to countenance some suicides, such as those of persons afflicted with incurable disease, or the very elderly and infirm, while suicides for religious purposes, such as *suttee* (the immolation of a widow), also escaped the general condemnation. In modern times passive resistance, which is praised in Hindu thought, has led to hunger strikes, such as those practiced by Gandhi, and there is no sin if, in a good cause, one starves oneself to death.[49]

Hindu thought, however, distinguishes between suicide and "freedom to leave," the idea that a person may will his or her death when the proper time has come. This "willing" might come in the form of refusing food or water, while at the same time engaging in certain types of meditation. Under these cir-

cumstances, which some Western writers view as akin to euthanasia, it is permitted for family members or disciples to "help"
one who has willed himself to leave.[50]

Most contemporary religions share basic assumptions against
suicide and active euthanasia, believing that when death ap-
proaches, one should let nature take its course, while providing
as much dignity and comfort as possible for the patient. But in
those societies where modern medicine is practiced, problems
have arisen that do not fit easily into traditional religious doctrine. As a result, theologians, ethicists, and others have engaged
in a continuous discussion over how modern, life-prolonging
technology can accommodate to religious belief. The debate has
been just as intense and soul-searching in the law.

CHAPTER TWO

Is there a "Right" to Die?

The debate that began with the Karen Ann Quinlan case involved legal issues as well as moral questions, for the law exists not only to ensure social stability but to protect individual interests as well. While in an ideal world there would be no conflict between these goals, in the real world the interests and responsibilities of the state often do collide with individual rights. Not infrequently the rights of one individual or group may run counter to that of another. In these instances, the courts are asked to interpret the law in order to resolve the conflict, a task they perform every day in countless cases covering an enormous variety of issues.

The Quinlan case, however, made it appear to the general public that the law on this subject had not kept pace with the breakneck technological changes then transforming the practice of medicine. Law in fact did exist, and the courts applied it in the Quinlan case, but by the mid-seventies a nation that had just lived through a civil rights revolution believed that there must be a *constitutional right* to die. After all, the Supreme Court had ruled that men and women enjoyed a constitutionally protected right to privacy; that women had a constitutional right to obtain an abortion; and that even those accused of terrible crimes had a constitutional right to decent and fair treatment. Surely, then, Americans had a constitutional right to die in peace and dignity if they so choose. They *must* have such a right!

In fact, they do, but the United States Supreme Court, which is the ultimate arbiter of what the Constitution says, did not say so until 1990. However, the right to die* is grounded in common law that goes back well before the Quinlan case and can also be found in more recent legislation enacted by many states. That is the law that governed, and continues to govern, nearly all the cases that arise in this area.

The common law is judge-made law, the accumulated wisdom of hundreds of thousands of cases over several centuries in which judges faced new conditions and problems and attempted to apply established legal rules to these questions. While in a democracy elected legislatures have the primary responsibility to establish public policy, only the most naïve person would believe that judges do not make law. Their obligation to interpret statutes or, in the absence of statute, to apply existing rules as best they can, means they make law as well as policy. Although there has been a vigorous debate in recent years over the limit of this policy-making function, the Anglo-American legal tradition has always looked to the courts for rulings when society is confronted by new and puzzling situations.

The common law right to be free from physical harm expressed itself in the various rules governing assault and battery. Historically this was transformed, among other things, into the idea that unauthorized medical treatment constituted assault and battery, and that a person could refuse treatment. "Under a free government," declared an Illinois court in 1905, "the free citizen's first and greatest right, which underlies all others—the right to the inviolability of his person—is the subject of universal acquiescence, and this right necessarily forbids a physician or surgeon

---

*By this time the phrase "right to die" has become so universally used that nearly everyone accepts it as a shorthand phrase for an individual's right to refuse medical treatment, the refusal of which will cause his or her death. But lawyers see the word "right" as occupying a high, almost sacred, status, while health care professions at times equate "right" with "duty," a situation that when applied to death may be confusing. The President's Commission for the Study of Ethical Problems in Medicine and Biomedical and Behavioral Research chose to use "forgoing life-sustaining treatment," a phrase that is only slightly more accurate and that has definitional problems of its own. The unwieldy definition never caught the public's attention, and people continue to talk of a "right to die."

... to violate without permission, the bodily integrity of his patient by . . . operating upon him without his consent or knowledge."[1] In a 1905 Minnesota case still studied by first-year law students, the court ruled that a doctor could not, in the absence of an emergency, perform an unauthorized procedure. "If the operation was performed without plaintiff's consent, and the circumstances were not such as to justify its performance without, it was wrongful; and, if it was wrongful, it was unlawful."[2] Benjamin Cardozo of New York, who served on the U.S. Supreme Court in the 1930s and is considered by many the finest common-law jurist of this century, declared that "Every human being of adult years and sound mind has a right to determine what shall be done with his own body."[3]

Common law spoke less to the idea of a right to die than to the question of individual autonomy, the control that a person has over his or her body against unwanted action, be it brute physical attack or medical intrusion. A person has a right to consent to treatment and thus a corollary right to refuse treatment. However, in this as in so many areas of the law, what appears simple on the surface is hedged about by conditions. The law recognizes that there may be times when a right, no matter how important, may be circumscribed. Oliver Wendell Holmes once commented that the right of free speech does not allow a person falsely to shout "Fire!" in a crowded theater; similarly, there are times when a person should be unable to exercise a right to refuse treatment.

At the heart of the law is the idea of informed consent. If a person is to make intelligent decisions about whether to accept or decline particular treatments, there must be adequate information upon which to base that judgment, and this requires that the physician talk to and consult with the patient. While today this sounds reasonable, not so many years ago doctors did not feel it necessary to discuss medical decisions with their patients, or even, in many instances, to seek their permission. Even today, many doctors view the idea of informed consent as no more than a duty to warn about any possible negative effects of treatment in order to avoid malpractice suits. One still finds doctors who claim that patients are incapable of understanding medical issues, and that trying to explain complicated procedures in lay terms is a waste of time that could better be devoted to treatment.[4]

While doctors and hospitals routinely require consent forms for almost any procedure, these forms are worthless unless it can be shown that certain other conditions have been met. A signature on a piece of paper does not by itself prove informed consent. As we have noted, for consent to be informed, it must be *voluntarily* given by a *competent* person who *understands* what is involved. These ideas are not novel to health care, but have evolved in many areas of law, including contracts and torts.

Permission given by one person to another to perform some act, whether it be surgery or selling certain goods, is not valid unless it has been given freely, without duress or coercion. There is no bright-line test in this area, and the limited case law acknowledges that it is often difficult to determine what is truly voluntary. This is especially true in medical care. A doctor will not hold a gun to patient's head to secure a consent form, but a dark description—even if true—of the terrible things that might happen should the patient refuse treatment is certainly a form of duress almost as compelling as physical force.

Valid consent may be given only by someone who has the mental capacity to make that decision. By this the law does not mean intelligence, or that a person has to make the "correct" decision, since what is "correct" will depend upon each individual's beliefs and attitudes. For one person, consenting to chemotherapy may be a good choice; for another, declining the treatment may be the better option. Most courts have moved toward the definition of capacity given in the *Restatement of Torts*: the ability to appreciate the nature, extent, or probable consequences of the physician's conduct for which consent is sought. The *Restatements* are the periodic attempts by the American Law Institute to define what the current legal consensus is in major areas of the law. While they have no legal standing *per se*, judges often rely on *Restatements* when seeking workable definitions of particular issues.[5]

The person must understand that to which he or she is consenting, and here the complex nature of medical treatment, as well as the uncertainty of results, makes understanding a most difficult criterion. How much does a doctor have to tell a patient in order for the patient to understand what a procedure will entail and what is at risk? How technical must the explanation be, or must the information be given in a form that any layperson can grasp? Is it possible to predict with accuracy the risks from certain drugs or treatments?

By now nearly all states have imposed upon physicians a duty to inform a patient of the risks and benefits associated with treatment, as well as what that treatment implies, and there is a clear legal duty to do so in a comprehensible manner. Not only must a patient consent to treatment, but a patient's consent must be informed consent. There is no legal defense to battery based on consent if a patient's consent to touching [treatment] is given "without sufficient knowledge and understanding of the nature of the touching."[6] Physicians who fail to carry out the duty to inform leave themselves open to malpractice suits.

But jurisdictions differ over what test they will use to determine if sufficient information has been given. About half the states use what is known as a customary professional practice test, in which expert witnesses testify as to whether the amount of information a doctor had offered, and the manner in which it had been given, comported with customary practice. Recently there has been a shift toward a legal or "reasonable person" standard; namely, whether the doctor provided sufficient information and in such a way as a reasonable layperson would understand the risks involved, and this would be determined not by expert witnesses but by the factfinder, the judge or jury.

Ideally, doctors and their patients ought to collaborate in a decision-making process, the doctor spelling out his or her judgment on proper treatment and explaining what it involved, and the competent patient voluntarily making an informed decision to accept or decline the treatment. But since this scenario cannot always occur, the law has spelled out four exceptions to the informed consent rule.

The first is *emergency* care, when in a critical situation requiring immediate action, a doctor may treat an injured or ill person without the consent of that person or of those authorized to give that consent, such as parents of a minor. Here the law recognizes that delay may cause the loss of life, and common sense tells us that if there is time to describe treatment and discuss risks and benefits, there probably is no emergency. But because emergencies do not allow for discussion, and in many cases for even securing information, decisions may be made that the patient, had he or she been competent, might have opposed.

If a patient is *incompetent*, then informed consent is by definition impossible to obtain, and the doctor's duty to inform is negated as well. However, it is not always easy to determine when someone is incompetent. Patients who are unconscious obviously are unable to involve themselves in any meaningful decision making, as are those who are inebriated, delirious, or in some form of toxic stupor. The hard cases are those in which a patient is conscious but somehow impaired so that it is difficult to tell if he or she understands what is happening.

Another exception is the *therapeutic privilege*, which permits a physician to withhold information if the disclosure would not be in the patient's best interest or would prevent the doctor from providing appropriate care. While at first glance this seems an open invitation for a doctor to deny information on the subjective judgment that it would be harmful for the patient to know, this is not the way the privilege has been interpreted by the courts.[7] This exception, which has not been the subject of very much case law, is addressed primarily to those instances where the emotional shock of the news might trigger the very crisis the doctor is trying to avoid.

Finally, as with all rights, a person may *waive* the right; however, as with informed consent, waiver must be voluntary and informed, and the person must be competent. Given the current emphasis on self-determination and collaboration with the doctor in treatment, it may seem strange that anyone might not want the information needed to make such decisions. But as Alan Meisel points out, it may be a manifestation of autonomy. Giving patients the information they need to make decisions is one form of self-determination. "However, compelling them to receive information they do not want or to make decisions they do not wish to make is a paternalistic denial of the right of self-determination. Waiver is the patient's counterpart to the therapeutic privilege."[8]

Just as patients have the right to consent or withhold consent, so they have a right to participate in decision making and a right to put their trust, and their lives, in the hands of another.

During the 1970s, as the public debate over the right to die expanded, doctors found themselves in something of a legal dilemma. On the one hand, they could be sued for malpractice if they forced treatment on an unwilling patient or failed in their duty to inform a patient of the risks and benefits associated with particular treatment. On these issues the law seemed clear enough. At the same time, doctors worried that they might be liable to criminal action if they halted a treatment already begun, such as removing a respirator or a feeding tube. It is one thing to withhold life-sustaining treatment, especially if a competent patient makes it clear that he or she does not want it. Legally, that would be the equivalent of passive euthanasia, allowing nature to take its course and death to bring its peace. Turning off a respirator, however, might be viewed as active euthanasia, which morally and legally could be considered murder.[9]

That this concern worried doctors could be seen in the oral argument before the New Jersey Supreme Court in the Quinlan case. Judge Sidney Schreiber asked the Quinlans' attorney, Paul Armstrong, whether he wasn't requesting the court to declare that if the doctors terminated treatment, they would be subject neither to civil nor criminal consequences. When Armstrong agreed, Chief Justice Richard J. Hughes leaned forward and asked him a question:

HUGHES: "Mr. Armstrong, doesn't it come down to this, the long and short of it being that you ask the Court to declare the law to be—there having been no precedent in any part of the common law that I can figure—that the Court is to declare now that if the doctors stop this procedure and cause death that it will not result in any civil or criminal sanctions as to such doctors, or indeed as to such family members."
ARMSTRONG: "Yes, Your Honor."
HUGHES: "So that, in effect, you're asking the Court to make new law."

ARMSTRONG: "On these facts, that's correct."

HUGHES: ". . . In that case, Mr. Armstrong, wouldn't the Court be legislating?"

ARMSTRONG: "No, Your Honor. It would be reflecting the majesty of the evolution of the common law, as it has since its inception in England. *I genuinely think that the Court is fully competent to address itself to these types of problems.*"[10]

The difficulty in the context of the criminal code was well described in a Washington court several years later. State law defined homicide as "the killing of a human being by the act, procurement or omission of another," and it classified murder in the first degree when "with a premeditated intent to cause the death of another person, one causes the death of such person." As the court noted, "the potential for criminal liability for withdrawing life-sustaining mechanisms appears to exist."[11]

Some commentators believe that a number of right-to-die cases in which the doctors and family both believed it would be best to terminate life support went to court not to resolve questions of personal autonomy but to ensure that neither the medical professionals nor the hospitals faced civil or criminal liability. As far as we know, there has been only one instance in which there has been a prosecution for stopping life-support treatment, and that indictment was ultimately dismissed.[12]

In May 1981 Clarence Herbert, a fifty-five-year-old security guard, underwent surgery in a Los Angeles hospital to correct an intestinal obstruction. In the recovery room he suffered cardiopulmonary arrest and lapsed into a coma from which he never regained consciousness. Three days later his physicians, Robert Nedjl and Neil Barber, adjudged his condition "hopeless" and informed his family. Herbert's wife and eight children all agreed that he should be taken off the machines, since he had indicated to them that he did not wish to be kept alive by a respirator. The doctors disconnected Herbert from the respirator, and, like Karen Quinlan, he remained comatose but was able to breathe by himself. After further consultation, the family and the doctors agreed that intravenous feeding should be stopped, and Herbert died six days later.

Subsequently the Los Angeles county prosecutor charged Nedjl and Barber with murder, claiming that they had cut off the respirator and feeding in order to cover up their malpractice and save money for a prepaid health plan. The doctors claimed that they did no more than follow the wishes of the family in an irreversible coma case. The magistrate who initially heard the case dismissed the charges, a superior court reinstated them, only to be reversed by the court of appeals.[13]

The appellate court, while recognizing the emotional distinction often made between a respirator and a feeding tube, considered both to be forms of medical treatment. In this case, the court ruled, the doctors—in consultation with the family—had withdrawn "heroic" life supports, and the court viewed this not as an act of commission but of omission, allowing nature to take its course. The court asked what is, or should be, a central question in all such cases: What is the duty that a physician owes to the patient? Obviously a doctor should do nothing positive to hasten death, such as injecting a patient with a poison, for that would be a deliberate act of murder. But a doctor does not owe a patient the duty of heroic treatment, nor is there a duty to impose or continue treatment against the wishes of the patient or of the family.

In fact, despite wording in criminal codes that would, on the face of it, make physicians liable for acts of omission as well as commission, no court has ever ruled that withholding or withdrawing life support constitutes a criminal act. A doctor will be protected, the Massachusetts Supreme Judicial Court noted, "if he acts on a good faith judgment that is not grievously unreasonable by medical standards."[14]

Why should this be so? If a doctor turns off a resuscitator, and the patient dies as a result, is this any different than if the doctor had taken a gun and shot the patient?

Some courts have argued that the real cause of death is not the termination of life-sustaining treatment, but the underlying illness. The disease, and not the doctor, killed the victim, so there can be no homicide. This is the reasoning ultimately adopted by the New Jersey court in *Quinlan*. Yet both medical and legal ethicists have problems with this rationale, since it could, if taken literally, allow any patient to refuse any treatment, and allow any physician to withhold any treatment, even a procedure that might save the patient's life. Such a policy would go against the state's long recognized power (*parens patriae*) to protect the interests and well-being of its citizens, and to intervene on their behalf when necessary.

Other courts have reasoned that there can be no homicide if a patient exercises his or her right to forgo treatment. This is the underlying philosophy of the Uniform Rights of the Terminally Ill Act, §10(a), that "death resulting from the withholding or withdrawal of life-sustaining treatment pursuant to a declaration and in accordance with this [act] does not constitute, for any purpose, a suicide or a homicide."

This or a similar provision can be found in the natural-death acts adopted by most states. Such acts provide a statutory framework in which patients can determine their treatment, and which shields physicians from liability for respecting these decisions. Uniform acts are proposals made by the State Commissioners for Uniform Legislation, a body that has now been meeting for over a century, and that drafts model acts on issues of common concern. While the states are free to adopt, reject, or amend the proposed legislation, many states do in fact adopt them, thus providing uniformity from one state to another on a number of important matters.

These laws also hold surrogates free of liability, an issue that arose in the Quinlan case and that confronts the problem of those who, like Karen Quinlan, could not make an informed decision because of legal incompetency. The law has for decades dealt with "persons under a disability," be it because of age or mental or physical infirmity, through the appointment of guardians. It has also recognized the right of people to name their own surrogates to act under certain conditions, the most common example being the appointment of executors to carry out the terms of a will.

Family members of a legally disabled person are normally accepted by the courts as surrogates. As the Florida Supreme Court noted, "if there are close family members such as the patient's spouse, adult children, or parents, who are willing to exercise this right on behalf of the patient, there is no requirement that a guardian be judicially appointed."[15] There are, however, some judges who believe that only a court-appointed guardian, acting together with the doctor, should be allowed to make life-and-death decisions, even if the guardian is a close member of the family. Most jurisdictions, though, are willing to leave the process to family, with judicial intervention only in exceptional circumstances.[16]

It is through surrogates that the law has extended to incompetent patients a right to refuse life-sustaining treatment, and it did this starting with *Quinlan*. There the New Jersey court declared that "our affirmation of Karen's independent right of choice . . . would ordinarily be based upon her competency to assert it. The sad truth, however, is that she is grossly incompetent and we cannot discern her supposed choice. . . . Nevertheless we have concluded that Karen's right of privacy may be asserted on her behalf by her guardian under the peculiar circumstances here present."[17]

As a result, right-to-die cases have from the start assumed that incompetents have the same right as competent patients, but that informed consent must be secured in a different manner, either through previous declaration or through the decision of a surrogate or guardian.

In addition to well-established common-law rules on informed consent and guardianship, by the time the New Jersey Supreme Court heard the Quinlan case in 1976 it could also look to a new constitutional basis, the right to privacy first enunciated by the U.S. Supreme Court in the landmark decision of *Griswold* v. *Connecticut* (1965)[18] and expanded in the high court's abortion ruling in *Roe* v. *Wade* (1973).[19] New Jersey Chief Justice Richard J. Hughes drew upon these two cases to conclude that the federal Constitution guarantees certain areas of privacy, and "presumably this right is broad enough to encompass a patient's decision to decline medical treatment under certain circumstances."[20]

Cases since *Quinlan* have drawn upon both the common-law right of personal autonomy and the constitutional right of privacy. In recent years, however, conservative denial of a federal constitutional right of privacy[21] as well as opposition to the *Roe* decision permitting abortion on the basis of a right to privacy has led many courts to back away from reliance on *Griswold* and to rely on the older common-law rights.[22] While some state courts, relying on state-guaranteed rights of privacy, continue to uphold such a right, federal courts, and especially the Supreme Court, are talking more about autonomy than privacy.

We can thus see that although right-to-die cases are relatively new, a sufficient body of legal precedents existed for judges to confront these cases with the assurance that the law they expounded relied on established principles. In many instances the courts admitted that they were making new law and invited the legislature to clarify the issues and enunciate the state's interests in these decisions. Most states did respond with so-called living-will or natural-death statutes, but these did not by themselves create new rights; rather, they codified already existing common-law rights and spelled out more precise procedures for dealing with legally incompetent patients.[23] What we find, then, is a series of decisions that intertwine common-law principles, statutory regulations, and constitutional principles.

The year after *Quinlan*, the Massachusetts Supreme Judicial Court heard the case of Joseph Saikewicz, a sixty-seven-year-old man with an IQ of ten who suffered from acute myeloblastic leukemia. Doctors said that without treatment Saikewicz would live for a few months at most and probably without great pain or suffering. With chemotherapy, he had a 30 to 50 percent chance of remission for up to fifteen months, but the treatment itself would be painful and produce uncomfortable side effects. The patient himself would not understand the reason for the treatment and, because of the pain, probably would not cooperate.

The court-appointed guardian recommended against the treatment, and the probate court agreed that it would not be in the patient's best interest. The probate judge noted, among other things, the patient's right to privacy, his age and condition, and the poor quality of life available to him even if the treatment proved successful.

The state's high court affirmed the ruling but rejected the idea that quality of life should be a consideration; neither intelligence

nor social standing had any bearing on the value of life insofar as
the law was concerned. Judge Paul J. Liacos based his decision on
a cost / benefit analysis; he weighed the pain and suffering of the
treatment against the limited benefits that would accrue and
concluded it would be in Saikewicz's best interests not to be
treated. As in *Quinlan*, the court emphasized the importance of
personal autonomy and the right of the patient to determine his
own fate or, as in this case, to rely on substituted judgment.[24]

Where *Saikewicz* differed from *Quinlan*, however, is in the
Massachusetts court's insistence that the ultimate authority in
deciding for incompetents rested with the judiciary. While the
wishes of the family or of a guardian, or the recommendation of
a hospital ethics committee would be given serious consideration, the final decision would be in the hands of a court and
would thus require some form of adversarial hearing in which
the interests of the patient would be represented.[25] Doctors, of
course, objected to this decision, since it would make them defend their medical decisions in a highly sensitive area and bring
in one more party to the decision-making process.

Recognizing at least some validity in their complaint, a Massachusetts appellate court later held that hospitals and doctors did
not need court permission for No Code and Do Not Resuscitate
orders. The case involved an elderly woman, Shirley Dinnerstein,
who suffered from Alzheimer's and the results of a massive stroke
that had left her in an essentially vegetative state. Both her adult
children argued that if a cardiac or respiratory arrest occurred,
she should not be resuscitated. Following *Saikewicz*, the family,
the attending physician, and the hospital joined in a suit to determine if DNR orders required court approval, and the court ruled
that such decisions remained in the realm of medical judgment
and the family's wishes.[26]

Next to Karen Ann Quinlan's, probably no other case attracted
as much public attention as did that of Brother Charles Fox of
the Catholic Order of the Society of Mary. Brother Fox, eighty-
three, suffered a hernia while tending his garden in August 1979;
during surgery at Nassau Hospital he went into cardiopulmonary
arrest that led to anoxia, the loss of oxygen to the brain, and the
doctors placed him on a respirator. A few years earlier, while

discussing the Quinlan case, Brother Fox had told his close friend and spiritual advisor, Father Philip Eichner, that should he become terminally ill and incompetent, he did not wish to be kept alive by extraordinary means. Father Eichner, attempting to carry out his friend's wishes, asked that the respirator be removed.[27]

Two neurosurgeons agreed that Brother Fox would never recover, but the hospital refused to disconnect the respirator. So Father Eichner went to court seeking appointment as Brother Fox's guardian. The trial court agreed to the request, and while denying the relevance of any constitutional right of privacy, it found that common-law rights of bodily self-determination would allow termination of treatment. Father Eichner, as guardian, could now exercise that right for his friend.

The local district attorney, Dennis Dillon, decided to appeal the decision, but before the Court of Appeals, New York's highest court, could rule, Father Fox died of congestive heart failure on January 24, 1980. Although the high court could have declared the case moot, that is, no longer a controversy, it decided to take the appeal on the grounds that such a question was likely to recur. In its ruling, the Court of Appeals wrote what was until then the strongest judicial support of a right to die.

Speaking for a near-unanimous court, Judge Sol Wachtler held that life support could be withdrawn from an incompetent who had, when competent, clearly and convincingly declared that he or she did not want to be kept alive in a terminal illness by heroic measures. Further, in carrying out such wishes, neither judicial hearings nor any other special procedures were necessary, provided there was clear and convincing evidence of the patient's wishes. However, Wachtler and his colleagues were not willing to infer such intent in the absence of evidence, nor were they willing to allow others, even family members, to make that decision, no matter how persuasive the claim that termination of life support would be in the best interests of the patient and of society.

The court did not use quite these words, but it made its position very clear in this and in an accompanying case it ruled on at the same time. Fifty-two-year-old John Storar was mentally retarded and suffered from advanced cancer of the bladder and a related loss of blood. His mother asked that the transfusions be stopped. In denying her request, the court said: "Although we understand and respect his mother's despair ... a court should not in the circumstances of this case allow an incompetent patient to bleed to death because someone, even someone as close as a parent or sibling, feels that this is best for one with an incurable disease."[28]

While the Brother Fox case strongly reinforced the common-law right of self-determination, it required the person's wishes to have been made known clearly and convincingly. But the ruling also seemed to close the door on any hope for incompetents, especially the mentally retarded who had never been in a position to make their desires known, even shutting out parents or guardians from acting for them. Throughout the decade, courts and legislature would differ over who should make these life-or-death choices and what evidence, if any, would be needed to support those decisions.

Karen Quinlan, Joseph Saikewicz, and Brother Fox could not, at the time of their ordeals, participate in the decision making. But Abe Perlmutter could, and when the Florida Medical Center refused to honor his choice, he went to court.

Perlmutter, a retired cabdriver, suffered from amyotrophic lateral sclerosis, commonly called Lou Gehrig's disease, a progressive deterioration and hardening of the portions of the spinal cord leading to loss of muscle control and, ultimately, paralysis. Perlmutter relied on a respirator to sustain his breathing, and while his body may have been ravaged, his mind remained clear; he easily met the law's definition of competency. He knew that if taken off the respirator he would live only a few hours; with it he might survive as long as two years. After consultation with his family and doctor, Perlmutter asked to be disconnected, but the hospital refused.

The circuit judge who heard the case, John G. Ferris, declared Perlmutter competent, defended his constitutional right to privacy, and ordered the hospital not to interfere with the patient's decision to disconnect. The hospital appealed, but the appellate court affirmed. While recognizing the hospital's legitimate fear of incurring liability, it ruled that Perlmutter's rights of privacy and self-determination outweighed those considerations. On October 6, 1978, the respirator was disconnected. An alarm sounded, and Perlmutter's son turned it off. With his family at his side, Abe Perlmutter died.[29]

During the decade of the eighties the public might well have become confused had it attempted to make some sense out of the welter of litigation confronting the courts.[30] But in fact some trends could be discerned.

First, a competent patient had the right to terminate treatment, although courts differed about whether this right derived from common-law rules of self-determination, the constitutional protection of privacy, or both.

Second, if a formerly competent person had made a clear and convincing statement of intent, those wishes would be honored, and in most jurisdictions there would be no need to involve the courts in the decision-making process. The adoption by most states of living-will or death-with-dignity statutes had made it possible for a person to make choices against the contingency of future disaster with a reasonable certainty that such wishes would be honored.

Third, the hard cases, the ones that caught the headlines, involved incompetent patients who either had never been competent or if formerly competent, had left no indication of their wishes.[31] Here courts had to grapple with the most difficult of legal and moral questions, trying to balance the state's interest in preserving life with what would be best for the individual, while also taking into account the judgments and fears of the health care providers.[32]

Activists on all sides of the right-to-die issue have been upset at the results. At the core is the question of who decides if the patient is unable to do so—the family, the doctor, the hospital and its ethics committee, a judge, or some other party? What criteria should they use? What if their own beliefs run counter to those of the patient? How great a role should courts, as opposed to state legislatures, play in the process? When, if ever, is it more beneficial for the patient or for society to "pull the plug"? What happens if the best interests of the patient do not coincide with the best interests of society? Is society best served by preserving life in all instances? Is there a slippery slope, so that allowing a person in severe pain to die today may lead to allowing less-afflicted people to die tomorrow, and the merely elderly or infirm the day after?[33]

While a few courts have indicated that extensive judicial involvement is either necessary or desirable in such cases, for the most part judges have not been eager to intrude into what they see as a legitimate function of family and doctors. At the same time, courts, as protectors of individual rights and construers of legislation, must be concerned that such decisions meet legal and statutory requirements, that adequate information is available, that due concern has been given to the dignity of the patient.

For most people, a key consideration is the "quality of life," yet here indeed one does find a slippery slope. People have greatly varying views on what is an acceptable quality of life. Thus in the case of Earle Spring, a seventy-eight-year-old senile patient dependent on dialysis treatments, the family petitioned the courts to end the treatment, claiming that were he lucid, such would be his choice. In opposition, a court-appointed guardian argued that no evidence existed to support this contention. Ultimately the Massachusetts high court sided with the guardian, although in doing so it did not dismiss the value of substituted judgment by family. The opinion, however, even while ordering treatment continued, spoke of the patient's irreversible mental deterioration which, aside from kidney failure, would never be restored to a "normal, cognitive, integrated, functioning existence."[34] This led George J. Annas to charge that the court's view, "phrased another way, [is that] there are some categories of people who are so abnormal or ill-functioning that the state has no interest in seeing to it that their lives are preserved."[35]

Almost all of these cases, and many others involving termination of treatment, were appealed to the United States Supreme Court, on grounds that a federal right—privacy—was implicated. But the high court consistently refused to grant certiorari, and since the Court rarely indicates why it turns down a petition, one can only surmise the reasons. Nearly all cases arose in state courts, and in most of them the court reached its decision on either common-law principles or state constitutional or statutory grounds. Unless there is a clear violation of federal law, federal courts will not normally review state court decisions based on "adequate state grounds."

However, many state court decisions referred to a right to privacy which, after *Griswold*, seemed to be grounded in the federal constitution. But in the 1980s, the Supreme Court grew increasingly distrustful of a constitutionally protected right of privacy, and the conservative justices appointed by Ronald Reagan had, for the most part, expressed reservations about *Griswold* and especially *Roe* v. *Wade*, the abortion decision. They questioned whether, in the absence of a specific provision, a right to privacy actually existed in the Constitution.

Ironically, even as the public accepted the idea of a constitutionally protected right of privacy, the Court sought other legal grounds to support self-determination. Court opinions spoke less and less about privacy, focusing instead on the notion of autonomy. With the increasing litigation and publicity surrounding right-to-die questions, it was only a matter of time before the Court agreed to hear a case. The justices took that opportunity in the case of Nancy Cruzan.

On January 11, 1983, coming home from her job on the night shift at a cheese factory, twenty-five-year-old Nancy Beth Cruzan lost control of her old Nash Rambler on an icy road near the small town of Carthage, Missouri. The car slid off the road and flipped over, throwing her some thirty-five feet out of the car and facedown into a ditch. Emergency help came promptly, but not soon enough. As her father, Joe Cruzan said, "If only the ambulance had arrived five minutes earlier—or five minutes later." The rescue squad resuscitated Nancy Cruzan, but by then her brain had been deprived of oxygen for too long.

Nancy, who in so many ways resembled the once-vivacious Karen Quinlan, now suffered a similar fate. She never regained consciousness, and she sank into a persistent vegetative state, seemingly awake, but totally unaware of her surroundings. From time to time there would be reflexive movement, but despite the hours that her parents Joyce and Joe Cruzan spent at her bedside hoping for some sign of cognition, they could not see any. For seven years Nancy Cruzan lay curled in a fetal position at the Missouri Rehabilitation Center in Mount Vernon, kept alive by a tube inserted into her stomach that provided nutrients and water. She had been a healthy person before the accident, and her doctors said that her heart and lungs could function for thirty years.

The Cruzans, however, did not consider this half-existence to be life, and they went to court asking that the feeding tube be removed to allow Nancy to die. The case differed from earlier ones primarily in the fact that no machines kept Nancy alive; her heart beat and she could breathe on her own. She, like some 10,000 other people in persistent vegetative states, needed only food and, in essence, removing the feeding tube would mean that she would starve to death. Although the American Medical Association and many medical ethicists consider artificial feeding and hydration a medical treatment that, like a respirator, could be withdrawn from a terminally ill patient, the idea horrified many people. Food and water, even through a tube, are the basic necessities of life and evoke a far more emotional response than do respirators.

The Cruzan case brought together many of the strands of earlier decisions—questions of personal autonomy, surrogate decision making, the interests of the state in preserving life, and the growing conflict between medical technology and humane values. Daniel Callahan, the director of the Hastings Institute, which has been the center for much of the research into ethical issues associated with the right to die, noted that in *Cruzan* and similar cases, one sees the clash of two basic values. "One is the sanctity of life, with its religious roots," which emphasizes individual autonomy; the other is "the technological imperative to do everything possible to save a life."

But while Nancy was technically alive, did she have a life? Her parents did not believe so; they considered their daughter trapped in a cage, and they had the obligation, and the right, to free her from that prison. If Nancy were alive, Joe Cruzan said, she would say "Help, get me out of this." George Annas of the Boston University Medical School, agreed. "The technological imperative obliterates the person altogether. It acts as if the person doesn't exist—that she has no personality, no family, and that no one who loves her can make decisions about her."[36]

When it became clear that Nancy would never recover, the Cruzans went into local probate court in their hometown of Carthage and asked Judge Robert E. Teel to authorize them to have the feeding tubes removed. William Colby, the Cruzan lawyer who donated his services to the family, later recalled that when he went before Judge Teel to make the request in the summer of 1988, he thought it would be a one-day hearing, since the law as expounded in other jurisdictions seemed to support the parents acting as surrogate decision maker. Because of Nancy's incompetence, the court appointed a guardian, Thad C. McCanse, to represent her interests; at the initial hearing, he also sided with the family. Judge Teel heard the petition, asked some questions, and granted the request.

But Missouri Attorney General William L. Webster decided to appeal the case and claimed that under Missouri law there had to be clear and convincing evidence that Nancy Cruzan had earlier indicated that in such circumstances she would want all medical assistance terminated. Although her parents had said this was her wish, Webster claimed that they had not met the burden of proof required under state law. The state, in its role as special guardian of incompetent persons, placed a high value on life. Webster did not dispute that people had the right to stop treatment; he argued that the state had an equally compelling right to insist that there be clear evidence of the patient's wishes. In fact, in January 1990, Webster proposed legislation to the Missouri legislature to establish clear guidelines on who would be able to make decisions in cases like Cruzan, and what criteria should govern the decisions. Joe Cruzan immediately endorsed the proposal, saying "It's just what we've been fighting for."[37]

The Missouri Supreme Court, by a vote of 4 to 3, reversed Judge Teel and upheld the attorney general.[38] The Cruzans appealed to the Supreme Court, which accepted the case and heard oral argument by the two sides in December 1989. The Court issued its decision the following July. Chief Justice William H. Rehnquist's opinion upheld the right to die, but balanced it against the state's interest in preserving life. While acknowledging that the Cruzans were "loving and caring parents," the Court regretfully rejected their plea. Because the *Cruzan* decision is the first statement of the nation's highest court on the subject and will therefore govern subsequent decisions, it is worth examining in some detail.

In an extremely cautious opinion the majority ruled that there was indeed a right to die. Chief Justice Rehnquist, however, emphasized that this right did not derive from any constitutional guarantee of privacy, but from the Fourteenth Amendment's Due Process Clause. "The principle that a competent person has a constitutionally protected liberty interest in refusing unwanted medical treatment may be inferred from our prior decisions."[39]

The key word is "competent" and the Court noted that this is an area normally assigned to state jurisdiction, not federal law. Although only two other states, New York and Maine, require the same high level of proof as Missouri does, under a federal system a state's powerful interest in protecting life gives it the authority to establish such a test. Missouri law, the Chief Justice concluded, did not unduly burden the individual's constitutionally protected right to autonomy.

Perhaps the element of the majority opinion most disturbing to civil libertarians was the discussion of this balancing of an individual's liberty interest against countervailing state concerns. Stating that a liberty interest exists merely begins the judicial inquiry; before a person can fully enjoy that interest, courts must determine whether the liberty interest outweighs the claims of the state. Rehnquist seemed to indicate that the courts should use little more than a "rational basis" test, the lowest standard of constitutional review, in weighing individual liberty interests against state concerns in this area. Thus, if the state can show a rational basis for depriving an individual of his or her liberty interest, such as the state's desire to preserve life, the courts will, under *Cruzan*, uphold that state claim. Moreover, it places the burden of proof on the family of an incompetent to "prove" that the patient, if competent and able to make his or her wishes known, would want medical treatment or artificial feeding terminated. In those states with high evidentiary standards, this may be a difficult or even impossible demand.

That, of course, is what Missouri wanted—not that Nancy Cruzan should live forever as a vegetable, but that there be clear and convincing evidence that she would have chosen death in these circumstances. While it might appear that Missouri acted in a heartless manner, in fact it carried on a long and honorable tradition, that of the state legitimately seeking to protect the lives of its citizens, even the life of a person in a persistent vegetative state.

The wording of the minority opinion by Justice William H. Brennan suggests that it might have originally been written as a draft of a majority opinion and that Justice Sandra Day O'Connor held the key vote. The four justices in the minority, Brennan, Thurgood Marshall, Harry Blackmun, and John Paul Stevens, would have struck the balance more in favor of the individual than of the state. The Missouri rule, Brennan charged, "transforms human beings into passive subjects of medical technology" and in essence gives the final power to decide to the state and not to the individual. The majority decision, he claimed, "robs a patient of the very qualities protected by the right to avoid unwanted medical treatment. His own degraded existence is perpetuated; the memory he leaves behind becomes more and more distorted . . . [and] the idea of being remembered in their persistent vegetative state rather than as they were before their illness or accident may be very disturbing."[40]

Despite the lengthy and numerous opinions, two things stand out in the decision. Most important, the Court for the first time formally acknowledged a right to die and grounded it in the old common-law notion of self-determination, or autonomy, as confirmed in the Due Process Clause. Second, the Court allowed Missouri to establish the "clear and convincing" rule of evidence, but it did not require other states to adopt it. Too many people merely read the headlines that the Cruzans had lost and jumped to the conclusion that there was no right to die or that people in Nancy Cruzan's condition had to be kept artificially alive for years, perhaps decades.

Even Justice Scalia, who was least sympathetic to the notion of a right to die, agreed with the majority's ruling; his main concern seems to have been that these issues are primarily questions of state law, and should not be decided in federal courts, a position that reflected his strongly held views regarding distribution of responsibility in a federal system. Justice O'Connor's concurrence almost shaded over into the Brennan view, and it appears that she was far more sympathetic to the idea than her colleagues in the majority. But she, too, has firm views on federalism, and urged that the rights of incompetents be worked out in "the laboratory" of the states.

In the end, it is possible that the more liberal view expressed in Justice Brennan's dissent will have greater influence on the law than the majority holding. *Cruzan* was not an ideal case in which to explore the boundaries and bases of a right to die, because while Missouri's application of its law certainly appeared harsh and unfair to the Cruzans, it also fell well within the state's power as *parens patriae* to protect life, and to look after the interests of incompetents.

Since only three states have the high evidentiary level, and the Court quite explicitly did not condition a right to die on adoption of such a test, in essence it left the states to devise their own procedures, and it also confirmed that a constitutional right did exist.[41]

The cases discussed in this chapter have, for the most part, been the "easy" legal questions. Although different courts have adopted differing notions of how a right to die may be expressed and what its bases are, there is a clear line from Karen Quinlan to Nancy Cruzan: *Competent patients, and lawful surrogates for incompetents, may terminate medical treatment, even if that termination will result in their death.*

Following the Supreme Court decision, Nancy Cruzan's parents went back into Judge Teel's probate court with "new" evidence, testimony from friends that Nancy had said she would never have wanted to be kept alive by machines or feeding tubes. Attorney General Webster had won his legal point but, aware of the immense sympathy generated for the Cruzans, withdrew the state from the case. "The public sentiment has shifted," said Ronald E. Cranford, a neurologist who advised the family. "It's not politically advantageous to be against the Cruzan family any-more." George Annas agreed. "It's hard to find anyone who thinks that Nancy Cruzan should not be disconnected from the feeding tube."[42]

Judge Teel heard the new evidence in early November 1990, and Thad McCanse, still acting as court-appointed guardian, also brought in evidence to support the Cruzans in their claim that disconnecting the feeding tube would be carrying out Nancy's wishes. Judge Teel gave them what they had so long sought on December 14, 1990, and the hospital removed the feeding tube less than two hours later. It soon became apparent that not every-one shared Professor Annas's view. Nurses in the Missouri Reha-bilitation Center hospital felt betrayed and angry at having to stop taking care of the young woman who had been their patient for nearly eight years. "The Humane Society won't let you starve your dog," said Sharon Orr, and another nurse noted that "They don't starve death-row inmates." The head nurse of the unit, Jeanette Forsyth, bitterly attacked the decision, and said "We don't want her blood to be on our hands."[43]

Protesters tried to get into the hospital and, when turned back by guards, mounted a prayer vigil outside with signs demanding "Help Save Nancy!" and "How Would You Like to Be Starved to Death?" A group opposing euthanasia went to court seeking to overrule Judge Teel, but various state courts, the Missouri Su-preme Court, and a federal district judge all denied their peti-tions.[44] Mobile television units parked outside the hospital, while Nancy's family sat at her bedside.[45] Twelve days after removal of the feeding tube, Nancy Beth Cruzan died quietly at 2:55 A.M. on the day after Christmas 1990, unaware of the controversy that had swirled around her for so long.

CHAPTER THREE

Suicide

A few years ago I visited a friend in Vermont and found him grieving and angry. A close friend and neighbor of his named Bruce had recently committed suicide. Bruce had given up a successful career in advertising to write novels. He had published six books, but while they were competent works, neither he nor the critics considered them first rate. Then everything turned sour. Bruce could not find a publisher or an agent for his latest manuscript, and a lucrative deal, in which he would have done the screenplays for a television miniseries based on his novels, fell through. He could no longer write and went through his savings to pay his daily expenses.

Then one day Bruce sat down and wrote several letters. He directed that his unmortgaged house be sold and the proceeds given to his daughters. He also wrote to my friend, who is a philosopher, and in that letter recalled some of their conversations about life and death and the values that matter. "I was an artist," Bruce wrote, "and an artist needs an audience. . . . A writer is someone with a vision, and when that vision goes, so the meaning of his existence also goes." Bruce then shot himself in the head.[1]

To many people, it is one thing for a terminally ill person who is suffering great pain and loss of dignity to request that life support be withdrawn; the resulting death is, in many ways,"natural," even a "blessing." But they do not understand how someone who is not suffering from the ravages of an incurable disease, who may have months—perhaps even years—of life left to live, can deliberately elect death.

Suicide puzzles and scares people; life, after all, is so precious, how can anyone not at death's door wish to open and pass through that portal? As Shakespeare asked: "Then is it sin / To rush into the secret house of death / Ere death dare come to us?"[2] Western religions and law have both frowned on suicide for centuries, yet it now appears that the miracles of medical technology that can prolong life have also triggered a new debate: Is it acceptable to allow a person to choose death, and, if so, how may it be done and who, if anyone, may assist?

Although some ancient Greek philosophies supported suicide, in general the popular attitude viewed taking one's own life as unnatural. In Athenian law the hand that committed the suicide would be cut off and buried apart from the rest of the body, which itself would be denied normal funeral rites. Yet many Greek writers acknowledged the legitimacy of suicide under certain circumstances, and the Romans accepted it even more: Roman law never included any general prohibition of suicide. There were, however, some special provisions. If a person committed suicide to avoid forfeiture of property for a crime, the property would still be forfeit. A soldier could also be punished for attempted suicide, on the ground that this constituted a desertion of duty, itself a crime against the state.[3]

Prohibitions against suicide made their way into Christian thought beginning with St. Augustine, who in *The City of God*, written in the early fifth century, condemned self-murder as "a detestable and damnable wickedness." Augustine, whose views were soon incorporated into canon law, interpreted a number of different biblical sources to "prove" that God had forbidden suicide.[4]

Since medieval secular authorities recognized canon law as binding in religious matters, the various pronouncements of the Catholic Church regarding self-murder quickly crowded out earlier pagan toleration of suicide. The edicts of the Council of Orleans in 533 implied that suicide was worse than any other crime, and the Council of Braga in 563 denied to suicides normal funeral rites, such as the singing of psalms. In England, the Council of Hereford in 673 adopted canon law, and King Edgar in 967 specifically affirmed the denial of burial rites; in 1284, the Synod of Nîmes ruled that suicides could not be interred in holy ground. Dante, in *The Inferno*, put suicides with murderers and blasphemers in the seventh circle of Hell.

The growth of the common law in England saw the canonical rules, including the practice of dishonoring the corpse, absorbed and strengthened. An early seventeenth-century writer noted that the suicide "is drawn by a horse to the place of punishment and shame, where he is hanged on a gibbet, and none may take the body down but by the authority of a magistrate." A century and a half later the English jurist Sir William Blackstone wrote that suicides were buried at a crossroads, with a stake driven through the heart and a stone placed over the face. Other cultures that considered suicide taboo also treated the body in a manner designed to keep it from contaminating the tribe. Alabama Indians, for example, threw the corpses into a river, while people in Dahomey carried the body out where it would be food for carrion-eaters.[5]

The last known crossroads burial of a suicide in England took place in 1823, after which Parliament passed a law calling for private burial in a churchyard, but at night and without religious rites. In 1882 an amendment allowed daytime interment, although still without the Church of England ritual. Only a verdict by a coroner's jury that the deceased had been mentally unbalanced, and therefore not responsible for his or her actions, would allow a normal church burial to proceed.[6]

The early settlers of New England brought with them both legal and religious proscriptions against suicide. In 1660 the Massachusetts General Court, in "bear[ing] testimony against such wicked and unnatural practices," ruled that self-murderers "shall be denied the privilege of being buried in the common burying place of Christians, but shall be buried in some common highway where the selectmen of the town . . . shall appoint, and a cartload of stones laid upon the grave, as a brand of infamy, and as a warning to others to beware of the like damnable practices."[7] Although the practice fell into disuse, the statute itself was not repealed until 1823. The United States, however, did not adopt English common-law crimes, so suicide is considered criminal only in those states that have specifically made it so by statute.[8]

The self-murderer, being beyond the reach of the magistrate, is not concerned with the law. But what of those who fail in their attempts, who do not take sufficient poison or sedatives, whose aim is off, whose boobytraps fail to work? In many states where suicide is not a crime, attempted suicide is, and the person who wakes up after a failed attempt may face criminal prosecution.[9]

These statutes also trace back to English common law. The courts reasoned that every attempt to commit a crime is punishable; suicide is a crime, and therefore attempted suicide may be punished. But when and how did suicide itself get to be a crime? Self-murder violated canon law, but the church, while condemning it as mortal sin, called only for a denial of burial rites. In the tenth century King Edgar ruled that a suicide's property would be forfeit to his feudal lord; somewhat later the rule changed so that a suicide's estate would be forfeit to the Crown. In order to justify this change, the royal courts noted that every felon forfeited his goods to the king; by making suicide a felony, the general rule could be applied to suicide as well.

In *Hales* v. *Petit* (1562), one of the first cases to equate suicide with other felonies, the court condemned suicide as a criminal act, an offence against nature, against God, and against the king.[10] Blackstone denounced suicide as "a double offence: one spiritual, in evading the prerogative of the Almighty, and rushing into his immediate presence uncalled for; the other temporal, against the king, who hath an interest in the preservation of all his subjects."[11]

The first known case involving the legal punishment of attempted suicide dates to 1854, when the learned judges held the criminality of attempted suicide a self-evident truth.[12] Within a few years other decisions confirmed the rule, and what began as a moral indictment, enlarged by the monarch's greed for property, became an accepted rule of common law—suicide constituted a felony, and if the successful felon escaped the law's punishment, the failed suicide would certainly stand in the dock.

The idiocy of this rule, both in England and America, seems obvious. As Glanville Williams wrote:

> Quite apart from the general debate on the ethics of suicide, the punishment of attempted suicide has to meet the twin objection that it is cruel and inefficacious. The prime fact about suicide is that legal sanctions cannot stop it. No country has ever succeeded in repressing suicide by this method; the threat of punishment for attempted suicide can only make the offender more likely, if anything, to make sure of succeeding at the first attempt. But for most persons the threat will have no effect one way or the other, because people who are bent on throwing their lives away are not likely to consider the possibility of punishment on failure.[13]

Not until the Suicide Act of 1961 did Her Majesty's Government finally stop making suicide or its attempt a crime.

Other countries had taken that step long before. The writings of the eighteenth-century Italian criminologist Beccaria led to the decriminalizing of attempted suicide shortly after the French Revolution, and most of the other countries of the continent followed suit in the early nineteenth century. Even when Germany, Italy, and Russia fell under the rule of totalitarian governments in the twentieth century and introduced strict population policies, they did not reenact criminal laws regarding suicide or its attempt.

In the United States today, even in those few jurisdictions where statutes still make attempted suicide a crime, there are no prosecutions. At worst, a failed attempt may lead to mandated therapy or perhaps incarceration in a mental hospital. The criminal stigma has for the most part disappeared, although many religions and many people still condemn self-murder as morally wrong.[14]

Following the Enlightenment, the Western world became less dominated by religious thought, and the absolute moral condemnation against suicide partially dissipated. Even as English judges criminalized suicide, philosophers began considering that not all suicides might be bad or even immoral, and the act might be defended on both rational and moral grounds.

In 1516 Thomas More allowed for suicide in his *Utopia*. A century later John Donne, in *Biathanatos* (published posthumously in 1644), argued that contrary to classical Christian teachings, the taking of one's life is not incompatible with the laws of nature, of reason, or of God. Perhaps the most famous of the early justifications is David Hume's essay, *On Suicide* (also published posthumously in 1777), in which he reasoned that a suicide is wrong only if it offends God, one's neighbor, or one's self, but such consequences are not always the case. Other writers of the Enlightenment, including Voltaire, Rousseau, Montesquieu and d'Holbach, endorsed Hume's argument.

The sheer number of volumes on library shelves dealing with suicide from ethical, sociological, psychological, religious, and metaphysical viewpoints shows conclusively that it is far from a moot issue today. For some people, taking one's own life, no matter what the circumstances, is wrong and even if not in violation of secular law is an affront to God's law. For others, one's life is one's own, and each person must determine whether it is worth living. To tie the matter of suicide to contemporary law, the issue must be cast not in religious terms but in the framework of personal autonomy, and the questions are far more complex than the often heard "Whose life is it anyway?"

Two leading students of biomedical ethics, Tom Beauchamp and James Childress, have suggested criteria for determining whether or not a particular suicide is moral. They list three principles, human worth, utility, and autonomy, and the latter is particularly apposite when it comes to the law.[15]

The idea of human worth, referred to by some as the "sanctity of human life," raises the question of whether life is so intrinsically valuable that its self-destruction is an act of murder and therefore wrong. The great humanitarian Albert Schweitzer wrote: "The ethics of respect for life does not recognize any relative ethics. It admits as good only the preservation and advancement of life. All destruction and harming of life, no matter what the circumstances under which this may occur, it designates as evil."[16] On the other side is the argument that existence must be meaningful, that the quality of a life is important, and that if that quality is eroded, through debilitating illness or great despair, then it no longer has any worth.[17]

Although suicide is intensely personal, it affects other people in a variety of ways; it left my friend angry and aggrieved, for example, because he had been deprived of Bruce's continuing friendship. Beauchamp and Childress argue that would-be suicides must look beyond their own reasons for ending life, and see how great a harm, if any, this act would cause other people. Without a family or obligations to others, a utilitarian calculus has no negative items to balance the desire to end pain, suffering, or any other condition the person finds intolerable. If, on the other hand, there is a dependent family or if the person has talents the absence of which would deprive society, then Beauchamp and Childress would put this into the balance against suicide.

There are, of course, many factors that could enter the calculations, such as whether the stigma of suicide might be injurious to relatives, especially children. The Beauchamp-Childress proposal is not meant to be exclusive, but merely to point out that various considerations must be taken into account. In its starkest form, the "utilitarian demand [is] that the greatest possible amount of value or at least the smallest amount of disvalue be brought about by the person's actions."[18]

But the strongest argument in favor of allowing individual discretion is that of autonomy, which has become a major issue in modern law. The right to refuse treatment is, in large measure, located in the right to privacy.[19] As noted earlier, however, the Supreme Court's new conservative majority has moved away from referring to privacy, and has emphasized the right of personal autonomy, which it finds embedded in the liberty interests protected by the Fourteenth Amendment. Under this line of reasoning, people have, within very broad parameters, the right to govern their own lives and to decide, if competent, when to end their lives. If one truly believes in the autonomy of each individual, it would be, according to Beauchamp and Childress, "a showing of disrespect to deny autonomous persons the right to commit suicide when, in their considered judgment, they ought to do so."[20]

The decision is individual, and former Chief Justice Warren Burger, while still a circuit court judge, pointed out that it is the individual, and not the society, that determines what is best for himself or herself:

> Mr. Justice Brandeis, whose views have inspired much of the "right to be let alone" philosophy, said: "The makers of our Constitution . . . sought to protect Americans in their beliefs, their thoughts, their emotions, and their sensations. They conferred, as against the Government, the right to be let alone— the most comprehensive of rights and the right most valued by civilized man." Nothing in this utterance suggests that Justice Brandeis thought an individual possessed these rights only as to *sensible* beliefs, *valid* thoughts, *reasonable* emotions, or *well-founded* sensations. I suggest he intended to include a great many foolish, unreasonable, and even absurd ideas which do not conform. . . . [21]

Each of these three notions, human worth, utility, and above all autonomy,[22] are powerful arguments, and should be binding upon all those who, for whatever reason, would seek to interfere. "If a suicide were genuinely autonomous and there were no powerful utilitarian reasons or reasons of human worth and dignity standing in the way, then we ought to allow the person to commit suicide, because we would otherwise be violating the person's autonomy. . . . The morality of suicide cannot be determined in abstraction from the facts of a person's own situation."[23]

Obviously there are limits on autonomy, and no one suggests that it should mean unbridled self-interest. For example, if a person decided it were in his best interest to get a lot of money by robbing a bank, that would be morally unacceptable, because other individuals, as well as society, would lose. But in talking about suicide, ethicists who support autonomy are concerned only with the individual and others with whom he or she closely relates.

Many people argue that there is never a right to commit suicide, since public policy imperatives to preserve life outweigh any considerations of personal autonomy.[24] But even if we are willing to grant that a person has such a right, we then face a far more difficult problem. People with severe emotional or physical problems may not be able to commit suicide by themselves; they may need help, and this raises highly complex moral and legal issues concerning "assisted suicide."

On June 4, 1990, in a van parked in a public park outside Detroit, Dr. Jack Kevorkian hooked up what he called his "Mercy Machine" to fifty-four-year old Janet Adkins, a Portland, Oregon, schoolteacher suffering from the early stages of Alzheimer's disease. Ms. Adkins had read about Kevorkian, a longtime advocate of physician-assisted suicide, and she had contacted him in the fall of 1989. After some correspondence and phone calls, Kevorkian agreed to help her end her life, and Janet Adkins and her husband, Ron, flew east to meet with him. To provide evidence that she understood exactly what she was doing, Kevorkian set up a video camera in a hotel room, and recorded a forty-minute conversation with the woman:

KEVORKIAN: "How was your life before, and how is it different now?"

ADKINS: "My life was wonderful before, because I could play the piano. I could read. And I can't do any of those things. . . ."

KEVORKIAN: "Janet, you know what you're asking me to do?"

ADKINS: "Yes."

KEVORKIAN: "You realize that. You want help from me. . . . You realize that I can make arrangements for everything, and you would have to do it. That you would have to push the button."

ADKINS: "I understand."

KEVORKIAN: "Janet, are you aware of your decision, and the implications of your decision?"

ADKINS: "Yes."

KEVORKIAN: "What does it mean?"

ADKINS: "That I can get out with dignity."[25]

The next morning, Kevorkian showed Janet Adkins his device, three vials suspended over a metal box containing a small electric motor. Once the doctor had inserted an intraveneous tube into her arm, she could press a button that would start the flow of

saline solution; then it would open the valve to the second vial,
releasing thiopental, which would induce unconsciousness; finally, the contents of the third vial, potassium chloride, would
cause her heart to stop. Kevorkian again asked Janet Adkins if
she understood what would happen, if she wanted to go ahead, if
she knew what to do. She assured him she did, and Kevorkian
then attached her to an electrocardiograph; he left the van[26] and
when he came back a little while later, Ms. Adkins was dead.
The retired pathologist then called the police and reported the
death.

The story of "Dr. Death," as the media quickly labeled him,
exploded all over the nation's newspapers and television stations.
Doctors, ethicists, and laymen alike all had something to say,
and so did the law. Oakland County Assistant Prosecutor Michael
Modelsky sought a first-degree murder charge, but after a two-
day preliminary hearing, Judge Gerald McNally ruled that the
state had failed to prove that Kevorkian had planned and carried
out the death of the woman. Ms. Adkins, McNally noted, had
caused her own death, and since Michigan had no law against
assisting in a suicide, Kevorkian had broken no law. But obviously appalled at the event, McNally called upon the state legislature to address the issue.[27]

Then in January 1991, Modelsky filed a civil suit to stop Kevorkian from using his device in the future. The four-day trial fea-
tured testimony from doctors, who denounced Kevorkian for
violating medical ethics, as well as from people who praised the
"Mercy Machine" and wanted the legal opportunity to use it.
Dr. Arthur Caplan, of the University of Minnesota Center for
Biomedical Ethics, said Kevorkian's actions fell "well outside
acceptable practice for physicians," and that they would under-
mine the public's view of "doctors as people they can trust, who
will not abuse their power and take life unnecessarily."[28] Actually, opinion within medical circles seemed to be split on the
case. Although many doctors criticized Kevorkian's handling of
the Adkins situation, they did not necessarily disapprove of his
intent. A survey by the New York–based *Medical Tribune* found
about 45 percent approving of Kevorkian.[29]

To defend Dr. Kevorkian's actions as humane and compassionate, defense attorney Geoffrey Fieger called Sherry Miller to the stand. Mrs. Miller, a forty-two-year-old mother of two teenagers, had been battling the crippling effects of multiple sclerosis for more than a dozen years, and she could not even lift her hand to take the oath. She described the ravages of the disease. "I went from a cane to a walker to a wheelchair. I can't walk. I can't write. . . . I can't function as a human being. What can anybody do? Nothing. I want the right to die."

Medical science had been unable to help her, and Kevorkian's machine now seemed her only hope. "I should have done something sooner when I was more—when I was capable of doing something on my own." When asked if she could not do something on her own now, Mrs. Miller said no. "I can't take a bunch of pills because I can't get to them," and she did not have the strength or the coordination to use a gun.

The attorney then asked what she thought of the statements by some of the medical ethicists who had testified that people who are in pain or have terminal illnesses can be made more comfortable through medical treatment, so there is no need to end their lives. "You sit in this chair for a year," she said, "not being able to do anything, and being made comfortable, and then tell me. You know, the quality of life after you sit in here—in my chair."[30]

The defense called other witnesses who related how Kevorkian's machine offered them hope out of a nightmarish situation. Virginia Bernero told of her son Victor's pain and suffering during his four-year battle with AIDS. They saw a story about Kevorkian on television, and Victor said he wanted to use the machine. Victor had died in November 1990, and his family said he suffered needlessly; to them, as her other son Virgil said, Kevorkian is "a hero and a trailblazer in a field of processionary caterpillars."[31]

Although a Michigan lawmaker had promised to introduce legislation to govern such cases, Judge Alice Gilbert had no state law in place to guide her decision. But law libraries contain considerable information and cases dealing with aiding, abetting, or counseling suicide. Under common law, if one counseled another to commit suicide, that person could be held guilty of aiding and abetting murder. The advisor, if present at the time of the actual death, could be charged as a principal in the second degree; if not present, then he or she in all likelihood would go free, even though technically an accessory before the fact. The reason the advisor would escape punishment lies in the common-law rule that an accessory cannot be tried for a crime unless the perpetrator has been convicted, and obviously, one cannot try a successful suicide.[32]

The great English jurist Blackstone believed, however, that "if one persuades another to kill himself, and he does so, the advisor is guilty of murder," and a few states have adopted that view. Also, in so-called suicide pacts, if two persons agree to kill themselves together and only one dies, the survivor is considered guilty of the murder of the one who dies.[33]

In a federal system such as ours, it is possible for acts that are legal—or at least noncriminal—in one state to be outlawed in another. Jack Kevorkian escaped criminal charges because Michigan had no statute addressing assisted suicide, but had he set up his machine in Missouri or Oregon he might well have been indicted and convicted as an accessory to murder.

Judge Gilbert eventually issued an injunction against Kevorkian using the machine to help other people commit suicide. "His goal is self-service rather than patient service," she charged, and his fellow physicians "look upon him as a menace that threatens the existence of the medical profession." Although Kevorkian pronounced himself saddened by the ruling, he initially promised to abide by it, although "I can still speak out and promulgate ideas."[34] One day later, however, he was counseling a cancer-stricken dentist about suicide, and announcing that he would test the limits of the injunction. In October 1991 as one news magazine reported: "Dr. Death Strikes Again."

One can hardly describe the two women involved as murder victims. If anything, they saw themselves victimized by cruel diseases and a society that denied them the one release they sought. Marjorie Wantz, fifty-eight, suffered from a painful pelvic disorder; she had endured ten operations, none of which had helped, and had been housebound for more than three years. Neighbors said that her cries of pain could often be heard at night.

She had met Kevorkian on a Detroit talk show and then had read the surprising runaway bestseller, *Final Exit,* a how-to-do-it suicide manual by Hemlock Society–founder Derek Humphrey.* She had tried to follow the instructions in the book and had failed; so she turned to Kevorkian and his machine. The other woman was Sherry Miller, forty-three, who had testified at Kevorkian's trial. She no longer had the strength even to push the button, so Kevorkian arranged for her to breathe carbon monoxide through a mask, while her best friend sat at her side. Kevorkian was present at the cabin in Bald Mountain park, about forty miles north of Detroit, and after both women had died, he called the police. When the county sheriff arrived, the bodies were still hooked up to the machines. Kevorkian's lawyer, Geoffrey Fieger, noted that his client "provided the expertise. He provided the equipment."[35] Asked whether he expected Kevorkian to be prosecuted, Fieger said "No. . . . it's a humane, ethical, medical act."[36]

Kevorkian remained free of criminal charges, since the state assembly, despite the extensive publicity surrounding the death of Janet Adkins, had failed to enact any legislation on assisted suicide. Prosecutors attempted to indict him on murder charges for aiding Marjorie Wantz and Sherry Miller, but those efforts also failed. Whatever moral judgments one wishes to make about him. Dr. Kevorkian did not violate existing Michigan law.

Kevorkian's case is unique in that he sees himself as an advocate and seeks publicity for his cause. The fact of the matter is that doctors assist their patients to commit suicide every day of the year. Most of them do so quietly and indirectly, with perhaps only the family knowing or guessing the truth. The columnist Anna Quindlen recalled a conversation she had once had with a friend whose mother suffered from the pain of ovarian cancer. Her friend spoke of the wonderful oncologist treating her mother,

---

*The book generated a great deal of controversy among ethicists, but relatively little in the law professions. One thing most commentators agree upon is that the sales of the book indicate a profound shift in public attitudes. Many of the people who buy the book are neither sick nor elderly; as one middle-aged woman put it, "When I'm dying, I want to be in control."

and how kind and patient and considerate he was, but none of these was his greatest virtue: "He told me how many of my mother's painkillers constituted a lethal dose."[37]

Many doctors admit that the rate of suicide among the elderly is far higher than the reported statistics indicate, and the known suicide rate is twice that of younger groups. Elderly people who are sick often are prescribed powerful medicines which, if taken improperly, can cause death; the warnings indicating what is improper use can also serve as a guide to suicide.

One doctor, speaking anonymously, said: "So the sick old man dies at home in his own bed last night instead of next fall in some intensive-care unit. He was in pain. He was suffering a lot. What good would come from an autopsy that finds some lethal dose? I'm not suspicious of the family. So I sign the death certificate for 'natural causes.' "

Another doctor, who had treated more than four hundred AIDS patients, told each of them that whenever they thought treatment or pain had become too much, he would provide medicine for a painless suicide. Only four accepted his offer, but he reported that they all felt that they had regained some control over their lives. In 1989, when the doctor himself developed AIDS, he took his own prescription, and his death certificate did not list suicide.[38]

Doctors are sworn to protect life, but far more than most people in society, they see death. They see people so diseased and wracked with pain that death is preferable to life, and they are unique in having the power and the resources to bring that release. Although some newspapers condemned Kevorkian for "disgracing" the medical profession, doctors may, both legally and ethically, help patients to die.

The doctor who agrees to refrain from treatment, or to help patients avoid further treatment, is not assisting in suicide. Courts have consistently ruled that forgoing treatment is not suicide, because the act of refusing treatment is not the cause of death; people die from their illnesses, not from withdrawal of treatment. Suicide is self-inflicted death; the illness that leads to death is not self-inflicted.[39]

To some people, this appears as sophistry, the drawing of fine lines to disguise or rationalize murder. But the law is made of fine distinctions, not just in the criminal area but in civil law as well. One has to take into account the facts of the situation, the motives of the actors, the rights of both society and of the individual. Nor is the law immune from morality or compassion, and that is as it ought to be.

Courts also distinguish forgoing treatment from suicide on the basis of intent. In suicide the person's specific wish is to die, while patients declining treatment do not necessarily wish to die so much as relieve their suffering. One can find this most clearly stated in the case of Abe Perlmutter, that victim of Lou Gehrig's disease who petitioned the court to have his respirator removed. The court noted that Perlmutter's testimony showed "he really wants to live, but to do so, God and Mother Nature willing, under his own power. The basic wish to live, plus the fact that he did not self-induce his horrible affliction, precludes his further refusal of treatment being classified as attempted suicide."[40]

Because doctors can help their patients die as well as live, it is not surprising that people turn to them for assistance. Some doctors are affronted by such requests; they have sworn to heal people, not to kill them, and they refuse to be accessories to suicide because of their own deeply felt moral convictions.[41] On the other hand, many doctors will one way or another quietly assist their patients to commit suicide. Shortly after the Kevorkian story broke, one doctor came forward and admitted that he had done just that.

Dr. Timothy Quill practices medicine in Rochester, in upstate New York. In March 1991 he was ready to publicly discuss his role in assisting a patient commit suicide, and he did so in an article in the prestigious *New England Journal of Medicine*.[42] Quill had known his patient, whom he called "Diane," for eight years and had watched her overcome alcoholism and depression and begin to enjoy life. Then she fell ill, and Quill diagnosed her ailment as acute leukemia. "Together we lamented her tragedy and the unfairness of life," but he urged her to start chemotherapy as soon as possible, after which she would have a bone-marrow transplant. Quill also told Diane that the bone-marrow treatment would be painful, and that at best it offered a one in four chance of survival.

Diane refused the treatment. She was convinced, she told Quill, that she would die during the treatment and would suffer unspeakably in the process. "There was no way I could say this would not occur," he recalled. "In fact, the last four patients with acute leukemia at our hospital had died very painful deaths."

Aware that her death would be only a matter of time, Diane came around to the idea of suicide and asked Quill to prescribe something that would end her life with as little pain as possible when the time came. Quill discussed the matter with her but initially would not agree. He referred her to the Hemlock Society, and a week later she called and asked him for a prescription for barbiturates—sleeping pills—because she was having trouble sleeping. The doctor knew this to be true, but he also recognized that if she had the pills, she would have some security, some control over her life, and could thus live what was left to her without the fear of a lingering and painful death. So he wrote the prescription. "I made sure that she knew how to use the barbiturates for sleep and also that she knew the amount needed to commit suicide."

Diane's condition grew worse. She made her farewells to family and friends and asked Quill to come over to say goodbye. Two days later her husband called to say that Diane had died quietly on the couch; Quill reported the cause of death as acute leukemia. It was the truth, but not the whole truth, and he did it to protect both the family and himself from investigation and possible prosecution for assisting in suicide.

Up until this point, the story of Dr. Quill and his patient is similar to that of hundreds, perhaps thousands, that occur in the United States every year. But then Timothy Quill decided to talk about it, in part to relieve the intense emotional stress the experience had produced, but also to lift the lid on a widespread practice, bring it into the open, and make it more honest. He consulted with attorneys for the state before deciding to publish his account and was told he probably would not face prosecution. While Quill prescribed the barbiturates, he had done so for legitimate reasons, and Diane had taken the overdose by her own hand.

Because assisting a suicide is a felony in New York, punishable by a 5-to-15-year prison sentence, local prosecutors did bring the case to a Rochester grand jury, but the jurors refused to indict Quill.[43]

Medical ethicists Arthur Caplan and George Annas, both of whom criticized Kevorkian, found Timothy Quill's case altogether different. Annas put it quite simply: "I want this guy as my doctor. The vast majority of people . . . would want somebody like this."[44] (Polls taken within the last few years find that out of every ten American adults, five to seven believe that people suffering from incurable disease should be allowed to commit suicide.[45]) Kevorkian, Caplan explained, worked with someone he barely knew, and was not medically competent to make a judgment of her mental condition or even of the progress of her illness. Diane's situation was completely different, and Quill did nothing wrong.

> He knew his patient. I think he felt he could not control her pain anymore. He knew that she was terminally ill. And in a sense, all he did was provide her with the means to activate a choice, but it was her responsibility to decide when and if to use the drugs that she ultimately did use to take her life. The doctor in this case behaved in a a very ethical manner.[46]

One could argue with the distinctions Caplan draws; both Quill and Kevorkian knew that their actions would have particular consequences. If Kevorkian had prescribed pills, and then left Janet Adkins to take them, would that have been more ethical or humane? Possibly, once hooked up to the "Mercy Machine," Janet Adkins might have felt pressure to go ahead, but by all accounts she had been the one to approach Kevorkian. She had already decided to end her life. Not everyone has a loving, caring family member or spouse willing to help. Should doctors, who have the knowledge and training in this area, be allowed to help their patients out of life?

It is nowhere legal for doctors to assist in suicide. In the Netherlands, the penal code forbids such practice, but courts and the medical profession tacitly allow active euthanasia. In early May

1991, a committee of the European Parliament quietly recommended that doctors be permitted to assist competent patients who have repeatedly asked for help in ending their lives.

Perhaps no other event demonstrates so vividly how attitudes are changing than Initiative 119, which appeared on the November 1991 ballot in the state of Washington. Called a death-with-dignity measure, the proposal would have authorized doctors to administer lethal injections to incurably ill patients. The patient had to make the request in writing, and had to have been diagnosed by two doctors as having less than six months to live. Two impartial persons, not members of the patient's family, had to witness the written request. If 119 had passed, the state would have become the first jurisdiction in the world to legalize a form of euthansia.

The Hemlock Society provided the major backing for 119, arguing that the proposal would provide terminally ill people with freedom of choice. Both proponents and opponents of the initiative flooded the state with media spots. In one ad, a hospice worker charged that "Initiative 119 would let doctors kill my patients," while in another a woman who had been diagnosed as having cancer seven years earlier told how glad she was to still be alive. Yes, there had been some rough moments, and if 119 had been in effect, she might have chosen death; but she was so happy to still be alive.

Supporters of the measure ran equally emotional ads, with stories of people who died agonizing deaths. One woman, Vera Belt, told how her mother had died in great pain from throat cancer after doctors had refused her pleas for help in ending her life. When Ms. Belt's sister became similarly ill, she knew what awaited her, so she killed herself by putting a gun in her mouth and pulling the trigger.

The proposal split religious and medical groups. The Catholic Church strongly opposed the measure, but more than two hundred Protestant ministers from mainstream and liberal groups endorsed it. United Church of Christ minister Dale Turner, a supporter of 119, declared that "We're on the frontier of the world," and he dismissed concerns that people would too readily choose suicide if it became so easily available. Turner, seventy-four said, "Nobody loves life like an old man. A person has to be pretty ill and desperate to want to leave."[47]

Many doctors bitterly fought the proposal. They had been trained to save lives, not to take them, and they saw 119 as opening the doors to a flood of abuse. When the Washington State Medical Society debated the issue, delegates voted 5–1 against it, but a poll of the general membership taken earlier in the year showed doctors split roughly evenly.

Although early signs indicated that Initiative 119 would pass, opponents gained ground as election day approached. Critics claim that American voters are apathetic, but 119 galvanized the populace, and voters came out in large numbers. The initiative failed by a 54–46 percent margin. Both sides agreed that the debate had been useful and that an important public policy issue had been raised, one that would not quietly go away. "If we don't deal with the problems raised by 119, we'll be facing this issue again and again and again," said Dr. Peter McGough, an opponent of the measure. "Saying 'No' to assisted death is not enough. Now we have a responsibility to deal with the problems that brought out this concern."[48]

Although lawyers and legal scholars played little public role in the 119 campaign, they too could not ignore the legal questions engendered by the measure. To begin with, proponents of 119 spoke not only of a right to die and death with dignity, both of which are now generally accepted notions, *but also of a right to physician-assisted suicide!* In a *New York Times*/CBS News poll taken in the spring of 1990 on the question of whether a doctor should help a terminally ill person die, 53 percent said yes, 42 percent said no, with the rest undecided.[49] Moreover, even before the vote on Initiative 119, courts had begun to hear arguments asserting a constitutionally protected right to assisted suicide.

In January 1987, lawyers for Hector Rodas filed a petition in Mesa County District Court in Colorado asserting that their client had a right to assisted suicide. In particular, his attorneys requested that Rodas "be confirmed as having the constitutional and privacy right to receive medication and medicinal agents, from a consenting health care professional or institution, which will result in a comfortable and dignified demise."[50]

At the time, Hector Rodas was dying of self-imposed starvation and dehydration, after having won a battle in the same court a week earlier to force the Hilltop Rehabilitation Hospital to withdraw his feeding tubes and allow him to remain in the hospital until he died. Rodas had not been considered terminally ill, but the thirty-four-year-old man was paralyzed from the neck down, and did not want to live anymore. The local court had no problem with disconnecting the feeding tubes on a theory of personal autonomy, even though it recognized that such an action would lead to Rodas's death. But the magistrate had great difficulty with the request for assistance, and must have breathed a sigh of relief when Rodas died before he had to rule on the question.

Supporters of a constitutional right to assisted suicide ground their argument on two basic premises. On the moral side, they argue that the normal public policy rules opposing suicide should not apply to severely disabled people or those suffering from terminal illness. On the legal side, they try to find support in the nonenumerated rights supposedly protected by the Ninth Amendment. This argument has some limited support, and one can find it in the order of the California appellate court to remove a feeding tube from Elizabeth Bouvia. In a concurring opinion, Judge Lynn D. Compton wrote:

> The right to die is an integral part of our right to control our own destinies so long as the rights of others are not affected. That right should . . . include the ability to enlist assistance from others, including the medical profession, in making death as painless and quick as possible.[51]

In some ways, this is the reciprocal of the right to refuse unwanted medical treatment, namely, the right to secure desired treatment, even if that treatment consists of a lethal injection.

Few courts or scholars have accepted this argument, and the results in the Washington referendum suggest that neither has a majority of the general population. Moreover, there is an enormous leap from saying that as a question of personal autonomy a person may elect death, either through withdrawal of life-sustaining technology or even through suicide, to saying that there is a right to enlist others to take positive steps to assist in one's own death.

Even when courts have found a constitutional right to refuse life-extending treatment, they have also, as a matter of public policy, recognized a compelling state interest in preventing suicide, and they go to great pains to distinguish between the refusal of treatment (which is protected) and suicide (which is not). Certainly the Anglo-American legal tradition has not shown any sympathy to the notion of either suicide or assisting in the act, and most states would subject the assistant to criminal prosecution.[52]

Should there be such rights? Should a person who wishes to die be allowed to demand legal protection and indeed to request assistance for an act that nearly all religions and societies condemn? The cases of sick and disabled people certainly warrant our compassion. Just as "natural" death may be a blessing and release for the very ill, so hastening that process, shaving off hours, days, or even weeks of pain, may also be a blessing, and the law has recognized that in its assertion that personal autonomy protects people in taking actions that may lead to their deaths.

But the law is far from clear on questions of assisted suicide, and in this regard, if we can use the Washington referendum and the reactions to Drs. Kevorkian and Quill as a guide, the law is probably reflective of current public sentiment. It is not an easy question, and there are no easy answers. But as many people noted on the day after Initiative 119 failed, the question will be around for a long time.

CHAPTER FOUR

On Death Row

A few days after Christmas in 1987, in the small city of Russellville in west central Arkansas, a man named R. Gene Simmons, wielding two pistols, killed two people, wounded four others, and briefly held a hostage before surrendering to the police. The attack initially confounded local officials, but what they found next turned the shooting spree into a horrific nightmare. When police went to search the Simmons farm in nearby Dover, they found five more bodies—Simmons's wife, a son, their daughter and her husband, and a grandchild. The next day searchers found nine more bodies in a shallow grave and in abandoned cars near the farm, all relatives or former coworkers of the forty-seven-year-old man.[1]

In the ensuing investigation, police could find no motive for the mass killing, and Simmons refused to say whether he had committed any of the killings or why. Neighbors reported that Simmons had never been very friendly and often seemed hostile to them. Police also produced evidence that one of the dead children had been fathered by Simmons on his oldest daughter. After a psychiatric examination found him capable of standing trial, the state tried him on two counts of capital murder. The defense called no witnesses, and the jury took little more than an hour to reach a guilty verdict; then in a separate hearing it recommended the death penalty.

Judge John S. Patterson asked Simmons if he had anything to say, and Simmons requested that the sentence be carried out as soon as possible. He did not want to make any appeals, nor did he want any person or organization to interfere in his behalf; he asked that the governor set an execution date immediately.[2]

The trial ended May 12, 1988, and just as Simmons wished, the state quickly set a date for his execution, June 27. Despite Simmons's request, however, people did interfere. A few days before his scheduled execution, the Reverend Joseph Franz, a priest opposed to capital punishment, filed motions contending Simmons was incompetent, that his decision to waive appeals had not been a knowing and intelligent act, and that an appeal was mandatory. The Arkansas State Supreme Court rejected all three arguments, but a federal court in Little Rock agreed to hear arguments on whether the waiver had been a knowing and intelligent act.[3]

While the case awaited a hearing in federal court, the state put Simmons on trial in February 1989 for the other fourteen deaths. In the midst of the trial Simmons, who again offered no witnesses or testimony in his own behalf, punched the prosecutor, an act for which he gave no explanation. The jury found Simmons guilty of all counts, and recommended the death penalty. Judge Patterson set a new execution date for March 16. But one day before the scheduled execution, the United States Supreme Court issued a stay.

Jonas Whitmore, a fellow inmate on Arkansas's death row, had filed a motion contending that Simmons's execution would have negative repercussions for other prisoners under the death sentence in the state. Arkansas had not executed anyone for more than a quarter century, and Whitmore claimed that if the state were allowed to proceed, it could trigger a wave of executions. The state supreme court rejected the Whitmore petition,[4] which his attorneys then sent to Justice Harry Blackmun, who brought it to the entire court the day before Simmons was due to receive a lethal injection.

The Court heard oral argument in the case on January 10, 1990, and handed down its decision on April 24. Chief Justice Rehnquist, speaking for a 7–2 majority, held that since Simmons was competent and had made his wishes known, Whitmore had no standing to intervene in the case.[5] The court lifted the stay, Arkansas set a new date, and R. Gene Simmons finally got his wish. At 9:02 P.M. on June 21, 1990, Simmons received a lethal injection; doctors pronounced him dead seventeen minutes later, two years after he had pleaded with the judge at his first trial for a swift execution to "let the torture and suffering in me end."[6]

In most of the cases considered in this book, men or women have been struck down by age, disease, or accident, and they seek release from a condition they never sought and over which they had no control. In nearly all instances, society empathizes with them and attaches no stigma to their longing for death. But there is one group of people seeking death who have placed themselves in this horrible position and for whom society has little sympathy. These are the condemned prisoners awaiting execution on the nation's death rows.

There are currently over two thousand persons in American prisons under sentence of death. The vast majority of them want to live, and they and their lawyers will use the elaborate processes of state and federal appeals to delay execution months, years, perhaps indefinitely. For some on death row, however, the darkest fear is not execution but the prospect of living out their natural years confined to a six-by-nine cell, under constant surveillance, with little or no hope of regaining their freedom. For them death may well be preferable; they want to hear the executioner's song.

The United States Supreme Court in 1972 held that the death penalty, as then applied, violated the Eighth Amendment ban against cruel and unusual punishment.[7] The Court did not hold capital punishment as such unconstitutional. Rather the majority ruled that this ultimate form of punishment could not be applied arbitrarily and that there had to be rules assuring fairness, proportionality, and adequate review. Opponents of capital punishment, or abolitionists as they are known, had hoped that this decision would lead many states to abandon capital punishment, but in fact every state that had previously imposed the death penalty retained it, revising its laws to meet the Court's guidelines. In 1976, in the first of a series of cases, the Court approved Georgia's revised capital punishment statute.[8]

Since then there have been a number of executions, and within these there is a small group that is termed voluntary, that is, where the condemned prisoners cut short their appeals in order to hasten their punishment. These cases are unique in some ways, but within a broader context they raise the same right-to-die issues confronting terminally ill cancer victims or those who have been diagnosed with AIDS—at what point does death become preferable to life, and what role, if any, should the state have in making that decision?

The difference, of course, is that here the state and not some caprice of nature has condemned them to death. The state seized them, tried them for one or more crimes, and a jury of their peers found them guilty. To say that the issue for a condemned prisoner on death row is the same as that of a person awaiting death in a cancer ward may seem farfetched, and it is true that the issues of personal autonomy are different. But there are still questions of personal autonomy and of whether we, as a society, wish to acknowledge the humanity and the personal dignity even of those whom society, acting through the criminal justice system, has condemned to death.

This is not a book about the capital punishment debate, just as it is not a book about the debate over euthanasia. But we are concerned with a specific aspect of both issues, how the law treats those who, for reasons of their own, wish to die. Because this question cannot neatly or easily be separated from the larger debates, some of the arguments by both opponents and proponents of capital punishment must be heard. I am aware of the argument by many people that because of racism and other factors, the criminal justice system is seriously flawed in its treatment of capital crimes. Many authorities can be found who will argue that the system is so unreliable that we should never execute anyone because the chances are so great we will be taking the life of an innocent person.[9]

Given the broader implications of this debate, the effort by some prisoners to abort the appeals process raises not only legal but moral questions as well; indeed, some opponents of capital punishment argue that there is no legal or moral right to terminate appeals because this leads to state-abetted suicide. Advocates of the death penalty, of course, do not consider it an issue, while abolitionists often find it an embarrassing dilemma.[10] I would argue that so long as capital punishment is maintained, the same legal and moral justifications that support a right to die in general ought to apply to competent prisoners. They should be allowed to die.

Although there have been very few such cases, in general the law supports the right of a prisoner to terminate appeals if the person is currently competent and knowingly and voluntarily undertakes that course. The leading case is that of Gary Mark Gilmore, the first person executed in the United States after the Supreme Court reinstated the death penalty in 1976. Gilmore had been tried and convicted for the murder of a gas station attendant during a holdup.

As Chief Justice Warren Burger noted: "This case may be unique in the annals of the Court. Not only does Gary Mark Gilmore request no relief himself, but on the contrary, he has expressly and repeatedly stated since his conviction in the Utah courts that he had received a fair trial and had been well treated by the Utah authorities. Nor does he claim to be innocent of the crime for which he was convicted. Indeed, his only complaint against Utah or its judicial process . . . has been with respect to the delay on the part of the State in carrying out the sentence."[11]

Gilmore not only sought death, but carried on his campaign with the help of a literary agent and a media eager to exploit this unusual story.[12] "Don't the people of Utah have the courage of their convictions?" he asked in a letter to the Utah Supreme Court. "You sentenced a man to die—me—and when I accept this most extreme punishment with grace and dignity, you, the people of Utah want to back down and argue with me about it. You're silly. Look, I am sane, rational and more intelligent than the average person. I've been sentenced to die. I accept that. Let's do it and to hell with all the bullshit."[13]

Actually, Gilmore did not have a problem with the state, which wanted to carry out the sentence, but with abolitionists who, after Gilmore rebuffed their efforts, persuaded his mother, Bessie, to file a next-friend petition seeking review of the case. A "next friend" is one acting for the benefit of an infant or another person who is either unable to act for themselves or who is not *sui juris*, a legal person. Unlike a guardian, who enjoys a legal status as the representative of the person under the disability, the next friend is not a party to an action, and can be self-appointed.

The U.S. Supreme Court granted a stay of execution on December 3, 1976, and after receiving responses from Utah and from Gilmore's attorneys, vacated the stay ten days later. In its brief order, the Court stated that it had been convinced that Gilmore had "made a knowing and intelligent waiver of any and all federal rights he might have asserted," and the execution could go forward.

As in the Gilmore case, it is common for one justice of the Court to issue a temporary stay of execution if he or she finds possible grounds to conclude that the prisoner, at some point in the trial, did not receive due process of law. This will delay the execution until the full Court can review the matter. If a majority then votes to vacate the stay, it will usually do so in a brief memorandum opinion. But the Court at this time was badly split over what to do with death-sentence cases, and instead of a short memo, four opinions accompanied the Court order.

Chief Justice Burger voted with the majority, arguing that Bessie Gilmore had no standing to file a next-friend petition so long as her son remained competent to assert his own rights. Justices Byron White, William J. Brennan, Thurgood Marshall, and Harry Blackmun dissented. Justice White argued that the consent of a defendant does not authorize a state to impose an otherwise unconstitutional punishment, and the legitimacy of the death penalty had not yet been fully resolved. Justice Marshall believed Gilmore incompetent in the light of a failed suicide attempt and dismissed the state's psychiatric evidence as inadequate. Justice Blackmun believed that sufficient constitutional issues existed to warrant a full hearing by the Court.

With the justices thus split five to four, Gilmore and Utah got their wish, and in the early morning of January 17, 1977, a firing squad executed Gilmore.

Although *Gilmore* has remained the most publicized of these cases, there have been others.[14] Jesse Walter Bishop, from the time police arrested him for a murder he committed during a robbery, attempted to waive one right after another. He told the Nevada trial court he wanted to represent himself, and after three psychiatrists pronounced him competent, he entered a plea of guilty. At the sentencing stage of his trial, he refused to allow court-appointed standby counsel to introduce mitigating evidence that might have led to a lesser sentence. Bishop even tried to abort the mandatory review of all death-sentence cases by the Nevada Supreme Court, but that only made the justices of that panel look more closely at the record; they found no error in the trial.[15]

At this point, just as in the Simmons and Gilmore cases, third parties attempted to save the prisoner despite his wishes. After the review by the state's high court, the trial judge relieved the public defenders, whom Bishop had consistently ignored, from any further responsibility. But, as Justice Marshall later characterized it, "referring to their moral and ethical obligations, they filed [a] habeas corpus petition against Bishop's wishes." Bishop appeared in person in district court and reaffirmed that he did not wish to pursue any appeals, and the local judge, while applauding the efforts of the public defenders to avoid what they perceived as a miscarriage of justice, nonetheless denied them standing. "Bishop is sane," Judge Joseph Sneed decided, "and he has made a knowing and intelligent choice to forgo his federal remedies."[16] Bishop went to his death on October 22, 1979.

The problem of the "meddlesome intervenor" comes up in each case of a condemned prisoner seeking execution of sentence, and the analogy to doctors trying to keep terminally ill persons alive, despite their wishes, is in some instances striking.

A former policeman and seminarian, Frank J. Coppola, had been convicted of killing a woman during a robbery of her home by beating her head against the floor in order to force her to tell him where she had hidden her money. Coppola insisted on his innocence, but after the Virginia Supreme Court had found no error in his trial and U.S. Supreme Court had denied review, [17] Coppola decided to drop his appeal. He was ready to die, he said, "to preserve his dignity and spare his family further agony."

Coppola then fired his attorney, J. Gray Lawrence, Jr., but Lawrence refused to accept. Lawrence believed that Virginia's capital punishment statute, which had never been tested in federal court, was unconstitutional, and that neither Coppola nor anyone else should be executed until the law had been judicially examined. Other civil liberties lawyers also wanted the appeal continued and suggested that Coppola's death wish indicated mental imbalance.

Less than thirty-six hours before the scheduled execution, Lawrence petitioned for a stay of execution in federal district court. At the hearing before Judge D. Dortch Warriner, Coppola, his head already shaved, declared: "I adamantly stand by my decision to seek execution, and it is my sincere wish that it be carried out." Judge Warriner rejected Lawrence's petition, and compared the efforts to keep Coppola alive to attempts to keep terminally ill patients from dying. "We are performing the legal equivalent of inserting tubes . . . into him so that we can satisfy the quite appropriate urge to save his life, not so much for the good it does the client but for the good it does us."

However, following Warriner's decision, Lawrence secured a stay of execution from Judge John D. Butzner of the U.S. Court of Appeals for the Fourth Circuit, who noted possible constitutional defects in the Virginia statute. Lawyers from the Virginia attorney general's office immediately flew to Washington to seek review by Chief Justice Burger, who had jurisdiction over the Fourth Circuit, and they carried with them a handwritten plea from Coppola asking that he be allowed to die. The Chief Justice then arranged a conference call with seven of his colleagues. (Justice O'Connor was out of the country.) Only Justices Brennan, Marshall, and Stevens objected to lifting the stay. Burger reinstated the sentence at 10:26 P.M. on August 10, 1982, and the state executed Coppola one hour later in the electric chair at the Virginia State Prison in Richmond.[18]

These and other cases raise both moral and legal questions, but the place to start our examination is not in the courtroom, but on death row itself. Doris Ann Foster is one of a dozen or so women currently awaiting execution, and she is confined to a small cell in the Maryland Correctional Institution for Women for stabbing a seventy-one-year-old woman to death during a robbery. She has put the matter quite bluntly: "Death is my only route to freedom." Foster has written to both the Maryland Court of Appeals and the U.S. Supreme Court asking them to ignore the efforts of her public defender to reduce her sentence to life. "If the court says you're guilty and you're going to die, why spend all this money to fight it? Let them carry it out. They will be satisfied and I will have peace." Continuing in a legal limbo while confined "is ruining my body and eventually would ruin my mind. . . . I have no desire to continue on in such an inhumane existence."[19]

Foster's attitude is not uncommon among condemned prisoners. Robert Lee Massie pleaded guilty to first-degree murder during a 1965 robbery and received the death sentence. Four times execution dates were set, and four times lawyers for the NAACP, acting without Massie's consent, secured stays, claiming Massie was mentally incompetent. Massie considered this on-again, off-again condition worse than death, and in a widely noted article asked:

"Would [Christ] condemn me to a four-by-ten cell year after year, giving me dates of execution, and bringing me from the brink of death each time the sentence was about to be executed? Would He subject me to this kind of mental torment? Since we all know He would not participate in these atrocities, then how are Christians able to justify the laws which permit such inhumanity to man? If you are adherents to the Mosaic law, which advocates 'an eye for an eye and a tooth for a tooth,' then my question is: Would Moses subject me to years of mental torment before putting me to death? I did not confine my victim for years in prison under the constant threat of death before killing him, so why is it being done unto me?"[20]

Following the *Furman* decision in 1972, Massie received another reprieve and was eventually paroled. He then committed another robbery and murder, for which he received the death penalty in 1979. Once again he asked the court to carry out the sentence, but lawyers convinced the court that Massie lacked mental competency, and he remains on death row, his case still unresolved.

The longtime warden of San Quentin prison, Clinton Duffy, acknowledged that conditions on death row had to be horrible: "The men of death row live in fear and hopelessness, and their thoughts are never off the glass-walled enclosure that waits for them six floors below. This is not justice but torture, and no court in the land will deliberately sentence a defendant to that."[21] Even before the *Furman* decision focused attention on capital punishment, the horrible conditions in some state prisons led researchers to conclude that confinement on death row produced mental suffering that violated the constitutional ban against cruel and unusual punishment.[22] It is unlikely that courts will find confinement awaiting execution unconstitutional, because the long waits are often due to appeals initiated by the prisoners themselves, but there is no doubt that the very conditions inherent on death row can cause extreme mental anguish.

A number of studies document the stress faced by prisoners awaiting death and not knowing when or if it will come.[23] A few samples from these studies will give an idea of the environment these men and women face, week after week, month after month, year after year. Moreover, because of the special security requirements, death-row prisoners rarely mix with other inmates and are often unable even to socialize with each other. Their only company consists of prison officials, their lawyers, and occasional visitors.

A study of Alabama's death row found it "a prison within a prison, physically and socially isolated from the prison community and the outside world. Condemned prisoners live twenty-three-and-one-half hours alone in their cells, punctuated by thirty minutes devoted to private exercise in a closely guarded outdoor cage designated for high-security-risk inmates. Only passive recreation is available to prisoners on death row. The inmates try to fill empty time with exercise, reading, reverie, television, or conversation with their neighbors. Strategies vary. For some men, a tightly patterned sequence of private activities and accomplishments is required to reduce anxiety and maintain self-control."

As an example of how death row prisoners in Alabama pass their time, Johnson reports the following exchange:

PRISONER: "I have got so bored at times, I used to hook cockroaches together, sort of like they was a team of mules, to drag a matchbox around on the floor to pass time. I mean that may sound weird to you or somebody else, and it might be. Matter fact I just flushed a little frog down the shit jack the other day that I had back there. It came up through the shit jack. I kept him back there a couple of weeks and I kicked roaches and things to feed him. Just any little old thing."

INTERVIEWER: "Just to keep you busy."

PRISONER: "To more or less keep your mind off the damned chair and the things that you're seeing around you. Anything to occupy your mind."[24]

Given such conditions, which are apparently endemic to all death rows, it becomes more understandable for a California inmate to say: "I would rather go downstairs to that gas chamber than to have to spend the rest of my life here. Being free is being alive. If a person goes down to the gas chamber he's escaped. It is going to cost him his life, but he's escaped."[25]

Thirty years ago Jacques Barzun, one of the most perceptive social critics of our time, wrote a controversial article in favor of capital punishment, in which he argued that life in prison might well be a fate worse than death. To abolitionists who believed a life sentence preferable to execution, Barzun responded:

They read without a qualm, indeed they read with rejoicing, the hideous irony of 'Killer Gets Life'; they sigh with relief instead of horror. They do not see and suffer the cell, the drill, the clothes, the stench, the food; they do not feel the sexual racking of young and old bodies, the hateful promiscuity, the insane monotony, the mass degradation, the impotent hatred. They do not remember . . . that Joan of Arc, when offered 'life,' preferred burning at the stake. . . . For my part, I would choose death without hesitation. If that option is abolished, a demand will one day be heard to claim it as a privilege in the name of human dignity.[26]

Obviously not all or even a majority of death-row inmates would elect death over lengthy imprisonment, just as many people would opt for life in a nursing home or tied to life-support equipment rather than death. But the issue is the same: What is the quality of the life that one has? Barzun concluded that "I shall believe in the abolitionist's present views only after he has emerged from twelve months in a convict cell."

Death row is by nature nothing more than a warehousing operation, storing condemned prisoners until the appeals process has either freed them from the threat of death or run its course and delivered them to the execution chamber. One need not go as far as Robert Johnson, who argues that "a death sentence amounts to death with torture," to recognize the depressing and degrading conditions in these units. Perhaps locking them away in such an environment is fitting retribution for their crimes, more terrible in its severity than the finality of death. But that is not the punishment society supposedly has chosen. So long as imposition of the death sentence is permitted, prisoners should not be denied the opportunity of asking the state to implement its justice.

Gary Gilmore's lawyer summed up this attitude when he wrote: "Mr. Gilmore had sufficient experience of prison life to estimate . . . what it would be like for him to languish in prison. Historical, religious, and existential treatises suggest that for some persons at some times, it is rational not to avoid physical death at all costs. Indeed the spark of humanity can maximize its essence by choosing an alternative that preserves the greatest dignity and some tranquility of mind."[27]

The Supreme Court has never addressed the issue of suffering attached to the death sentence aside from the actual mode of execution, and that case came down in 1890 when the Court approved the use of the electric chair. Punishments are cruel, the Court noted, "when they involve torture or a lingering death; but the punishment of death is not cruel, within the meaning of that word as used in the Constitution. It implies something inhuman and barbarous, something more than the mere extinguishment of life."[28] Not until 1958, in a noncapital punishment case, did the Court hold that a person's humanity must be respected regardless of guilt or crime.[29]

Abolitionists consider capital punishment in itself violative of the Eighth Amendment ban on cruel or unusual punishment, but even those who favor the death penalty ought to concede that months or years on death row is for some individuals "more than the mere extinguishment of life." If one is going to argue that

even condemned murderers retain some spark of humanity, some
rights of individual autonomy, then one should also concede that
condemned prisoners may opt for execution.[30]

In order to hasten execution of sentence, some condemned prisoners must waive certain rights of appeal. In contrast to the
majority who want to use every opportunity the law allows in
order to stay alive (and very often do so successfully through
years of appeals), people like Gilmore and Coppola want to skip
that process. Although the Supreme Court has on a number of
occasions described the death sentence as "qualitatively different
from a sentence of imprisonment," the legal doctrine of waiver
in this area does not differ substantially from general rules of
waiver in criminal law.

Under early common-law doctrine, an accused person could
not waive any rights intended for his or her protection; this had
less to do with protection of the accused than with assuring the
integrity of the process. Later on, an accused could waive those
rights personal to himself or herself, but not those in which the
state maintained an interest. Today, an accused may waive any
privilege. This does not, however, mean that by waiving one right
an accused may insist on another; for example, waiver of a right
to jury trial does not imply a right to insist on a bench trial.

The key to waiver is the determination that the accused is
mentally competent to make such a decision, is aware of the
choices, and has knowingly made the decision. The law will not
infer a waiver of rights from a defendant's silence; in fact, every
reasonable presumption will be made against waiver. When a
defendant does waive rights, then the courts will step in to determine competency and knowledge.[31]

Once competency is established, a judge will seek to determine
that a waiver is voluntary, undertaken knowingly, and with an
understanding of the likely consequences. In a confession case
(which is a form of waiver), the Supreme Court set down the
following guidelines: "The ultimate test remains that which has
been the only clearly established test in Anglo-American courts
for two hundred years: the test of voluntariness. Is the confession
the product of an essentially free and unconstrained choice by its

maker? If it is, if he has willed to confess, it may be used against him. If it is not, his will has been overborne and his capacity for self-determination critically impaired, the use of his confession offends due process."[32]

Once a court determines that a person is competent and has acted in a knowing and voluntary manner, then the defendant must bear the consequences. The right to terminate appeals in death-sentence cases, however, is partially circumscribed because of the extreme nature of the penalty. The state's concern that so severe a punishment is not imposed arbitrarily or unjustly requires an automatic first-stage appeal that cannot be waived. Moreover, if at any time a condemned prisoner has a change of mind about appeal, various legal routes still remain open.

In all cases concerning competency and voluntariness, there is no doubt that judges pay close attention to these issues. In the case of Charles Rumbaugh, a convicted murderer protesting efforts by his parents to appeal on his behalf, the district judge conducted his own examination of the prisoner:

Q. "Is there anything you would like to tell us . . . about the testimony of the doctors relating specifically to the depression that they believe you're experiencing now?"

A. "Well, I don't feel I'm depressed now. I haven't been taking any medication for approximately thirty days. I was taking medication, an antipsychotic drug, and I haven't experienced any problems since I quit taking it. And I think I understand my situation very well and I believe my decision is a logical and rational one."

Q. "Are you anxious for some kind of resolution of this case one way or the other?"

A. "Yes. There has to be an end to it. You know, it's gone on and on for eight years and that's long enough."

Q. "And is it your desire at this time to waive your further appeals available to you?"

A. "Yes, it is."

Q. "And are you fully aware that if you decline to pursue your appeal and the Court finds that you are competent to do so, that you will be executed by the State of Texas?"

A. "I'm aware of that."
Q. "Is this a decision that you've come to over a lengthy period of time?"
A. "Yes it is."[33]

In this case, the court found Rumbaugh competent and refused to allow his parents to intervene on his behalf. In other cases, however, where there was even the slightest question of the defendant's competency, courts have denied waiver.[34]

For the most part, courts have not taken a defendant's desire to terminate an appeal as evidence of either incompetency or lack of understanding. Opponents of capital punishment, on the other hand, believe that prisoners should not be allowed to terminate appeals, and that a desire to do so is prima facie evidence of mental imbalance. The most common argument they put forward is that acquiescence in the sentence amounts to state-abetted suicide. For abolitionists, the death penalty is no less barbarous "on those occasions when a murderer welcomes his own legal execution" than when a prisoner is involuntarily dragged to death.[35]

Hugo A. Bedau, one of the leading opponents of capital punishment, has set out four arguments against permitting condemned prisoners to terminate their appeal in order to bring on their own executions. First, by terminating an appeal, a prisoner may be jeopardizing the lives of other death-row inmates because it might trigger a "national avalanche of legal slaughter." Second, this "death wish" should be considered "prima facie evidence of mental disturbance and, therefore, that others have a duty of care to intervene." Bedau's third argument is that even if a condemned prisoner had a right to take his or her own life, "it would not follow that he had the right to compel the state to take it for him in the name of punishment." Finally, although Bedau grudgingly concedes a right to die for those who are incurably ill, he denies a comparable right to those on death row because he does not consider them "terminal" in the same sense.[36]

Bedau's arguments do not, however, rely on legal principles relating to individual autonomy. Rather, they are an intuitive response to a practice abolitionists find intolerable, namely, that if they condone cases of voluntary execution, then their entire argument against capital punishment fails; one cannot selectively condone murder. For the abolitionist, there is apparently no middle ground; any execution by the state must be resisted.

If one takes a closer look at these arguments in the light of both legal and ethical considerations, their logic fails. First, ever since Gary Gilmore ended a ten-year moratorium on executions in this country, each new execution has brought dire warnings of a bloodbath. With so many people on death row, the nation would have to execute ten persons a week for four years just to catch up with the backlog. Despite a growing dissatisfaction with seemingly endless appeals, the courts have continued to insist on individualized considerations of each case, because the death sentence is different. Even Bedau concedes that the avalanche has failed to materialize.

The second argument, that the "death wish" is prima facie evidence of mental incompetence, has little factual or legal basis and, as we can see elsewhere in this book, may be the most rational response to an intolerable situation. For the abolitionists, however, if suicidal inclination can be labeled as incompetence, then prisoners could be prevented from dropping their appeals. Lester Maddox, while governor of Georgia, favored abolition of the death penalty; he commuted one prisoner's sentence to life imprisonment after hearing that the man, William Clark, had said he wanted to die. "He must be nuts," concluded Maddox. "Even animals want to live. I don't believe any person who has any sense at all would want to die."[37]

Even if one granted condemned prisoners a right to take their own lives, Bedau's third argument is that they cannot compel the state to do it for them in the name of punishment. Bedau is especially furious at Gary Gilmore and the media circus that surrounded his execution. But while it is true that no one can "force" a state to execute someone, logic dictates that if there is going to be a system of capital punishment, then the state, the public, and the condemned prisoner all must have a reasonable expectation that the system will act in some consistent manner.[38]

One response to Bedau's argument, although one he would not

accept, is Martin Gardner's suggestion that condemned prisoners be permitted the option of taking their own lives, perhaps through lethal injection. Gardner is not being facetious; he considers such an option more humane than the electric chair, hanging, or the firing squad, and consistent with the prisoner's human dignity and freedom of choice.[39]

Bedau's final argument seems most at odds with the general abolitionist view of granting human dignity to prisoners. If, as the abolitionists argue, capital punishment is an inhumane deprivation of rights as well as degradation of the individual, then why should death-row inmates not be allowed—if they themselves so choose—to accept their punishment with dignity. It is ironic that in the Gilmore case, the American Civil Liberties Union fought passionately to prevent the execution of a convicted murderer who wished to die, claiming that Gilmore had no right to do so. It then turned around and argued that a right to die existed for Karen Ann Quinlan, who could not express her wishes one way or the other.

The ACLU would distinguish between the two cases on the grounds that Quinlan's family, rather than a court, should have been able to speak for her, while its position in Gilmore's case derived from a principled campaign against all capital punishment. The problem, from the abolitionist standpoint, is that of line-drawing. If you oppose capital punishment, then for the sake of both principle and consistency, you have to oppose it in every instance, even if it does, at times, create inconsistencies. Because of the great chance of error, abolitionists are willing to impose some limits on individual autonomy in order to avoid the greater evil they see in the death penalty.[40]

One can infer from Bedau that although society may not exact retribution from convicted murderers by taking away their lives through execution, they may punish them by locking them away for life and denying them a right to die, no matter how terrible the conditions of imprisonment. But these conditions are such that for some the electric chair or the lethal injection may provide release, just as the removal of life-support systems may provide release for the terminally ill from another kind of intolerable situation.

*   *   *

To the abolitionists, waiver of appeals equates to state-abetted suicide. For some prisoners, the atmosphere on death row has proven more than they could bear, and they have bypassed the system to take their own lives. A short time before he overdosed on antidepressant pills that he had been hoarding, Alexander Bowling, a condemned murderer on Kentucky's death row, wrote to his attorneys: "Being alive means nothing if there's nothing in your life to do. You have to have something in your life to look forward to each day."[41]

In his study of Alabama's death-row population, Robert Johnson found this imagery pervasive, with many prisoners characterizing their existence as a living death, and themselves as the living dead. Even a reprieve with commutation to life is not always attractive because it usually does not include a chance of parole. "If it's either living in prison or dying in that chair, I'm going to go ahead and be exterminated. There ain't no way I'm going to die in a penitentiary, unless they execute me." Even if they retain a chance at parole, many current inmates would be fifty or sixty years old before they would get out of prison. "Don't make no sense to get out then. What you gonna be able to do to make a livin'? Might want to kill myself then anyway. . . . It's better off all the way around to get it over with than it is to go out there."[42]

If we assume that voluntarily going to one's execution is a form of suicide, we can attempt to evaluate it within the framework that Beauchamp and Childress have suggested, and that we have used elsewhere in this book: autonomy, human worth, and utility.

Autonomy For the prisoner, convicted and condemned by society and restrained in a tiny cell with practically no freedom, the option of terminating appeals and being executed may represent the only opportunity to exercise any personal choice in order to affect his or her fate. For the abolitionists, this may be the most difficult aspect of the problem, for granting the condemned person the right to bring on death affronts their belief in the sanctity of human life.

What must be remembered at all times, however, is that the life involved is that of the prisoner; it is his or her life at stake, his or her personal autonomy, and not that of the abolitionist. The only argument that can be made is that a murderer, by taking the life of another person and denying the victim's autonomy, has invited retribution in the form of losing his or her own autonomy. Yet the abolitionists deny that such "an eye for an eye" rationale is consistent with the values of a progressive society or with the goals of punishment.

Human Worth For the condemned, the quality of life on death row has depreciated to nothing or little better than nothing. If we grant the terminally ill the right to die, it is because we recognize the distinction between being alive and living as free and autonomous individuals. We recognize that pain and suffering may reach a point where death brings release.

The problems in this area seem to be primarily with others: the abolitionists for whom human life is so sacred that none should be extinguished needlessly, or the lawyers who are faced with the express wish of their clients that appeals be dropped and yet who have their own commitment to humanizing the law and preserving life. In some instances there may be legitimate reasons to question whether the prisoner is mentally competent, but psychiatrists and others, as Glanville Williams has charged, "are too ready to assume that an attempt to commit suicide is the act of a mentally sick person."[43]

In the end, if the value of his or her life is of little value to the prisoner, do third parties, no matter how dedicated they may be to the sacredness of life, have a right to intervene?

Utility Unlike questions of autonomy and human worth, in this context, the desires of the individual may be balanced against the interest of others, including society, family, and persons affected by the decision. Yet it is just this concern for others that occasionally motivates the condemned prisoner. Frank Coppola, for example, wanted to die to end the shame and embarrassment he believed his family suffered because of his trial and incarceration. And there are those prisoners who believe they should accept their punishment in order to pay their debt to society and thus obtain absolution and forgiveness of sins.

Richard Hager, an Oklahoma inmate seeking execution, told a reporter: "I believe in Jesus Christ. In the last two, two and a half months, I've found something that's beyond words. It's brought a real peace to me. And it's brought a lot of peace to the other four men on Death Row. We've had something really fantastic happen back there. We're all pretty well behind it now. I tell you, Jesus Christ walked Death Row." For Hager and others, the walk to the electric chair is "the road to Glory Row" and expiation of their sins.[44]

For whatever reason a prisoner wants to die, there is no question that the state has an interest that overrides individual will. Above all, when imposing the death penalty there is need to be sure that no mistakes have been made, both for the sake of the condemned person and for society. Each case must be looked at individually, yet within a standardized context so that we can be sure that all are treated on an equal basis.

But once the appeals have been made, once the state is assured that justice has been done in a fair and equitable manner, then the state may well claim it has met its obligations. If a prisoner then wishes, further appeals may be taken, just as people with terminal illnesses may continue to seek new drugs in hope of a cure. But just as we respect a sick person's wish to be left alone, so regard for individual autonomy requires that the choice of the condemned also be respected.

There is one final argument put forward by the abolitionists, that the death penalty might be imposed by mistake and an innocent person executed for a crime he or she did not commit.[45] What if such a person, believing there is no hope for rectifying the error and confronted by the hopelessness of prison life, elects to terminate the appeal and accept death? Jack Potts, convicted of capital murder, had determined not to pursue his appeals and was less than thirteen hours from death when his girlfriend persuaded him to change his mind. Two years later, a federal judge ruled that the sentencing phase of his trial had been flawed.[46] Although the ruling upheld the guilt determination so that one cannot argue Potts's innocence, here we have a case in which the imposition of the death sentence seems to have been an error. Abolitionists would argue that even one such mistake undermines the integrity of the entire judicial system and the only means to rectify the error is to do away with the death penalty. Failing that, every prisoner should, voluntarily or involuntarily, take the appeals to the ultimate limit to defeat the death sentence.

No system is foolproof, and errors will creep in no matter how hard we try to avoid them. But should the possibility of error be balanced against all other values, or should it be considered as one of several values that must be weighed? Sanctity of life is an important—some would say the highest—value, but so is the need of society to punish those who break the social contract and deprive others of their lives. Life is important, but so is respect for individual autonomy, even if that leads to the extinguishment of one's own life. After the state takes all possible precautions to avoid error and protect the interests of society, the final decision on whether to appeal or not, to try to prolong life on death row or to bring an end and release, should be left to one person—the person whose life is at stake.

In the case of Jesse Bishop, whose public defenders tried to carry on an appeal against his wishes, federal judge Joseph T. Sneed summed up the entire case quite well: "Bishop is an individual who, for reasons I can fathom only slightly, has chosen to forgo his federal remedies. Assuming his competence, which on this record I must, he should be free to so choose. To deny him that would be to incarcerate the spirit—the one thing that remains free and which the state need not and should not imprison."[47]

CHAPTER FIVE

Baby Doe

Like countless other young couples, they could hardly wait for the birth of their first child. But shortly after the woman delivered on October 11, 1983, their joy became despair. Doctors informed the parents that their new daughter had not one but multiple serious birth defects. She suffered from spina bifada (an open spinal column), excess fluid on the brain, an overly small skull, and other problems.

Medical science could help alleviate the problems associated with some of these defects, but not the others.[1] The doctors told the parents that surgeons could join the spine and drain some of the excess fluid from the brain. Without these two operations, their baby probably would die within two years; with the operations, she might live into her twenties. But, they added, even with the surgery she would be severely retarded, epileptic, bedridden, and in much pain. The parents did not have to decide at that moment, the doctors said. Their infant was receiving the best medical treatment possible and no nursing staff could possibly provide more compassionate care than that at the University Hospital at Stony Brook, New York.

Mr. and Mrs. A., as they would be known, sought other medical opinions, but all the doctors confirmed the initial prognosis. They also spoke with social workers and clergy and, after much soul-searching, they decided not to permit the operations. If possible, they would bring their infant daughter home and care for her, but they would not impose a life of pain and suffering on the child.

The story up until this point, while tragic, is unfortunately one that a number of parents have faced,[2] and their decisions have varied depending upon the severity of the child's problems, their own religious beliefs, and their faith in their doctors. Those decisions and sorrows have for the most part been private; Mrs. and Mrs. A., however, found their case and the future of their daughter (now to be known in legal and press circles as Baby Jane Doe) at the heart of a wrenching political and legal debate over what level of care, if any, should be extended to babies born with such severe physical and mental defects.

Shortly after the couple had made their decision, someone in the hospital informed a conservative group called Birthright, which in turn contacted A. Lawrence Washburn, a Vermont attorney and antiabortion activist. Washburn did not notify any of the state or local child-protective agencies but instead went straight to court, claiming that the child was already in deadly peril. According to Howard Oaks, the vice president for health sciences at Stony Brook, a man identifying himself as a judge, followed by an entourage that included Washburn, showed up at the hospital on a Saturday afternoon, and ordered hospital officials to appear in his court the following Tuesday with the infant's medical records and to show cause why he should not appoint a guardian for the child.[3]

Before the hospital could respond, another judge, Melvyn Tanenbaum of the New York Supreme Court, announced that he had jurisdiction and had already appointed attorney William Weber as guardian for Baby Jane Doe. Despite its name, the Supreme Court is the lowest tribunal in New York's judicial system, and its judges are elected. Tanenbaum had been elected to the court largely through the efforts of right-to-life organizations that oppose abortion, and his highly unorthodox actions reached out far beyond the accepted parameters of judicial conduct. At the hearing, child welfare officials testified in support of the doctors' diagnosis and defended the right of parents to make such decisions regarding the welfare of their children. Weber in turn denied that family autonomy extended so far as to give parents "the freedom to bring about their children's death by deliberate medical neglect." Tanenbaum ruled the same day, ordering the hospital to perform the surgery.[4]

The hospital appealed immediately, and the appellate court promptly overruled Tanenbaum's decision on October 21, 1983. The court found no reason to question the evidence of expert witnesses that "the parents' choice of conservative treatment, instead of surgery, was well within accepted medical standards" and "would not place the infant in imminent danger of death."[5]

The case marched rapidly through the state courts. The New York Court of Appeals, the state's highest court, unanimously affirmed the appellate ruling on October 28, and severely criticized Tanenbaum for "an abuse of judicial discretion." The court also termed the original suit by Lawrence Washburn "offensive," and characterized him as a man who had "no disclosed connection with Baby Jane Doe or her family." The failure of Washburn, Tanenbaum, and Weber to follow accepted law and procedures in this case had subjected the infant's parents, already "confronted with the anguish of a child with severe physical disorders," to unauthorized and unnecessary litigation. The United States Supreme Court refused to accept an appeal by Weber.[6]

At this point the public agony of Mr. and Mrs. A. should have ended. They should have been allowed to care for their child and to do what they could to make her life as comfortable as possible, without any further meddling by people like Lawrence Washburn. But the Reagan administration, which had courted anti-abortion groups during the 1980 election and then had ignored them, decided that the Baby Jane Doe case provided just the opportunity to repair its bridges with the right-to-life lobby, which equated nontreatment of disabled infants with abortion. The drama of Baby Jane Doe still had several acts to play, but before examining those events, we need to understand the law as it applied to the treatment of severely ill newborns.

Very few right-to-die cases have involved children, but there is a solid common-law tradition regarding medical care and decision making for minors that is consistent with the larger body of case law concerning adults. The basic assumption is that an infant or child, defined as anyone below the age of majority, is legally incompetent for purposes of decision making. A second assumption is the logical correlative of the first, that parents are "natural guardians" who will normally act in their child's best interests and who have the authority to make medical decisions for the child. As the Supreme Court noted:

> The law's concept of the family rests on a presumption that parents possess what a child lacks in maturity, experience, and capacity for judgment required for making life's difficult decisions. More importantly, historically it has recognized that natural bonds of affection lead parents to act in the best interests of their children.[7]

This common-law rule has been slightly modified recently to give minors a greater voice in such decisions. These exceptions, however, apply primarily to emancipated minors, that is, those who live independently outside the family, and to teenagers seeking certain types of care, such as abortion, and in cases where there is parental neglect or abuse. In general parents still have the right and the power to act for their children, and the rules are the same as apply to adults—rules regarding informed consent and the right to refuse treatment. Doctors are expected to give parents full information about their child's condition, as well as what medical options are available. Both state courts and the United States Supreme Court have held that parents, with certain exceptions, have a constitutionally protected authority to make such decisions for their children, including the right to refuse treatment.[8] So if parents do choose to forgo life-saving procedures, courts normally will require a heavy burden of proof from medical or welfare officials before they will impinge on parental authority.

Religious beliefs are the most familiar reason why parents decline certain treatments, and normally that does not raise legal issues. But when the children die or suffer serious illness or injury as a result of their parents' beliefs, the law will intervene.

In July 1990 Ginger and David Twitchell went on trial in Boston on charges of manslaughter. The Twitchells, both Christian Scientists, had chosen to pray over their two-and-a-half year old son Robyn when he fell ill. Robyn died after five days from a bowel obstruction, a condition that doctors could have treated. A spokesman for the Christian Science Church, Nathan Talbot, claimed that the prosecution was really an attack on the religion, which believes in healing through faith. "We have never asked for the right to neglect children," Talbot said. "We have asked for the right to practice spiritual healing. That for us is what the free exercise of religion is all about." A jury of eight women and four men deliberated two days before bringing in a verdict of guilty, and it was the latest in a growing series of prosecutions and convictions of Christian Science parents whose adherence to the teachings of their religion lead to the death or critical illness of their children.

The issue raises two troubling questions. One is the problem of free exercise of religion, guaranteed by the First Amendment, and the other is the extent of parental authority. Both claims have been limited by courts and by statute under the notion of *parens patriae*, the police power of the state to intervene on behalf of the welfare of children. But it is one thing to intervene ahead of time, in order to require an operation or a blood transfusion against the parents' wishes; it is another to prosecute parents for manslaughter or child abuse after the fact.[9]

How is this different from saying that parents ought to have the right to determine appropriate medical treatment for seriously ill newborns? There would be no prosecution if the parents of a severely ill newborn decided to pray for its recovery and the child died. Nor would there be a prosecution for parents who declined medical treatment on nonreligious grounds. Should not the same argument for autonomy made throughout this book apply to people with strong religious beliefs?

The answer is *yes* for themselves. If Christian Scientists or adult members of any other faith that believes in spiritual healing want to forego medical treatment, that choice should be theirs alone. But in terms of children who could be saved from serious illness or death, the answer is *no*. In this instance the state has a legitimate reason to interfere.

The problem is obvious. Why should the state interfere when the child is healthy, but not when the child is born with a terrible problem that threatens not only life itself but the quality of future life should the infant survive? Do we value one type of life more than another? Aren't all lives sacred and worth saving? If we start by saying that one type of life is not as worthy as another, is this

the same slippery slope we saw the eugenicists of the 1920s and
then the Nazis traverse?

The answer, perhaps regrettably, is that society and individuals
do value some lives more than others. Critics who claim this is
wrong have strong arguments on their side, but the fact remains
that the law, and social norms, give greater weight to saving the
lives of those who are healthy than those who are terribly ill.
Perhaps logically and religiously one could argue that the lives
of Robyn Twitchell and Baby Doe are both equal, but that is not
the case in our society, an attitude that is reflected in the law.

Other than the special case of newborns, there is limited litigation where parents have argued that life-support equipment
should be turned off so that children in a hopeless condition could
die. One reason may be that parental authority is normally so
clearly accepted in these matters that hospitals or doctors rarely
oppose such decisions. Courts have held that children have the
same right to forgo life-sustaining treatment as adults, even
though that substantive right may have to be exercised for them
by their parents. When a child is terminally ill, the Massachusetts
high court noted, "the question is not of life or death but the
manner of dying," and parental decisions override any interest of
the state.[10] If a child is in a persistent vegetative state, parents
also have a greater interest than the state in determining whether
to terminate treatment.[11] (Thus if Mary Beth Cruzan had been a
minor, courts would have accepted her parents' decision; but
because she was of age, they no longer had the authority, at least
under Missouri law, to make those decisions for her.)

It should not be inferred, however, that parents have an unlim-
ited right to make medical decisions for their children. The state,
and courts themselves, may under certain conditions circum-
scribe parental authority. Although it is not a precise standard,
the assumption is that parental decisions will always be mea-
sured by the best interest of the child.

But what is the best interest of a newborn, one who has been
born with severe physical or mental disabilities? Should parents
alone be allowed to make life-or-death decisions for them, or can
outsiders interfere on the grounds that death is never in the best

interests of a child? Do the rights associated with individual and family autonomy come into conflict with the powers of the state in matters of neonatal euthanasia?

Critics of Mr. and Mrs. A termed their decision "infanticide," calling to mind the practice of ancient Greece and many other cultures of exposing unwanted newborns and letting them die from the elements and neglect or even of actively killing them.[12] In part, exposure represented one manner of dealing with sickly or malformed children who might be a burden not only to the family but to society as well. Even in the absence of such practices, until recently medicine did not have the means to treat infants such as Baby Jane Doe; they would have died within a short period of time, and about all the parents or doctors could do was to make their brief lives as pain-free as possible.

With the amazing leaps in medical science in the last quarter century, a whole new range of questions has arisen for which there are no simple ethical or even medical answers. If doctors can save the lives of severely impaired children, for what kind of future are they saving them? If, of course, one sees any life as sacred, then the fact that a person is physically or mentally retarded makes no difference. But if one believes that life is valuable only if it has some minimal level of quality to it, that at the least a person must be able to function physically and mentally so as to interact with others and derive some satisfaction from life, then a whole other set of imperatives comes into operation.

The decision that Mr. and Mrs. A. made, to allow their baby to die, is, and was, not that uncommon. Doctors will privately admit that they have allowed severely disabled infants to die, usually through acts of omission—they did not order certain procedures, they did not administer certain medicines, they withheld nutrition. Sometimes they did this unilaterally, without consulting the parents, so as to spare them the pain; in other instances parents and doctors reached the decision jointly. With the development of sophisticated testing procedures within the last decade, it is now possible to identify whether a fetus has congenital defects and, as a result, for the mother to choose to abort the pregnancy. While this issue is certainly related to the problem of neonatal euthanasia, it is also one of the divisive questions in the debate over abortion in general.

Just how common these practices were became known with the publication in 1973 of two articles in the same issue of the highly respected *New England Journal of Medicine*.[13] According to one study, one-third of the deaths in a special-care nursery over a thirty-month period resulted from withholding treatment. Other studies a few years later indicated that doctors rarely went against parental wishes, even to treating correctable problems in newborns with Down's syndrome.*

In 1977 Anthony Shaw suggested that objective criteria might be developed to assist in determining which disabled infants should be treated and which allowed to die. Shaw suggested a formula, $QL = NE \times (H + S)$, the "quality of life" equals "natural endowment" multiplied by the "contributions of the home" together with the "contributions of society." The factors would include the parents' intellectual and financial resources, the child's potential to live without a wheelchair, availability of specific social services and suspected mental retardation. Later that year a medical team at the Oklahoma Children's Hospital began testing Shaw's theory on babies with spina bifida. In the next five years, all of the twenty-four infants who, with their parents' consent, had been marked as not worth saving, had treatment withheld and died, while of the thirty-six the doctors did treat, all but one lived, and that one died in an automobile crash.[14] Other doctors have written about "managing" the severely disabled, with treatment withheld from those showing the least promise of enjoying anything resembling a normal life. "If physicians are going to play God," Paul Ramsey commented, "let us hope they play God as God plays God."[15]

At the heart of the issue is a question of worth, human worth, and a number of studies indicate that doctors and other health

---

*Down's syndrome, or what many people call "mongolism," is a congenital defect characterized by an extra chromosome 21, which can cause mental retardation, abnormal physical structure (including slanting eyes and a small round head flattened at the back), as well as other anomolies such as repairable defects in the heart and esophagus. In England, common medical practice as late as 1985 was to let Down's syndrome infants die.

care professionals do not place as high a value on children with severe mental and physical defects as they do on healthy infants. When there are multiple problems, doctors may recommend forgoing potential life-saving procedures if the other maladies diminish the quality of life. Alan Meisel notes the not-uncommon practice that when a child is born with life-threatening but correctable problems, such as esophageal atresia (an esophagus that does not connect to the stomach and therefore prevents the child from receiving food), the doctors will recommend against the operation if other problems, such as Down's syndrome, are present.[16] The parents of such an infant, who are usually in a state of shock, may often be unaware of what treatments are available or of what support may exist for them or for their child.[17]

Until the 1970s relatively few of these problems reached the courts. Early in that decade trial courts heard a handful of cases about whether medical treatment should be mandated. In 1979 a New York court considered a request that a guardian be appointed to authorize surgery for an infant suffering from myelomeningocele (a protrusion of a portion of the spinal cord and its enclosing membrane through a bone defect in the vertebral column). The parents had refused treatment and said they would "let God decide" if the child should live. The court overrode the parents' wishes on medical testimony that the operation would give the child a chance to lead a relatively normal life.[18] The next reported case was that of Baby Jane Doe, and then, with public attention growing, so did the number of cases.

In Florida a judge ordered surgery for a newborn with spina bifada, although even with the operation the child would still be partially paralyzed, incontinent, and most likely severely retarded. The parents, Albert and Jennifer Daniels, chose not to appeal the ruling, but as Mrs. Daniels said, "It's difficult for us to realize that we may be condemning our daughter to a life of surgical procedure after procedure."[19]

In a rather bizarre case, a Danville, Illinois, couple gave birth to Siamese twins, so joined that they could not be surgically separated. Robert Mueller, a physician, and his wife Pamela, a nurse, decided with the concurrence of the attending physician to allow the infants to starve to death. An anonymous complaint,

however, led the state to investigate, and Illinois officials filed a
negligence complaint and then took custody of the twins. At the
hearing family court judge John P. Meyer recognized the anguish
of the Muellers, but nonetheless declared:

> The juvenile court does not make philosophical judgments.
> The juvenile court must follow the constitutions of Illinois and
> the United States, each of which contains a Bill of Rights. The
> bills of rights give even to newborn Siamese twins with severe
> abnormalities the inalienable right of life.

Illinois later filed criminal charges against the parents and the
doctors for conspiracy to commit murder and endangering the
life and welfare of children. The twins survived, and when what
had been thought to be a fatal heart problem in one of the twins
improved, the state dropped the criminal charges, and the Muellers took the children home.[20]

But these are isolated cases, and while the law regarding children parallels that of adult decision making, there have been too
few decisions about children to develop the relatively mature
doctrines concerning adults that emerged between the Quinlan
and Cruzan cases. Most doctors and lawyers who work in this
field recognize the difficulty in trying to establish guidelines
for deciding when it is appropriate or inappropriate to withhold
treatment. Surgeon General C. Everett Koop, testifying before
Congress in 1984, emphasized that infants may be born with
problems that are not medically correctable. These babies face
imminent death, and nothing is to be gained by prolonging their
dying. But, Koop said, "We seek to guarantee that infants who
would live, given ordinary care, will not be denied the opportunity for life by those who would decide that their lives are not
worth living."[21]

But the Reagan administration did, in fact, want to remove the
decision-making power from parents and doctors, and to impose
bureaucratic rules, all in the name of preserving life. "We are
trying to protect the lives of a small group of newborns," declared
Surgeon General Koop in defending the policy, "whose civil rights

may be abrogated because somebody doesn't like the quality of life they may have."[22] Three cases in the early 1980s provided the springboard for the administration's plans.

First came the so-called "Baby Doe" case in April 1982. The baby had Down's syndrome and a malformed esophagus, which needed repair if food were to reach the stomach. After conferring with their obstetrician, the parents declined to have the esophagus repaired and also decided not to allow intravenous feeding, so that the child would soon die from starvation. The father, a schoolteacher in Bloomington, Indiana, had worked from time to time with Down's syndrome children, nearly all of whom have multiple handicaps, and he and his wife believed that such children could never attain "a minimally acceptable quality of life." They also felt that it would not be in the best interests of the infant, their other two children, or their family to treat the baby.

But the hospital, upon learning of the parents' decision, sought a judicial opinion from Munroe County circuit court judge John G. Baker, who immediately scheduled an emergency hearing. Judge Baker heard testimony from one set of doctors that even if the surgery proved successful, the child's severe mental retardation would preclude anything approaching a normal life. Two pediatric specialists, however, while agreeing with the prognosis, nonetheless recommended that Baby Doe be transferred to another hospital and that the court authorize the surgery. In a separate hearing, Bobby and Shirley Wright, the parents of a daughter with Down's syndrome, offered to adopt Baby Doe, and charged that the infant's parents had neglected him.

The attorney for the parents argued that far from neglecting their child they were following the course of treatment prescribed by the doctor, namely, denying him food and water in order to save him from a life not worth living. As Dr. Owen testified, "Some of these children . . . are mere blobs. . . . These children are quite incapable of telling us what they feel, and what they sense, and so on."[23]

The court decided to let the parental decision stand, since they "have the right to choose a medically recommended course of treatment for their child in the present circumstances." However,

Judge Baker also appointed the local child welfare agency as the infant's temporary legal guardian to determine whether to appeal his decision. The welfare officials decided not to appeal, but the district attorney then filed a petition in juvenile court asking for an examination of whether the baby had been neglected under state law. The court denied this motion, and the Indiana Supreme Court dismissed his appeal as moot, since Baby Doe had died on the sixth day of his life.[24]

The Baby Doe case received a fair amount of newspaper coverage, and a month after the infant died, the Department of Health and Human Services (HHS), acting on direct orders from the White House, issued a notice on "Discriminating Against the Handicapped* by Withholding Treatment or Nourishment." In this notice, the administration declared that Down's syndrome and other congenital defects constituted handicaps within the meaning of Section 504 of the 1973 Rehabilitation Act. In a press statement, Secretary Richard Schweiker noted that "the President has instructed me to make absolutely clear to health care providers that federal law does not allow medical discrimination against handicapped infants."[25]

To back up this new policy, the department threatened to cut federal funding to any hospital that withheld nutrition, medication, or surgical procedures from any infant if: "(1) the withholding is based on the fact that the infant is handicapped; and (2) the handicap does not render treatment or nutritional sustenance contraindicated." In other words, unless the baby was so severely handicapped that medical help could do little more than prolong the dying process, then everything had to be done no matter how severe the birth defects, so long as the child could live.

Ten months later, a Boston television station aired a sensational series entitled "Death in the Nursery," that included a segment on withholding treatment from newborns. The series, produced by Pulitzer and Peabody award—winner Carleton Sherwood had a chilling and graphic portrayal of the abysmal care

---

* Although the Reagan and Bush administrations have constantly used "handicapped," that term is frowned upon by those with disabilities, who prefer the term "persons with disabilities."

provided in Oklahoma for those spina bifida babies chosen to die. The series also included interviews with physicians who vigorously defended withholding of medical treatment from handicapped infants. That same week, on March 7, 1983, HHS announced its new regulations. In every hospital receiving federal funds, a poster had to be displayed conspicuously in each delivery ward, maternity ward, nursery, and intensive-care nursery announcing DISCRIMINATORY FAILURE TO FEED AND CARE FOR HANDICAPPED INFANTS IN THIS FACILITY IS PROHIBITED BY FEDERAL LAW. The poster also listed a toll-free hotline number that people could call to report instances of suspected abuse.[26] The new regulations also authorized HHS officials to take "immediate remedial action" to protect such infants and required hospitals to provide access to the wards as well as records to departmental investigators.

Under the Administrative Procedures Act (APA), publication of a proposed rule by a federal agency requires a thirty-day period in which the public can comment. The department, however, claimed that the waiting period was unnecessary, since the new requirements constituted no more than "minor technical changes . . . necessary to meet emergency situations." Any delay, it claimed, would leave lives at risk, and "for even a single infant to die due to lack of an adequate notice and complaint procedure is unacceptable."[27]

The American Academy of Pediatrics, the National Association of Children's Hospitals, and several other groups immediately brought suit against the department and its new Secretary, Margaret Heckler. They sought a temporary restraining order from federal district judge Gerhard Gesell on March 18, four days before the new rules were to go into effect, on the grounds that the department had not followed the procedures required by the APA. Although Gesell denied the request, he did agree to an expedited review and said he would hear the case upon submission of written arguments and documents on April 8. Six days later, he ruled the new regulations invalid on exactly the grounds claimed by the medical groups—the Department of Health and Human Services had clearly violated the law. Judge Gesell, however, refused to rule on the substantive question of whether such a rule, if properly promulgated, would be either illegal or unconstitutional.[28]

Commentators generally agreed that the government had the authority to issue such rules, even if they questioned the wisdom of the policy.[29] So the department started again, this time paying attention to APA requirements; it also strengthened the rules. The new version called upon federally assisted child-welfare agencies to utilize their "full authority pursuant to State law to prevent instances of medical neglect of handicapped infants." The regulations also listed a number of medical conditions, explicitly not meant to be exhaustive, for which treatment could not be denied. After receiving comments on the proposal, the department made some minor adjustments and issued its new final rule on January 12, 1984.[30]

Even before final publication of the new regulations the government decided to apply them. After the New York Court of Appeals had dismissed the Baby Jane Doe case, a group called the American Life Lobby complained to the White House and to Attorney General Edwin Meese. At a press conference on November 2, 1983, Surgeon General Koop announced that the Justice Department would intercede in the case. When the University Hospital refused to surrender Baby Jane Doe's records, the federal government took it to court.

Federal Judge Leonard Wexler, a Reagan appointee, had been on the bench barely five months when he had to decide the thorny issue of when the government can override parental wishes. Surgeon General Koop explained that the administration was attempting to "hammer out something that will protect children and satisfy the medical profession." Antiabortion groups as well as advocates for disabled persons supported the rules, but medical associations and the New York Civil Liberties Union denounced them as an unwarranted intrusion by the government into family autonomy. Dr. Harry Jennison of the American Academy of Pediatrics charged that the Reagan administration "rode into office to take big government out of our personal lives and then commits the most flagrant intrusion."[31]

Wexler denied the government access to the records, although he dismissed the hospital's claims that a right of privacy as well as doctor-patient confidentiality shielded the files from governmental scrutiny. The administration rested its demand to see the records on Section 504 of the Rehabilitation Act, which forbids discrimination against the disabled and explained that it needed to see the records to make sure that a physically impaired infant had not suffered discrimination in medical treatment. Wexler ruled that Baby Jane Doe had not suffered from discrimination, because the "hospital has at all times been willing to perform the surgical procedures in question, if only the parents would consent." The parents had made a "reasonable" choice, and therefore the hospital had not violated the law.[32]

The Justice Department appealed the decision, and while the hospital put Baby Jane Doe (now two months old) on the critical list, a three-judge panel of the Court of Appeals for the Second Circuit heard arguments in early December. Judge Charles Metzner showed more than a little skepticism as he questioned the government's lawyer, Charles Cooper.

METZNER: "Are you claiming the hospital has discriminated?"
COOPER: "Absolutely not."
METZNER: "Then why are you bringing this action?"
COOPER: "To investigate."
METZNER: "Just because you feel like doing it?"
COOPER: "We have a complaint."

The problem, as the Justice Department failed to understand, did not involve hospitals refusing to treat impaired infants. The University Hospital had, as Judge Wexler noted, always been ready to do the surgery on Baby Jane Doe. But her parents had chosen not to elect that treatment, and as the president's own commission had reported, "parents should be the surrogates for a seriously ill newborn unless they are disqualified by decision-making incapacity, an unresolvable disagreement between them, or their choice of a course of action that is clearly against the infant's best interest."[33] What the administration seemed to be saying in its rules and in this suit was that any course forgoing treatment constituted illegal discrimination, a view borne out by Carl Horn III, a lawyer with the Justice Department. "We've conceded that a degree of medical and parental discretion is appropriate, but as a matter of principle there have to be parameters. . . . It comes down to a basic attitude about life."[34]

Surgeon General Koop, himself a pediatric surgeon for more than four decades, recognized that at times such a decision made medical as well as emotional sense. But he too wanted to keep that option very limited. "I am distressed that in an era of moral relativism," he wrote, "the life of a handicapped child can be forfeited to alleviate suffering in the family."[35]

On February 22, 1984, the Court of Appeals for the Second Circuit also rejected the government's demand for the records.[36] The court held that although Baby Jane Doe was a "handicapped individual" under Section 504, the requirement that a person be "otherwise qualified" to receive the withheld service did not apply to her. The court interpreted the law as applying in situations where an individual's impairment had no relationship to, and therefore was an improper consideration in determining, such things as eligibility for housing, employment, education, and transportation. In case of medical treatment, however, the disability most certainly related to the treatment decision therefore did not come under the umbrella of Section 504. Congress, the court concluded, did not intend Section 504 to "apply to treatment decisions involving defective newborn infants."[37] The Department of Health and Human Services, therefore, lacked statutory authority to investigate hospitals and compel them to produce records of individual patients.

Thwarted at still another step in the judicial process, the Reagan administration appealed to the United States Supreme Court, which accepted the case in mid-1985 and heard oral arguments in early 1986. The justices, at least during the oral argument, showed little sympathy for the government's position. Thurgood Marshall indicated that he thought the regulations intruded into the domain of state authority. Sandra Day O'Connor pressed the government's lawyer as to why HHS felt the regulations of fifty states to be inadequate. Under questioning by

John Paul Stevens, the government conceded that even if the regulations had been in place in 1982, the parents of Baby Doe would still have had the right to refuse surgery on their child. Bryon White wanted to know if the new rules interpreting Section 504 would have the federal government "looking over doctors' shoulders at treatment decisions."[38]

The Court handed down its decision in June 1986, invalidating the new HHS rules on relatively narrow grounds. The plurality ruled, as did the lower courts, that the regulations exceeded the statutory authority granted to the department in Section 504. The high court did not, however, look at the broader question of whether HHS had the authority to promulgate any regulations concerning treatment of impaired newborns, although the lower courts had implied that the agency lacked such power.[39]

The key holding of the majority opinion, written by Justice Stevens, found that the hospital had not withheld treatment because of discrimination, but because the parents had not consented to treatment. Discrimination by parents on the basis of physical or mental impairment is beyond the reach of Section 504 because "without the consent of parents . . . the infant is neither 'otherwise qualified' for treatment nor has he been denied care 'solely by reason of his handicap.' "[40] The federal government, the decision said, should not intervene directly in decisions by parents and doctors about treating seriously ill newborns.

Although the administration had attempted to defend the rules in the courts, it recognized that HHS did in fact lack specific statutory authority, so in 1984 it turned to Congress. Since protecting newborns, especially those with severe disabilities, appealed to politicians from both liberal and conservative camps, the drive for some form of legislation rapidly gained momentum. Proposals to redefine child abuse picked up endorsements in the Senate from liberals such as Edward M. Kennedy of Massachusetts and Alan Cranston of California and conservatives Orrin Hatch of Utah and Jeremiah Denton of Alabama.

Support for the proposal saw the unlikely coalition of civil libertarians, [41] disability advocacy groups and the antiabortion lobby. Jan Carroll of the National Right to Life Committee called on Congress for "a strong signal . . . that handicapped kids deserve nondiscriminatory care." She denounced the American Medical Association for allegedly refusing "to admit that a child has any rights apart from its parents. That is an untenable position."[42] It is also, of course, the link between opposition to abortion and opposition to allowing parental decision making in the case of severely ill newborns; if one grants one position, one must grant the other as well.[43]

The 1984 Child Abuse Amendments to the Child Abuse and Treatment and Adoption Reform Act of 1974, which passed both houses of Congress by overwhelming votes, defined the withholding of treatment from infants with "life-threatening conditions" as a form of child abuse or neglect. The law did, however, define five exceptions in which heroic measures might legally be withheld:

- the infant is chronically or irreversibly comatose;
- the provision of such treatment would merely prolong dying;
- treatment would not be effective in ameliorating or correcting all the life-threatening conditions;
- treatment would otherwise be futile in terms of survival of the child;
- treatment would be virtually futile in terms of the survival of the infant and the treatment itself would be inhumane.

More than twenty national organizations, including such groups as the Down's Syndrome Congress, the National Right to Life Committee, and the American Academy of Pediatrics endorsed the final draft. The American Medical Association, however, objected because the act failed to consider the quality of life a severely disabled infant might expect after treatment.[44] And some objections also came from people who were sympathetic to the act but who saw it as a slippery slope in regard to hard-won rights of personal autonomy. Alexander Capron, who headed the President's bioethics commission, thought it unfortunate that a law designed to enable people to get the medical treatment they want could be used as a club to force undesired treatment. Why not use the same argument in regard to treatment of the comatose or terminally ill? "By the stroke of a pen," Capron warned, "they can call [such a condition] 'handicapped' and the federal government could intervene."[45]

The amendments called for HHS to draft implementing rules, and after the criticism by medical groups and the court decisions about its earlier regulations, this time the agency trod very carefully. It refused, as some right-to-life groups demanded, to go beyond the strict mandate of the statute and, in fact, held that the rules were intended primarily as guidelines rather than as ironclad regulations.[46]

There is no question, however, that the new law does impinge on the decision-making process, and to some extent limits the discretion of doctors and parents in how they choose to treat severely disabled newborns. In the case of Baby Jane Doe, who was still alive when the amendments passed Congress, medical treatment would have been mandated, since her problems, although severe, were not immediately life-threatening and could have been somewhat ameliorated by surgery. As for this particular infant, whose first name was eventually revealed to be Keri-Lynn, after passing through a critical period, she grew stronger. Her parents, whose identity remained anonymous, then agreed to the operation to drain fluid and relieve pressure on the brain. They took their daughter home with them in April 1984. It is not known what happened afterward.

At the heart of the new scheme is the concept of "medical neglect," that is, treatment must be administered if the failure to do so would constitute "medical neglect." Withholding treatment in the five exceptions mentioned above would not be neglect, nor would withholding treatment if it could be justified as a "reasonable medical judgment." The rules require hospitals to establish "infant care review committees" that would evaluate individual cases. But the bill clearly changes the ground rules in that it assumes treatment must be given and shifts the burden of proof to health care professionals who have to justify withholding treatment.[47]

It also limits the discretion of parents. If parents choose not to permit treatment, as they did in the Baby Jane Doe case, and the doctors say that under the new rules they cannot withhold treatment, the doctors may not proceed unilaterally, but instead are required to report the case to local child-protective services. That agency could then secure appointment as the child's guardian in order to override parental wishes and authorize the medical treatment.

One suspects that in the case of severely disabled infants, doctors and parents might still elect to allow the child to die, because it would be possible to justify withholding treatment under a broad interpretation of one of the five exceptions. But in other instances doctors and hospitals, already reeling under the barrage of malpractice suits, will elect to recommend treatment or to refer the decision to the child-protective agency, thus protecting themselves from either criminal or civil legal action. So far, however, there has been practically no case law resulting from the HHS rules. In one suit, that of "Baby Lance," a Minnesota juvenile court judge initially ruled that a ventilator could not be turned off for a child in a persistent vegetative state, since that did not come under one of the five exceptions provided for in the law. At a subsequent hearing, however, the court reversed itself after a doctor explained that a persistent vegetative state did, in fact, mean that the infant was "chronically and irreversibly comatose."[48]

The intent of the law is humane, and given the advances in medical science in recent years, it is very possible that new treatment will, in fact, not only alleviate some of the problems caused by congenital defects, but in fact make it possible for these infants to grow up and to live normal lives. But the law itself makes no reference to "quality of life," a term that strongly offends disabled groups and antiabortion lobbyists. For them, life is so precious that no matter how disabled or retarded a person may be, he or she is nonetheless alive and that is, if not *all* that counts, at least the prerequisite for any of life's other blessings. In a 1974 case in which he appointed a guardian for a severely handicapped newborn whose parents had refused their consent to surgery, Judge David Roberts of Maine said that "the most basic right enjoyed by every human being is the right to life itself."[49] Life is very precious, and there are amazing stories of people with severe disabilities who have overcome them to lead not only productive but truly creative lives. But one must also wonder whether some of these infants will grow up, like Sherry Miller, to want nothing more than release from imprisonment in tortured minds and bodies.[50] Would they thank their parents or doctors for "saving" them? It is a terrible and difficult question, and the law, like society in general, has no easy or straightforward answers.[51]

CHAPTER SIX

Mercy Killings

Bertram Harper and his wife, Virginia, believed strongly in an individual's right to die. Both belonged to the Hemlock Society, so when doctors diagnosed Virginia Harper with breast and liver cancer, the sixty-nine-year-old woman decided there would be no surgery; she would take her own life at what she considered the appropriate time. But she believed she would need help, and her husband promised to assist her.

The couple lived in Loomis, California, and under that state's law, assisting in a suicide is a felony punishable by up to five year's imprisonment. Then they read about Dr. Jack Kevorkian, and while they would have liked to have used his invention, he appeared to be under court order not to make it available to would-be suicides. But, the Harpers discovered, Michigan at that time had no law specifically barring or penalizing one person from assisting another to commit suicide.

So in August 1990, the Harpers drove from their home on the West Coast to Romulus, a suburb of Detroit, and checked into a Comfort Inn. Virginia's daughter, Shanda McGrew, knew that her mother had been planning suicide, and flew out to Detroit on August 18, not to talk her mother out of the act, but to provide her and her stepfather with moral support and comfort.

The next day Virginia Harper took what she believed to be a fatal dose of a tranquilizer along with some alcohol. She also took some medicine for motion sickness, in order to dampen the body's natural tendency to react to overdoses of any medicine by trying to regurgitate it. She then pulled a plastic bag over her head. But the tranquilizer did not take effect soon enough, and Mrs. Harper began clawing at the bag. Her husband and daughter removed it, and then Mrs. Harper put it on again; this happened three or four times before the pills finally took effect, and Virginia Harper fell into a deep sleep.

"At this point my stepfather pulled the bag over her head and secured it," Ms. McGrew said.

"We waited. I have no idea how much time passed. She stopped breathing."

Bertram Harper checked his wife and then said, "She's gone." He then called the police to report his wife's death.

For his efforts to help his wife end her life, Michigan officials arrested Bertram Harper and charged him with second-degree murder. At the trial in May 1991, Wayne County assistant prosecutor Timothy Kenney contended that Harper had murdered his wife, and that he had crossed the line between assisting suicide and murder when he pulled the plastic bag over his wife's face and tied it into place.

"You have a seventy-three-year-old man who is likable and admirable in a number of ways," Kenny told the jury in Detroit recorder's court, "but what he did is unacceptable in the state of Michigan."

In Harper's defense, his attorney, Otis Culpepper, asked the jury to remember that his client had acted out of his deep love for his wife. "This is not a crime of violence," Culpepper argued. "This is an act of love."

The jury debated two hours and found Bertram Harper not guilty.[1]

There is indeed a line between assisting suicide and murder, but it is often hard to know where to draw it. The law holds that a person who takes an active role in causing another person's death has committed homicide.[2] It is one thing for a loving son or daughter or spouse to accumulate a lethal supply of painkillers or tranquilizers, or even to procure a gun, and then step back and allow the suicide to ingest the pills or use the weapon. It is quite another to pull the trigger. In fact, that was exactly the case in one of the most famous of recent mercy-killing cases, that of seventy-five-year-old Roswell Gilbert in 1985.

Roswell and Emily Gilbert had been married for fifty-one years, and no one questioned the retired electronics engineer's deep devotion to his seventy-three-year-old wife. Throughout their married life he had catered to her every whim; the two were inseparable, and he used to say that they fit together like spoons. In 1978 they bought a condominium in Florida, and then what should have been golden years turned to sorrow instead. Emily's mental state gradually deteriorated from Alzheimer's disease; in addition, she suffered from osteoporosis, a bone disease that caused her much pain. Roswell became her caretaker, brushing her hair and teeth for her. Since he still had a small business as a consulting engineer, he took elaborate precautions never to leave her alone for more than a day.

The couple's only daughter, Martha Gilbert Moran, suspected that her mother had Alzheimer's as early as 1982, but her father refused to confirm it, trying to protect her from the knowledge. The following year Martha took her mother out, "and it was like taking a three-year-old to lunch. She couldn't even read the menu. She ordered tuna salad but didn't eat it. I took Mother to the ladies' room, and she wouldn't come out. I walked in to find her looking in the mirror vacantly. Later that afternoon she said that she hadn't seen me in over ten years."[3]

By late 1984 Emily Gilbert rarely remembered who she was; she would wake up in the morning and ask Roswell if they were married. She was in such pain that she could not even go across the street to the beauty parlor to have her hair done. "In better days," her daughter recalled, "she would have crawled to a beauty parlor. Daddy used to put on her makeup."

On March 4, 1985, Ros Gilbert, a gun collector, put a single bullet into a Luger decorated with an American eagle. He came out of the bedroom, walked up behind Emily, and shot her through the temple. He felt her heart, which was still beating faintly, so he went back into the bedroom, reloaded the pistol, and shot her again. This time she died.

He walked out of the apartment into the hall and met their

neighbor, Elizabeth Phillips. "Libby," he told her, "I just shot Emily." Mrs. Phillips ran to get her husband, a doctor, but nothing could be done for the woman. Roswell Gilbert then called the police, and when they arrived, reportedly told them that he was an engineer and he had come up with a solution to the problem.

Convinced that his action was justified he refused to plea bargain to a lesser charge of manslaughter and decided to leave his fate in the hands of a jury. It was not that easy to get a jury in Broward County, which is populated largely by retirees. Many of the prospective jurors, pensioners themselves, had watched members of their own families die slowly and said they would find it difficult to return a guilty verdict. Finally, however, ten women and two men were impaneled in early May 1985 to hear the case of the State of Florida against Roswell Gilbert, on charges of first-degree murder.

Although neighbors and his daughter testified to his love for Emily and her deteriorating condition, Gilbert himself, never an emotional man nor one given to sharing his feelings with others, calmly and stoically told his story, declining to go into details about his wife's illness. He told the jury exactly the same story he had told the police, his daughter, and his neighbors at the condo. His beloved wife was suffering; she had begged him to let her die; he had to put her out of her suffering.[4]

"He didn't cry," said one observer at the trial, he "didn't pour out his feelings in soap-opera fashion." The prosecutor, Kelly Hancock, argued that Emily Gilbert "was not that bad off. She was able to eat and walk. She was not on a life-support system. She was a functioning human being." The killing, Hancock charged, was not an act of mercy but cold-blooded murder, and he asked the jury to find Gilbert guilty of first-degree murder.

Much to everyone's surprise, after four hours of deliberation they did. "We gave him charity on the first shot," one of the jurors explained. "He was upset and overcome psychologically. But it was the second bullet that did it. That was premeditated." Although one of the jurors told the judge that they would like to recommend leniency, under Florida's sentencing law conviction brought a mandatory life sentence, of which twenty-five years had to be served before the prisoner would be eligible for parole.

Almost immediately, Gilbert's friends and family began a campaign to have the sentence commuted. The conviction and what
seemed to many a Draconian sentence caused outrage across
Florida and in much of the nation, especially in the light of other
recent mercy killings. Two years earlier, in the same Broward
County courthouse, a grand jury refused to indict seventy-nine-
year-old Hans Florian, who had wheeled his sixty-two-year-old
wife, Johanna, out of her room at a nearby hospital and then shot
her in the head. Mrs. Florian had also suffered from Alzheimer's
and screamed continuously except when heavily sedated. In San
Antonio, Texas, in 1982, Woodrow Wilson Collums, sixty-nine,
received a ten-year probationary sentence after shooting his sev-
enty-two-year-old brother who lay helpless in a nursing institution.[5]

On August 9, Harry Gulkin, one of the defense attorneys,[6]
petitioned Florida governor Bob Graham for clemency. Under
state law, such a grant required three votes from the Governor's
cabinet. Graham announced he would support clemency, as did
Commissioner of Education Ralph Turlington and Secretary of
State George Firestone, but the other four members—Insurance
Commissioner Bill Gunter, Attorney General Jim Smith, Comp-
troller Gerald Lewis, and Commissioner of Agriculture Doyle
Connor—voted against clemency.[7]

Over the next few years, Gilbert's case would stay in the national limelight. In 1987 Robert Young played Gilbert in a made-
for-TV movie based on the case entitled *Mercy or Murder*. Lawyers attempted several strategies to have the sentence overturned,
but none succeeded. Finally, in August 1990, Governor Bob Martinez, who previously had opposed clemency, changed his mind.
One factor may have been that Kelly Hancock, the prosecutor at
the original trial, had visited Gilbert in prison and reported that
the then eighty-one-year-old man was in failing health. Gilbert
is now a free man, but the ethical and legal issues raised by his
case have not been resolved.

Both Bertram Harper and Roswell Gilbert committed criminal
homicide, which is defined in the Model Penal Code as "purposely, knowingly, recklessly or negligently caus[ing] the death

of another human being."[8] Harper and Gilbert, and others involved in so-called mercy killings, acted "purposely" and "knowingly." Whatever their motives, they set out to, and succeeded in, ending another person's life. One may believe in an individual's right to die or commit suicide, but the law views homicide in an entirely different light.

Homicides are not treated identically by the law; the person who kills another in self-defense is obviously not in the same category as the cold-blooded professional who has taken a life for a fee. The drunken driver who causes a death is different from the jealous wife who kills her husband in a fit of passion. The law defines different degrees of homicide, but it has no special category called mercy killing, and when a Harper or a Gilbert comes along, the prosecutor, the jury and the judge are often faced with difficult and agonizing decisions.

A crime has two basic elements, the *mens rea*, "guilty mind," and the act itself. Since about 1600, judges have defined common-law crimes as requiring some sort of intent as well as an illegal act to constitute a crime. *"Actus not facit reum nisi mens sit rea"* ("An act does not make one guilty unless one's mind is guilty"). A person who has no idea that his or her actions are illegal, or that they will injure someone or cause property damage, cannot be held to have committed a criminal act.

There are, of course, crimes that do not require *mens rea*, so-called crimes of strict liability. These are, however, statutory crimes defined by the legislature, rather than the traditional common-law crimes. One example is the carrying of a firearm or other weapon onto an aircraft; under federal law the act by itself is illegal, even if the person is unaware that he or she is carrying an illegal object.

There are, however, differing degrees of knowledge, and the law books are full of cases in which subtle distinctions have been drawn between "intentional" and "knowledgeable," or between "reckless" and "negligent." The different levels of mental state, or *scienter* as it is also called, determine what type of homicide has been committed. Criminal homicide constitutes murder when it is committed "purposely" or "knowingly," or "recklessly under circumstances manifesting extreme indifference to the value of human life," or when death occurs during the commission of another crime, such as rape, arson, or robbery.⁹ Murder is a felony of the first degree and may be punished by lengthy prison terms, life imprisonment, or the death penalty.¹⁰ When death results from reckless behavior, or from mental or physical distress for which there is a reasonable explanation, it is called manslaughter and is considered a second-degree felony. The lowest level of criminal homicide consists of deaths caused by negligence; negligent homicide is a third-degree felony.

ʃMercy killing is rarely a spontaneous act; it requires some forethought, some knowledge of what the results of the act will be, some intention that death come to pass. Bertram Harper and his wife planned what they would do; he knew that tying the plastic bag over her head would suffocate her; and he made several efforts before she finally fell asleep and he was able to secure the bag. Roswell Gilbert knew what firing a bullet into his wife's head would do; he deliberately shot her again when he found her pulse still beating after the first round.

Prosecutors dread these cases because of the high emotional fervor surrounding them. Many people think the defendants ought not to be on trial at all, that they should be commended for acting as they did. Their attitude is very similar to that of a woman who told me about her husband, who had been stricken with a cancer that left his bones very brittle. He fell and broke both legs, and wound up in a hospital with his legs in traction. Between the sickness and the traction, he was in great pain, and the doctors could do little but keep him highly sedated until he died. As she and the doctor stood at her husband's bedside one afternoon, the doctor turned to her in frustration at his inability to help and said, "You know, if this were a dog or a cat, I could put it out of its misery. But it's a man, and all we can do is let him die slowly and painfully." For this woman, Roswell Gilbert and Bertram Harper were not criminals; they were men who acted out of love for their wives.

Although the definition of criminal homicide is strict, this does not mean that the law has no flexibility. Most prosecutors, like Kelly Hancock, prefer to plea-bargain; if the person pleads guilty to a lesser charge, the state will not press for first-degree murder and will often recommend probation or a suspended sentence. According to the Model Penal Code, when "a homicide which would otherwise be murder is committed under the influence of extreme mental or emotional disturbance for which there is reasonable explanation or excuse," it is manslaughter, a lesser crime.[11] Nearly everyone can understand how witnessing the physical or mental deterioration of one's spouse could produce emotional disturbance, and while it cannot be forgiven outright, prosecutors and judges have sufficient discretion to mitigate the harsh penalties normally associated with homicide.

Juries also have discretion, and from time immemorial, one form of discretion has consisted of a grand jury refusal to indict or a petit jury refusal to convict.[12] In some states, juries may choose to convict for a lesser crime than the one charged or recommend a lenient rather than a harsh sentence. Our criminal justice system is based upon judgment by one's peers, and in many cases, people cannot bring themselves to condemn a person who has obviously acted out of love.

Juries also get upset when they believe that prosecutors are persecuting people rather than seeking justice. While alleged mercy killers must face up to the legal consequences of their acts, juries refuse to cooperate when they believe a person, even if he or she has committed homicide, has been unfairly charged. Witness the case of pathologist Peter Rosier, tried in Lee County, Florida, on charges of first-degree murder, conspiracy to murder in the first degree, and attempted first-degree murder, as well as several lesser criminal charges.

In April 1985 Pat Rosier had been diagnosed as having lung cancer; within a few months the cancer had metastasized to her brain and adrenal glands. There was no hope of recovery, and as her pain increased she decided to commit suicide. On January 14, 1986, she and her family, dressed in formal evening wear, shared a final farewell dinner in their Fort Myers home. At midnight she took a massive dose of Seconal, an amount that should have killed her. But hours later she was still alive and gasping for breath. Her husband desperately called several physicians trying to locate morphine, which he then administered to her and which, he believed, caused her death.

With her body cremated, there was little to connect Peter to his wife's death, but about a year later, he went on television. Pat Rosier had appeared on several talk shows during her illness to help other cancer patients and their families cope with the disease. After her death, one of the program hosts, unaware of Peter's role in her death, merely wanted him to come on and talk as a surviving spouse of a cancer victim. Instead Peter talked about mercy killing and his role in his wife's death. His "confession" led to a grand jury indictment on the three charges, and Rosier contacted Stanley Rosenblatt, a flamboyant civil attorney whom Rosier had spoken to earlier about a possible malpractice suit against a doctor who had misdiagnosed his wife's illness. At first Rosenblatt did not want to take the case, pleading that he knew little about criminal law. But the more he learned about the circumstances, the more incensed he became. So, too, did his wife, Susan, also a civil attorney, and in the end she joined her husband to form Rosier's defense team.

It seems that Peter Rosier had not killed his wife; that despite the Seconal and the morphine, she was still alive when he left her bedroom for a few minutes. During those few minutes, her stepfather, Vincent Delman, and her two half-brothers entered the bedroom; while the two younger men watched, Delman smothered her with a pillow. The Lee County prosecutor granted them immunity and they, as well as the physicians who provided Rosier with the morphine, were the chief witnesses against him at the trial.

Perhaps aware that the facts of the case would not impress a petit jury, the prosecutor offered to plea-bargain. But the least the state would offer was seven years in prison, and Rosenblatt, who came to believe passionately in his client's cause, would not settle for any jail time at all. Because the case had made front-page headlines, Rosenblatt secured a change of venue to St. Petersburg. During jury selection he posed a hypothetical scenario, in which potential jurors had to choose between helping an old lady from falling and putting money in a meter to avoid a ticket. He dismissed those who chose the meter. "We didn't need people who mechanically follow the law."

Just as in the Harper and Gilbert cases, the prosecutor kept emphasizing that the law is the law, and however noble and loving Peter Rosier's motives had been, that did not justify his breaking it. Under Florida law, according to the prosecution, Rosier was guilty of murder, even though the morphine he gave his wife did not kill her. Moreover, even though Rosier did not know of Delman's act, the two men were guilty of conspiring to commit murder.

Rosenblatt had originally lined up several medical experts to testify to Pat Rosier's pain and her desire to end her life before the cancer ran its course. But Rosenblatt, whose reputation in part rested on his cross-examination skills, tore into the prosecution witnesses with such effect that he and his wife decided to forgo calling any witness for the defense. That also gave them, and not the prosecution, the right to make the last statement the jurors heard before retiring to deliberate.

Essentially, Rosenblatt had two major arguments, first that Peter Rosier had not committed any despicable act, but had tried to help his beloved wife carry out her wish to end her life and the pain she suffered constantly. Second, he attacked the state's effort to make his client a scapegoat, even allowing the actual "murderer" to go scot-free, while piling three major charges and ten lesser criminal charges on his client. Rosenblatt led the jurors to believe the district attorney was seeking publicity and not justice, and the jury agreed. The jurors may not have approved of what Peter Rosier had done, but they liked even less what the State of Florida was trying to do to him.[13]

A jury also did not like what a Chicago hospital had done to Rudy Linares. His infant son, Samuel, had swallowed a balloon and had stopped breathing. Linares rushed the child to a nearby emergency room where doctors quickly removed the blockage, but Samuel remained unconscious, able to breathe only with the aid of a respirator. The doctors determined that lack of oxygen during the time Samuel had been unable to breathe had caused brain damage; they told the family that the child would never recover. For the next several weeks the infant lay in a hospital room, kept "alive" by the aid of the respirator, until finally Rudy Linares asked the hospital authorities to turn off the machine and let his son die a natural death. The hospital refused and, in effect, told him that they were in charge; if he did not like it, he should get a lawyer and a court order.

In fact, under Illinois law the Linares family had the right to order discontinuation of treatment, but Linares, a laborer, did not know the law or his rights in the matter. He pleaded with the hospital and was shunted from one office to another, and no one seemed to pay him any attention.

Finally, after nine months Rudy decided to release his son from the machine. He came to the hospital armed with a pistol, and holding off the staff, disconnected Samuel from the machine. Then he held the child in his arms until he died, telling the doctors and nurses he held at bay that he was doing this because he loved his son. After Samuel died, Rudy laid down the gun. Police arrested him, and the district attorney charged him with murder.

The charge outraged friends and neighbors of Linares, who immediately raised bail money to get him out of jail. A few weeks later, a Cook County grand jury refused to indict him.[14]

The law, if it is to have any meaning, must be consistent, and while motive is an integral part of a crime, good motives do not necessarily excuse bad acts. Bertram Harper's wife wanted to commit suicide; he helped her, and the law is vague in many areas as to whether criminal culpability results from such assistance.[15] But Emily Gilbert did not decide to commit suicide; it is questionable if she even had the mental capacity to consider such an option. There is a significant difference, both legal and moral, between Virginia Harper choosing for herself, and her husband making sure that her wish was fulfilled, and Roswell Gilbert deciding on his own to end his wife's life.

Is the Gilbert case different from that a family member who decides to end life support for a comatose patient, of which the Linares incident is only an extreme version? If there is a living will, the answer is clear; the choice had already been reached by the patient when he or she had been competent to make such a decision. But, if the patient had never faced the issue, had never drawn up a living will, had never indicated even in casual conversation what he or she might wish, then is there a distinction between pulling a plug and pulling a trigger?

Morally one might argue the case, but in the law there is a clear distinction, and there are proper procedures. In the absence of a living will, statutes in all of the states allow the appointment of a guardian to look after the patient's best interests. If, as is usually the case, the guardian is a close family member, then the law assumes that a decision to end life support will not be made lightly, and that the guardian will do everything to determine what the patient would have wanted to do had advance provision been made.

But when one person decides to take the life of another, when the victim is not in an immediate life-threatening situation (such as being on a life-support system or in a coma), and when that decision is made and carried out unilaterally, then the law considers that action homicide. The reasons why a person acted may and should be taken into account as mitigating factors. But for the present, in the eyes of the law, mercy killings remain murder.[16]

CHAPTER SEVEN

Advance Directives

Hilda Peter knew about hospitals, having spent much of her working life as a secretary at the Irvington General Hospital in New Jersey. She knew about patients on life-support systems and how modern medicine could fend off death; her mother had been kept alive by medication, and the prolonged dying process had been a terrible ordeal for the both of them. She wanted none of that, and told her friends repeatedly that if anything ever happened to her, she did not want to be kept alive by heroic measures or machines. She went even further and executed a power of attorney giving her longtime companion, Eberhard Johanning, the authority to make all decisions regarding her health care if she should become incapacitated.

In October 1984 Mr. Johanning returned to the apartment they shared and found Hilda Peter collapsed on the kitchen floor. He called a rescue squad, and although the paramedics were able to resuscitate her, she never regained consciousness. Once in the hospital, she remained in a persistent vegetative state, fed by a nasogastric tube. After it became clear that she would never recover, Johanning went to court seeking to be named as Peter's guardian, with the express purpose of having the feeding tube removed so that the sixty-five-year-old woman could die a natural death. Hilda Peter's only surviving relative supported Johanning in the petition and in his decision that the tube should be removed. The court granted his request, but on condition that he take no action without consulting with the state ombudsman.

Following the Quinlan case, New Jersey had created an Office of the Ombudsman for the Institutionalized Elderly, with the responsibility to see that no decisions were taken in regard to the treatment of institutionalized older people that might be against their best interests. The legislature agreed that while it might be best to remove life support in some cases, there ought to be some representative of the state who would look after the welfare of the elderly, especially those now incompetent to look after themselves.

On March 6, 1986, Jack D'Ambrosio, the New Jersey ombudsman, announced that he believed Hilda Peter "would not have wanted to be kept alive by mechanical means in a persistent vegetative state." However, in light of the state supreme court's recent decision establishing criteria for removal of life-support, [1] D'Ambrosio concluded that he could not permit Johanning to order the feeding tube removed, Moreover, when Johanning appealed this ruling, D'Ambrosio changed his mind, and declared that not enough evidence now existed to "prove" that Hilda Peter would have wanted the nasogastric tube removed.

The New Jersey Supreme Court reversed the ombudsman's ruling, and in three decisions handed down on June 24, 1987, reaffirmed the right of individuals to control their own destinies through the use of advance directives. According to Justice Marie Garibaldi, "the cornerstone of our analysis" is that a competent patient has the right to refuse treatment, and that right is not lost because of incompetency.[2] Medical choices are "private, regardless of whether a patient is able to make them personally or must rely on a surrogate. They are not to be decided by societal standards of reasonableness or normalcy. Rather, it is the patient's preferences—formed by his or her unique personal experiences—that should control."[3]

The court went on to say that its *Conroy* criteria did not apply, since in that case the patient had been conscious and capable of making a decision. Here Hilda Peter could not speak for herself, and whether or not she could live with the help of a feeding tube for months or years to come made no difference. She had expressed her desires clearly, and neither the ombudsman nor the hospital had any right or power to deny her wishes. The court granted Johanning his petition, and within a few hours the nasogastric tube had been removed, carrying out Hilda Peter's instruction.[4]

The reader must wonder why this case ever went to court. After all, Hilda Peter had made her wishes clear and had named a surrogate to make the appropriate decision. Why should the ombudsman have interfered? Why should it have taken months of litigation to permit what the court finally declared to have been her right all along? The answer is that the law in this area is still extremely new, a mixture of common law and statute, and it has changed with breathtaking speed in the last decade. Doctors, hospital administrators, state health officials, and even lower court judges are extremely wary of proceeding without great caution, to the point of near-paralysis in some instances. It will take time to sort out all the nuances of these developments, but one should understand that, aside from fear of lawsuits, caution is warranted because death is involved. Once a respirator or a nasogastric tube or any other kind of life-support device is removed, the decision is final. Death will occur, and that is irreversible.

Living wills or, to be more precise, advance directives,[5] are relatively recent phenomena,[6] arising from the development of modern medical technology capable of sustaining the bodily functions of people who otherwise would die. An Illinois attorney, Luis Kutner, is given credit for proposing a formal advance directive in 1969, although the idea did not immediately catch on.[7] Following the Quinlan case, interest in some form of advance directive grew enormously, and the growth itself created legal problems that took time to straighten out. Although many people think that a living will solves their problem, that may not be the case. It depends on the state in which one resides, the statutory and common law of that state, and the type of advance directive one has executed.

Although the phrase "living will" is in common use, such documents normally incorporate one or more types of advance directives. To understand how a living will may or may not apply in certain circumstances, we must first explore what the rationale is behind the instrument and what the different types of advance directive are.

The law starts with the assumption that each individual is the person best able to make decisions about his or her health care. In normal circumstances, a competent individual, informed about specific treatments or procedures, will make the decision as to whether to proceed or not. This type of informed consent, however, takes place contemporaneously with the need to agree to or forgo treatment. A person becomes ill or is injured, a doctor prescribes a certain therapy or perhaps an operation, and the decision is made. While the time frame may extend over a few days or even weeks depending on tests or the severity of the problem, for practical purposes all of the events happen contemporaneously.

Advance directives, on the other hand, are anticipatory. A person says, in effect, "Something might happen to me, and I might not be able to decide for myself what to do. In that case, if the following circumstances are present, this is the choice I would make if I could." The directions are contingent upon certain types of events occurring, and because one cannot anticipate the future, it is impossible to be entirely precise in the type of instructions one gives. Moreover, because such events may not happen for a long time, or ever, a person can change his or her mind in the interim.

In some of the cases testing the limits of advance directives, courts have said that for the directions to be effective, they have to meet the same criteria as those of informed consent. Future refusal of treatment, according to an Ohio court, "must satisfy the same standards of knowledge and understanding required for informed consent" by a currently competent person.[8] This criterion, fortunately, has not been widely adopted, since it would negate the effectiveness of nearly every form of advance directive. The purpose of a living will is to take precautions against whatever type of illness or accident might leave one unable to make decisions; informed consent requires a person to understand both the nature of the malady and the proposed treatment. How many people can predict that they will incur a particular type of debilitating disease or be injured in an accident so as to leave them in a particular helpless situation?

For such directives to be useful, both to the individual making

as well as to the person or persons charged with their
ation, there must be a certain generality, so that all of the
ed contingencies are included. At the same time, the directive
st not be so broad that it is unclear exactly what is desired.
Most judges have recognized this reality, and what we find in
their decisions are efforts to ensure that the wishes of the person
involved are accurately determined and then carried out.

There are several types of advance directive, some of which
may be very specific and others more open-ended. They may be
written or oral, and they may be made in pursuance of specific
statutes or of common-law decisions. A **living will** is the popular
term given to a written directive. It may be a handwritten letter,
or it may be a form, and such forms are distributed by a number
of organizations concerned with the issue. One typical form is
appended at the end of this chapter.

A more circumscribed document is a **natural death act directive.** Many states have now adopted some form of statute spelling
out conditions under which individuals may direct that treatment be forgone or stopped and requiring health care providers
to obey these wishes. In some instances the application of these
documents is limited by the terms of the statute; in other states,
there is little difference between the statute-based declaration
and the common-law-based living will.

While not technically an advance directive, a **durable power of
attorney** is often used to implement a living will. Although used
for many other purposes, a durable power of attorney is quite
helpful as a form for establishing one's wishes and for naming a
particular person to carry out these instructions.

The most effective form of advance directive is one that com-
bines a statement of the person's wishes with the naming of
an agent or proxy to be responsible for making the appropriate
decision. A statement of desire by itself may be useless if the
hospital has policies that require something more specific;[9] a
delegation of authority to a person without a statement of intent,
either oral or written, may place an intolerable strain on the
proxy if he or she has no guidance.

Because advance directives may take such a variety of forms,
health care providers are understandably cautious in their re-

sponse. We are not talking here of doctors who deliberately ignore the expressed wishes of patients, but of the fact that in a society as litigious as ours, doctors and hospitals must take every reasonable precaution to stay out of court. From a legal point of view, it is better for them to err on the side of caution, since delay in accepting an advance directive means only that death will be delayed; one can always terminate treatment following a court order. On the other hand, if they accept a directive that is less than clear, death is final, and no decision of any court can reverse that fact.

While there are many horror stories of arrogance and insensitivity on the part of doctors and hospital administrators, the trend is toward greater respect and deference to patient wishes. Nearly all major hospitals now have ethics committees that pass on the validity of advance directives, and they also have counsel to advise on the legal requirements. Doctors who have questions about advance directives and their personal liability in respecting them, can be reassured. It is the responsibility of both ethics committees and lawyers, however, to be cautious and to err on the side of life. From the patient's point of view, this makes it imperative that the advance directive meets all of the state's requirements.

But even when the advance directives are clear, the fact is that given the rapid changes in the law in this area, there are legitimate questions. Under what circumstances are such advance directives legal, in the sense that they are valid? When are they invalid? Who is required to abide by these directives?

The legal basis for advance directives derives from the same common-law and constitutional source as that supporting the right to die: the right of individual autonomy. Competent people should be able to make their own decisions, with substituted judgment permitted for incompetent patients. The basis of substituted judgment, as we have seen, is that the guardian or parent should attempt, to the best of his or her ability, to determine what the patient would have wanted, based on whatever knowledge is available of the person's expressed wishes, personality, and other evidence. Advance directives permit the surrogate to have a clearer and more definite understanding of the patient's intent.

A major concern, as we have noted throughout, is the question
of who decides. There is, however, a growing body of normative
legal precedent on the legitimacy of advance directives, and the
means by which they can be executed should the principal become incapacitated. In terms of statutory law, a number of states
have adopted so-called natural-death acts. California passed the
first such law in 1976 following the Quinlan case, in order to
head off similar litigation in the state as well as to legitimate
advance directives. Since then nearly every other state has passed
similar legislation, although the provisions vary significantly.
Missouri, for example, has such a statute, which also allows for
the acceptance of other forms of evidence. A central issue in the
Cruzan case was whether Missouri could impose such a heavy
burden of proof as to the intent of a currently incompetent patient.[10] Had Nancy Cruzan executed an advance directive,
though, the state courts would have honored it.

An advance directive that meets the requirements of the state
statute is valid and enforceable; at most, the agent named in the
document may have to go into local court and secure a judicial
order validating the directive, a relatively simple procedure. In
many states even this is not necessary; hospitals may accept a
valid document directly from the patient, his or her family, or a
named surrogate.

However, what if the directive does not meet the statutory
requirements? What if it is neither witnessed nor notarized, and
instead of following the language prescribed in the act, it is handwritten in lay terms? Here one has to rely on the common law,
that body of judicial decisions made in the absence of specific
and relevant legislation. The common law has been the means
by which society and the courts have kept the law apace of social
change, and this area has proven no exception. As Florida circuit
court judge George B. Hersey wrote: "Since man, through his
ingenuity, has created a new state of human existence—minimal
human life sustained by manmade life supports—it must now
devise and fashion rules and parameters for that existence. That
is the business this court is faced with. It is not an easy question
. . . [h]owever, it is a question that must be answered."[11] Moreover, the passage of natural-death acts does not replace the com-

mon-law and constitutional rights of autonomy, but merely provides a statutory means for their expression. Statutory law overrides common law, but it cannot negate constitutional protections. Thus, it might be possible for a state to prescribe that advance directives must take particular forms or that, as in the Cruzan case, that a certain level of evidence be produced as to intent. But since the Supreme Court held in *Cruzan* that a constitutional right to self-determination exists, a state cannot declare all forms of advance directives or substituted judgment illegal.

Whether a state has a particular law on the books or not, the right remains. The first case to test the validity of living wills—and one that remains the leading case on the subject—made that quite clear. It occurred in Florida.

In April 1981 an extremely ill Francis B. Landy entered John F. Kennedy Hospital in Palm Beach, Florida; within two days he could no longer breathe on his own, and doctors placed him on a ventilator. He continued to deteriorate and suffered brain damage; his doctor told his wife that no hope existed for recovery. Mrs. Landy then handed the doctor a piece of paper entitled "Mercy Will and Last Testament," which her husband had written out and signed, in the presence of two witnesses, on April 16, 1975. In it he specifically stated that "he did not wish to be kept alive through the use of extraordinary life support equipment such as a respirator." As recently as two months before he entered the hospital, Mrs. Landy had promised her husband that should he be hospitalized, she would make the "mercy will" a part of his medical record.

On April 23, Mrs. Landy went into probate court, which declared her husband incompetent and named her as his guardian; she immediately asked the doctors to turn off all life-support equipment. The hospital, however, unsure of the legal status of the "mercy will" or of its own liability in case it failed to comply, went into court seeking a declaratory judgment, a ruling by the court as to its obligations. Mr. Landy died the next day while still on the respirator, but the hospital asked the courts to continue the case because it had other patients on artificial life supports.

The trial court agreed that Mr. Landy's death had not mooted the issue, held hearings, and in its decision ruled that for a hospital to avoid potential civil and criminal liability for terminating life support, a guardian would have to be appointed to act on the incompetent patient's behalf, the guardian would have to file a petition with the court for authority to terminate treatment, and the court would have to give its approval. The court gave no indication of what criteria it would use, but said it would decide on a case-by-case basis. The case then went on appeal to the Florida Supreme Court, which issued a broad mandate for use of living wills.

Speaking for a unanimous bench, Chief Justice James E. Alderman started with the assumption that "terminally ill incompetent persons being sustained only through use of extraordinary artificial means have the same right to refuse to be held on the threshold of death as terminally ill competent persons." In order to ensure that this "valuable right" not be lost, the procedure for implementing it must not be too cumbersome. Requiring prior court approval, said Chief Justice Alderman, especially where there is an indication of the patient's wishes, is "too burdensome, is not necessary to protect the state's interests or the interests of the patient, and could render the right of the incompetent a nullity."[12]

The law had long recognized the concept of substituted judgment as one means by which an incompetent could effect decisions made when he or she had been competent. "If such a person, while competent, had executed a so-called 'living' or 'mercy' will, that will be persuasive evidence of that incompetent person's intention." To be relieved of potential civil or criminal liability, all a doctor or hospital had to do was "act in good faith" in following the patient's expressed wishes. "Under the circumstances of this and similar cases, prior court approval is not required." The courts would, of course, always hear the matter if requested by the family or other parties in the case of legitimate disagreement over meaning or other causes.[13]

The Landy case is not, of course, legally binding in any other state than Florida, but because there have been relatively few opinions on the subject, the judges' opinions in this and in cases such as Conroy[14] and Peter[15] carry a fair degree of influence. Moreover, there has only been one case in which a lower court has refused to exercise common-law judgment and ruled that the validity of living wills depended solely on legislative enactment.[16] In fact, even when confronted by oral directives, which normally carry less evidentiary weight than written documents, courts have been willing to accept testimony regarding the patient's wishes. The New Jersey Supreme Court, which had refused to accept oral proof of Karen Ann Quinlan's wishes, later specifically admitted that it had been in error. Oral evidence, it concluded in the Conroy case, "is certainly relevant to shed light on whether the patient would have consented to the treatment if competent to make the decision."[17]

Whether an advance directive is based on common law or on a natural-death statute, it will be easier to implement if it is accompanied by a durable power of attorney. A power of attorney is a simple instrument by which the principal grants to an agent the power to act in his or her behalf in certain matters. To illustrate by a simple matter, my son wanted to sell his car, but was going to be in Europe for a month. He signed a power of attorney authorizing me to dispose of the car and to sign any of the transfer documents required.

Traditionally, however, regular powers of attorney automatically lapse if the principal becomes incompetent, even temporarily, such as when recuperating from an accident or surgery. Since even these temporary conditions served to cancel a regular power of attorney, it would be useless for the purpose of implementing advance directives. The only remedy would be to seek a court-appointed guardian, a cumbersome procedure, but worse, it does not permit the patient to name the guardian.

These and other limitations led every state to enact legislation providing for *durable* powers of attorney that would survive the grantor's incompetence. These were not, it should be noted, designed primarily for health care, but rather to ensure smooth handling of financial matters. It quickly became apparent that durable powers of attorney not only met a need; they also had the advantage of lying latent until needed. A person designated would not actually assume the surrogate powers until the grantor had become incompetent.

Because durable powers of attorney derive from specific statutes, there has been little reason for courts or hospitals to question their validity. What few cases there have been have focused not on whether the surrogate could act, but on the scope of his or her actions as defined by the instrument.

As of 1992, all fifty states and the District of Columbia had adopted some form of living-will statute; forty-eight had provided for a health care proxy through durable power of attorney; and twenty-five had enacted some form of surrogate decision-making statute.[18]

These laws all have certain things in common. First, they define the condition the patient must be in for the advance directive to take effect or for the surrogate to exercise authority. Essentially, the patient must be unable to make a decision, and many of the laws use phrases such as "terminal condition"[19] or "permanently unconscious."

The laws often define the type of treatment that may be precluded either under the terms of the advance directive or at the behest of the surrogate. These may include use of respirators, feeding tubes, hydration, and surgery. The laws may require some form of notice, so that the grantee understands what sort of power he or she is giving to another, and they also include immunity, both civil and criminal, for the health care providers who follow the instructions of either the advance directive or the surrogate.[20]

While the statutes have, in general, gone a long way in helping to clarify the rights of individuals and the obligations of doctors and hospitals, there are some problems. The phrase "terminal condition" is scientifically imprecise; everyone is in some form of terminal condition. A patient who has been diagnosed with inoperable cancer, for example, is in terminal condition, but may have days, weeks, or months left in which to live. Doctors also have varying views on what constitutes a "terminal condition."[21] The same problem arises from those statutes that use the phrase "terminal illness."

For example, Estelle Browning suffered a massive stroke in November 1986. A year earlier she had executed an advance directive stating that if she ever became terminally ill, she did not want life-prolonging procedures, nor did she want to be fed or hydrated by tubes. She went on to instruct her physicians to withhold such treatment "when death is imminent," but unfortunately that phrase was not defined under Florida's Life-Prolonging Procedure Act. As a result, her court-appointed guardian could not convince a court that her condition had become terminal, and the court said that since no statutory definition existed, the will was in effect null.[22]

Other states have attempted to avoid this issue by referring to situations in which death is "imminent," but if the law stipulates that a terminal condition is one where death is "imminent" regardless of the application of life-support treatment, then, as the Conference on Uniform State Laws pointed out, there is "little point in having a statute permitting withdrawal of such procedures." The answer is not to try to be more precise, but to be flexible, and to phrase the stipulations in such a way that common sense and good faith on the part of all concerned will work to the best interests of the patient.

The Uniform Rights of the Terminally Ill Act was amended by the National Conference of Commissioners on Uniform State Laws at its annual meeting in August 1989, and approved by the American Bar Association the following February. The act is designed to serve as a model for states to follow in drafting their own laws, so that there will be some uniformity throughout the nation. In the Definitions section of the act, the key items are "life-sustaining treatment," "qualified patient," and "terminal condition."

The former is defined as "any medical procedure or intervention that, when administered to a qualified patient, will serve only to prolong the process of dying." A "qualified patient" is a person eighteen years or older "who has executed a declaration and who has been determined by the attending physician to be in a terminal condition." The last term means "an incurable and irreversible condition that, without the administration of life-sustaining treatment, will, in the opinion of the attending physician, result in death within a relatively short time." As the Comment by the Commissioners indicates, the terms "life-sustaining treatment" and "terminal condition" need to be read together, since they are interdependent.[23]

Is legislation really needed? The answer seems to be yes, and it is in the best interests of all the parties concerned—the patients, their families and surrogates, doctors, hospitals, and courts—that the appropriate procedures be spelled out. Even when courts and legislators acknowledge the existence of a right of personal autonomy that includes the right to refuse treatment, many problems can arise. Doctors differ on what constitutes a terminal illness or condition, and some have religious or moral scruples about not trying to do all they can to keep patients alive. Family members, beset by doubts and guilt in times of crisis, may wonder if the patient really meant what he or she said to them at dinner two years ago. Hospitals and doctors have every reason to fear civil and criminal liability, and know full well that the American people will go to court over every real or imagined harm. While courts do create law when necessary, and the right to refuse treatment is grounded in centuries-old common-law traditions, judges feel more comfortable if the elected representatives of the people have spoken as to appropriate procedures. And above all, the person most affected, the patient, can know with some certainty that his or her wishes will be carried out.

In a study of states that do have natural-death statutes, researchers discovered that the statutes led to increased discussion by doctors and hospital authorities, and often the creation of hospital committees to formulate policies, a distinct improvement over a situation in which no clear policy existed. The authors concluded that doctors should encourage their legislators to enact such laws if their states currently do not have one, and to update existing statutes so that they come closer to the models proposed by the Uniform Laws commissioners.[24]

Such legislation, however, is not a sure-fire answer to all the questions that may arise in these situations. There will always be exceptions to any statute, no matter how carefully drawn, because the circumstances differ from patient to patient, family to family, hospital to hospital. There will be times when, even with an advance directive and health care providers willing to follow its instructions, issues will arise that may have to be resolved in court or in some other forum. This will surely be the case in a federal system where each state may enact a statute of its own choosing; it would still be the case, I believe, even if all the jurisdictions within the United States adopted the uniform model.

The important thing, if the right of self-determination is to be honored, is for all those involved, especially health care providers, to honor the wishes of the patients. To do this, however, they must know what those wishes are, and also, they need to make patients aware of their rights. Here a significant step took place with the passage by Congress of the Patient Self-Determination Act in October 1990.

Sponsored by Representative Sander Levin (D-Mich.) and Senators John Danforth (R-Mo.) and Daniel Patrick Moynihan (D-N.Y.), the law requires all hospitals receiving Medicare or Medicaid funds to provide entering patients written information about their rights under state law to accept or refuse medical treatment, as well as their right to formulate advance directives and durable powers of attorney. The hospitals are obligated to record in each patient's records whether or not an advance directive has been provided, and to train their staffs on the subject. In addition, each state, if it did not already have one, had to develop a description of existing state law. The bill went into effect at the beginning of December 1991, and it is still too early to know if it has increased the number of patients expressing their wishes in some form of advance directive.[25]

Given the fact that most Americans do not have a regular will, much less an advance directive, [26] the bill may have less effect on the patient than it does on the hospitals, who now are required by law to enter such directives, when they exist, in the patient's records. Doctors and hospital authorities will now have a greater impetus to follow patient directives than to ignore them. Rather than worrying about the liability for following patient or surrogate wishes, they will now have to worry about the liability for ignoring them.

The interest in advance directives increased dramatically following the Cruzan case and peaked again after passage of the Patient Self-Determination Act, but there are still many issues that need to be resolved. According to Cathy Myer, a lawyer at the Beth

Israel Medical Center in New York, "advance directives are a very middle-class activity. A lot of our patients are from the Lower East Side or Chinatown, where you do not talk about death, much less sign documents about when you want life-support stopped." Even when someone has signed some form of advance directive, there is the possibility that he or she does not know the full implications of the document. One doctor reported that a woman came into a Chicago hospital with a card that said she should be allowed to die if she were severely ill or unable to speak on her own behalf, but it did not say anything about being irreversibly ill. She was, in fact, gravely ill, and her husband went up to the doctor sobbing, saying they had no idea it would be taken seriously in this type of situation. So they treated her, she recovered, and the couple left the hospital thanking the medical staff profusely.[27]

Doctors point out that the mere existence of an advance directive is, by itself, no guarantee of anything. "Families have an awful tendency to turn to the doctor," according to Dr. Steven Miles, a geriatrician at the Hennepin County Hospital in Minneapolis. "They ask what they should do instead of asking themselves what John would do if he were able to decide for himself."[28] Other doctors report that in a situation where a living will exists that says "Do not treat," and the children say "I don't care what he wrote, we want you to treat him," they will nearly always follow the wishes of the family. It remains to be seen whether state or federal legislation will change that response.

Many doctors, ironically, find it difficult to talk about advance directives. "I'd rather shoot myself in the foot," one physician at New York's Montefiore Hospital said, "than start a living will discussion." Others worry that patients coming in with treatable problems will be frightened. Dr. James Snyder, chairman of the ethics committee at Pittsburgh's Presbyterian University Hospital reported that at a meeting of the group following the Cruzan case, several doctors worried that if a patient came in with chest pains and you handed her a living will form, she might die of a heart attack.

It is unclear just how much credence doctors give to advance directives. Two studies undertaken in California shortly after the passage of that state's natural-death act reported that few doctors had even come into contact with advance directives. A recent study indicates that while doctors now appear to be more receptive to advance directives, the most important factors in the decision to continue or withhold treatment are the physician-family consensus and the doctor's perceptions of civil or criminal liability.[29]

The argument against accepting advance directives is the same as that against allowing substituted judgment—only the individual can make the decision; incompetent individuals cannot make informed judgments and no one else should be allowed to sign their death warrant; only God can give life, and therefore only God can take it. For example, in New Jersey where the whole debate began in 1975 with the Quinlan case, the legislature did not pass a statute until 1991 and then only over the strong objection of the state's Catholic Conference, which labeled the bill as "euthanasia." This response reflects the tie that some people see between the abortion debate and that over termination of treatment. Dr. Robert L. Pickens, chairman of the biomedical ethics committee of the New Jersey Medical Society, who testified in favor of the bill, said, "When I hear the right-to-lifers say this is a right-to-die bill, I disagree. It's a right to choose."[30]

While the debates over abortion and the right to die are significantly different, there is one area of the right-to-die issue in general, and the question of advance directives in particular, that relates directly to the abortion controversy. Over thirty state statutes contain clauses to the effect that a terminally ill or comatose patient's living will is suspended if the patient is pregnant. A majority of these statutes suspend the advance directive throughout the entire pregnancy, while others depend on whether the woman is carrying a fetus that could develop to the point of live birth if the patient were continued on a life-support system. So far no state court has ruled directly on the constitutionality of these statutes, and it is unclear whether such provisions conflict with the right of self-determination established in *Cruzan*.

Here again one confronts significant advances in medical science that raise complex and emotionally difficult issues, and the

law will be called upon to provide answers. At one time, the
death of a pregnant woman almost automatically meant the death
of the fetus she carried.[31] Just as it is possible to keep the body
functioning even if one is brain-dead, now it is also possible to
keep a fetus alive in such an environment until it reaches a point
of viability. The same emotionally charged issues that are present
in the debate over abortion are here as well. Does the woman's
right to privacy and to self-determination outweigh the state's
interest in preserving the life of the unborn? Does the right to die
with dignity disappear because one is pregnant?[32]

The little case law that exists on the subject would seem to
indicate that, at least in federal courts, such provisions would be
sustained. The 1973 decision in *Roe* v. *Wade*[33] gave a woman
near-complete autonomy to choose an abortion in the first two
trimesters of pregnancy. Since then, however, the Court has nar-
rowed the scope of that autonomy, and in the Webster and Casey
cases[34] it significantly expanded the power of the state to protect
fetal life. Some scholars believe that under these rulings pregnancy exceptions to advance directives could easily be upheld.[35]
On the other hand, David A. Smith, director of legal services for
Choice in Dying, believes some of the language in *Casey* indicates that the Court would uphold the living will except in those
instances involving a viable fetus.

The Supreme Court does seem determined to push the judicial
debate over abortion back into the state courts, and the chances
are that we will see a pattern in which some state courts validate
pregnancy clauses and others strike them down. The issue will
be on what grounds such decisions are made, and at least in
some states, privacy clauses in state constitutions may provide a
sufficient argument to elevate the interests of the patient over
that of the fetus. Both Florida and California have advance directive statutes that include an automatic suspension during the
entire term of pregnancy; both also have explicit privacy rights
in their state constitutions. The Florida court specifically relied
on the privacy clause in the case of Estelle Browning, and it also
struck down a parental notification bill on the same grounds,
completely ignoring Supreme Court rulings that would have upheld the measure.[36] Similarly, California's highest court has uti-

lized the privacy rights in the state constitution to take a far more liberal view of abortion rights than has the Supreme Court.[37]

Georgia's advance directive statute has a pregnancy clause and a lower court in that the state granted a hospital's petition to continue life support for a pregnant brain-dead woman, despite her husband's objections. The woman did not have a living will, and the court made no effort to determine what her wishes might have been. The judge rejected out of hand the argument that the woman had privacy rights to reject treatment because she was, under Georgia law, technically dead, and dead persons have no privacy rights. Although the constitutionality of the Georgia pregnancy clause was not before the court, the opinion seemed to indicate that even if she had had a living will, the pregnancy clause would have taken precedence.[38]

There are, of course, several possible scenarios in the tragic situation in which a pregnant woman has expressed a desire not to be kept alive by machinery. In some instances, where both the husband and wife wanted the child, the husband could agree—indeed insist—on procedures to keep his wife's body functioning until the child they both wanted could be born. One would suppose that in any situation in which the husband wanted the child, even if the wife had signed a living will, doctors would honor his wishes. The difficult cases will arise when there is an advance directive, and the husband does not want the child; that question so far has not reached the courts. When it does, the courts will be confronted with the key issue of the whole debate: Who decides?

ADVANCE DIRECTIVE
Living Will and Health Care Proxy

Death is a part of life. It is really like birth, growing and aging. I am using this advance directive to convey my wishes about medical care to my doctors and other people looking after me at the end of my life. It is called an advance directive because it gives instructions in advance about what I want to happen to me in the future. It expresses my wishes about medical treatment that might keep me alive. I want this to be legally binding.

If I cannot make or communicate decisions about my medical care, those around me should rely on this document for instructions about measures that could keep me alive.

I do not want medical treatment (including feeding and water by tube) that will keep me alive if:
- I am unconscious and there is no reasonable prospect that I will ever be conscious again (even if I am not going to die soon in my medical condition), *or*
- I am near death from an illness or injury with no reasonable prospect of recovery.

I do want medicine and other care to make me more comfortable and to take care of pain and suffering. I want this even if the pain medicine makes me die sooner.

I want to give some extra instructions: *[Here list any special instructions, e.g., some people fear being kept alive after a debilitating stroke. If you have wishes about this, or any other conditions, please write them here.]*

The legal language in the box that follows is a health care proxy.
It gives another person the power to make medical decisions for me.

I name _____, who lives at _____

_____ , phone number _____

to make medical decisions for me if I cannot make them myself. This person is
called a health care "surrogate," "agent," "proxy," or "attorney in fact."
This power of attorney shall become effective when I become incapable of
making or communicating decisions about my medical care. This means that
this document stays legal when and if I lose the power to speak for myself, for
instance, if I am in a coma or have Alzheimer's disease.

My health care proxy has power to tell others what my advance directive
means. This person has power to make decisions for me, based either on what I
would have wanted, or, if this is not known, on what he or she thinks best for
me.

If my first choice health care proxy cannot or decides not to act for me,

I name _____ , address _____ ,

phone number _____ , as my second choice.

(over, please)

I have discussed my wishes with my health care proxy, and with my second choice if I have chosen to appoint a second person. My proxy(ies) has(have) agreed to act for me.

I have thought about this advance directive carefully. I know what it means and want to sign it. I have chosen two witnesses, neither of whom is a member of my family, nor will inherit from me when I die. My witnesses are not the same people as those I named as my health care proxies. I understand that this form should be notarized if I use the box to name (a) health care proxy(ies).

Signature _____

Date _____

Address _____

Witness' signature _____

Witness' printed name _____

Address _____

Witness' signature _____

Witness' printed name _____

Address _____

Notary [to be used if proxy is appointed] _____

Reprinted by permission of
CHOICE IN DYING INC.—
the national council for the right to die.
(formerly Concern for Dying/Society for the Right to Die)
200 Varick Street, New York, NY 10014 (212) 366-5540

Who Decides?

Modern medicine has not defeated death, but it has made it possible for many to live longer, healthier, happier, and more productive lives. Modern drugs and technology save thousands of lives every day, and what only a few decades ago would have been considered miracles are routine procedures today. The modern hospital, with its monitors and machines and instruments, its surgeons and nurses and anesthesiologists and therapists, is a place of hope for millions. It is also where people die, and just as there are many people involved in curing the sick, so, too, are many voices heard in caring for the dying.

Up until World War II, the physician appears to have been closely connected to his patients and to the community. Most doctors had a general practice and made house calls, and while it now seems part of a romanticized past, doctors did know their patients well, they did care for them and their children, and sometimes even their grandchildren throughout a lifetime. Oliver Wendell Holmes, Sr., who taught a generation of Harvard medical students, wrote: "The young man knows his patient, but the old man knows his patient's family, dead and alive, up and down for generations." These personal ties aided doctors not only in caring for their patients' health, but also, in many instances, in quietly assisting them to a dignified death.

The hospitals of that era also differed enormously from our own. The high technology we now take for granted was absent, of course. But hospitals worked harder to make their patients feel comfortable. While men and women suffered many different types of ailments, medical science could treat only a few of them. So aside from relatively basic testing and surgical procedures, hospitals offered compassion and a sense that a patient, no matter how ill, still had connections to the community. In big cities Catholic and Jewish hospitals catered primarily to the special needs of ethnic enclaves and often acted as little more than an extension of the family doctor, who controlled the patient's testing and care.[1]

As we have noted, all this changed with breathtaking speed after World War II with the growth of medical specializations and subspecializations, the invention of new machines that could provide highly detailed information on a person's physical functions, miracle drugs, and surgery performed with microminiature tools. "Family" doctors no longer made house calls, and their offices came to resemble small and not so small clinics. Going to the general practitioner often meant little more than getting directions about which specialist to consult.

At least with a doctor one could at times feel connected to another human being. Hospitals, however, grew ever larger and ever more impersonal. After a stay in a medical center hospital, columnist Meg Greenfield wrote that she had just come back from a "foreign place" where she felt like "a tourist in an unfathomable, dangerous land."[2] Some of this, as many commentators have suggested, could easily be remedied by reminding doctors, nurses, and other health care providers that their patients are not merely objects to be examined, with the bill sent to a third-party provider, but human beings who have a right to know what is wrong with them, and what the doctors propose to do.* But much of this impersonalized institutionalism is due to the specialized nature of modern medicine, where a doctor may never even see the patient until he or she is wheeled into the operating room.

One reaction has been a demand by patients for greater autonomy, for sharing knowledge, perhaps even joining in deciding treatment, and, of course, in refusing treatment. Given the liti-

*Dr. Holmes, typical of the older generation, warned doctors not to tell patients too much. "Your patient has no more right to all the truth you know than he has to all the medicine in your saddlebags. . . . He should only get just so much as is good for him."

gious nature of our society, it seemed destined that patients, upset at their treatment, would resort to the law for relief. And once the law had been involved, medical personnel and organizations threw up all sorts of precautions to limit legal risk. People checking into hospitals had to fill out as many, if not more, legal permissions than medical forms. Dying thus became a legal as well as medical process.

"Doctors ha[d] always been in control," according to Ruth Macklin, professor of bioethics at Albert Einstein College of Medicine in New York, "but now it's not just doctors and patients. There are hospital administrators, in-house attorneys and risk managers. . . . These are the people who are *really* in control."[3] Not necessarily. Many people are trying to gain control over how they die. The most common effort is through living wills and other forms of advance directives, which hospitals and doctors must now honor, although as many physicians note, if the family wants them to try to save the patient, they will obey the family's wishes rather than the patient's. Tens of thousands of people bought Derek Humphrey's *Final Exit*, but how many will actually be able to take their own lives is unclear. More and more people are choosing to face terminal illness at home, to die in familiar surroundings in the company of friends and family, rather than subjecting themselves to what they consider the indignities of hospital care. Akin to this is the growth of hospices, where nursing care is available to make the dying person more comfortable.

All of these options raise the same basic questions we have been discussing throughout this work: Who decides? Who decides whether a cancerous growth should be removed surgically or left alone? Who decides whether to let a ventilator keep a comatose person breathing, or turn it off? Who decides whether heroic measures should be taken to keep a severely deformed infant alive, or to let the child die quickly? Who decides what is in each person's best interest, and who decides whether a man or woman is competent to make that choice? And if doctors and patients and parents and children cannot decide, should the courts intervene? Should legislatures enact blanket rules to govern what ought to be the most personal of decisions?

These are not idle questions, because how they are decided

literally determines life or death. If the physician honors a living will and does not provide massive medical intervention, death will result. Is that what the patient truly wanted? If the doctor believes the patient did not really mean what he or she said, or the family wants heroic treatment, or if there is suspicion that perhaps the patient had not been competent when the advance directive had been written, should the doctor ignore the patient's wishes, and in doing so, risk incurring legal liability for the results?

This is why the law is involved: not to make the critical decisions, but to provide a procedural framework in which the doctor, the patient's family, the hospital, public health officials, court-appointed guardians, judges, and above all the individual, can determine what should be done. Ideally, the law would never intervene directly, because in every state in the Union, the legal presumption is that if individual decisions have been properly made, then the patient, the patient's family, and the doctors should be left alone to work out the specifics.

If one were looking for a story of how, faced with the agony of deciding life and death, decisions ought to be made, then one might look at the case of Helen Reynolds, sixty-two, who checked into Boston's Beth Israel Hospital in January 1991 and then again in April to repair and then replace a faulty heart valve. But she had other circulatory problems, and in May she developed gangrene in her feet. Reynolds was determined to hold on to life, even if she were to be confined to a long-term facility and hooked up to a ventilator to help her breathing. Even after she lost both feet to surgery, she took pleasure from life, joking with the nurses, having her hair done, ribbing the younger doctors. On her sixty-third birthday, she and her family celebrated in the ninth-floor intensive-care unit with balloons, cakes, cards and a big HAPPY BIRTHDAY FROM US ALL sign from the staff.

Then one day one of the nurses, sensitive to Helen's mood, said, "Helen, it really stinks. You know if you don't want all this stuff done, we can stop it. We can let nature take its course." Reynolds shook her head and said, "I want to get home." But she did not improve sufficiently to get off the ventilator, and one day she began talking about her pain. She called over one of the younger doctors and laboriously scrawled a note: "I have decided to end my life as I do not want to live like this."

The doctor informed her daughters, one of whom said, "I think she hung on more for us than for herself." Asked if she wanted to see a priest, Helen declined, afraid he would try to talk her out of it. The staff understood her decision, but they could not grant her wish immediately. They wanted to hear the same message from her several days in a row. As Dr. J. Woodrow Weiss, the ICU director, explained, "We need to be certain this isn't a whim." Reynolds repeated her decision—to doctors, nurses, her family, and to a staff psychiatrist, who had the responsibility to determine if Reynolds was competent, or whether her decision resulted from temporary depression.

Finally Dr. Weiss met with the family and said the staff was satisfied that Helen Reynolds knew what she wanted, and that she was competent to make the decision. "Our feeling both ethically and legally is that we should respect her wishes." They would remove her from the ventilator and give her morphine to ease the pain. When her daughters suggested that she might want a few more days in which to say goodbye, she rejected the idea vehemently. She was ready, and her endurance had come to an end. Her family gathered around, the ventilator was unhooked, and she drifted off to sleep. As it turned out, she awoke the next morning, somewhat surprised. She clung to life for another three days and then died.

Helen Reynolds had been in control of her medical decisions throughout the ordeal. When she had wanted the doctors to act, even to amputating both legs, they had followed her wishes. When she had decided it was time to stop, they made sure she knew what she was asking, that she was competent and aware of the consequences. From a legal, medical, and moral standpoint, personal autonomy had been honored throughout. Just the opposite could be said of Brenda Hewitt's death.

Brenda Hewitt, a poet and editor, discovered in her mid-forties that her kidneys were failing; dialysis would allow her to live a limited but often painful life, and renal failure could occur at any time. She decided that when that crisis came, she did not want any heroic measures—no machines, no tubes, no indignities. She said, "If I want to die, I have only to go to a hospital. They'll kill me through incompetence and then revive me with brain damage."

Brenda communicated these wishes to her personal physician. She drew up a living will and expressed her wishes in a separate handwritten document. She told her friends what she had done. Most important, she signed a durable power of attorney naming her longtime companion, physics professor Engelbert Schucking, as the person to make medical decisions for her should she become incapacitated. Yet when renal failure did occur, all of these measures proved worthless, and Brenda Hewitt spent her last hours enduring the indignities she had wanted so much to avoid.

On March 28, 1984, the crisis came, and although Schucking did not want to take her to the hospital, she was in such pain that he called her physician, who sent an ambulance. When they got to New York Hospital, the intern in charge ordered a series of tests as if she were a new patient and totally ignored Schucking who kept trying to tell the staff about Brenda's wishes. Ninety minutes after they had arrived, Brenda Hewitt stopped breathing. As Schucking later wrote, "I began to realize that, unexpectedly, the moment that Brenda had been awaiting for such a long time had finally come: her deliverance from years of almost continuous, unimaginable pain. . . . She was free at last. Death, the Redeemer, had come."

Then someone yelled "Code," and the staff started to resuscitate her. Schucking attempted to stop them, to tell them that Brenda Hewitt did not want to be resuscitated, that he had legal authority to make decisions and he had her living will with him. A heavyset male attendant physically prevented him from entering the critical-care unit. Only after Schucking threatened to sue the hospital did someone finally pay him some attention.

A doctor came out to say that the patient was breathing again, that Schucking would be allowed to see her "for two minutes," and that the attending doctors had decided to perform a pericardiocentesis, a procedure to drain excess fluid from the bag surrounding the heart.

"They can't do that without consent," Schucking yelled; the doctor shrugged. Schucking decided he had best get a lawyer, but first he would spend the two minutes he had been allotted to see Brenda. He walked into the room to discover that they had hooked her to a respirator.

"You can't do that without consent. You've no right and you know it. She's legally authorized me to act on her behalf. This will be aggravated assault and battery. I'll sue you. Do you think you can cut her up as it pleases you like a piece of meat? Who gives you the right? Who do you think you are?"

The doctor forced him out of the room and told him that since they had been unable to contact Brenda's personal physician, a hospital administrator had approved the actions of the staff. Only after a lengthy altercation, in which Schucking loudly threatened to hold each person who treated Brenda personally liable and sue them for every cent they had, did a senior staff physician arrive. He took Schucking into another room, read the documents, and listened as Schucking explained why Brenda had reached these decisions. The doctors who had disregarded those wishes, the physician said, had been "erring on the side of life."

Brenda Hewitt's ordeal, and Professor Schucking's as well, went on for another two days. The doctors reluctantly agreed not to operate, but otherwise ignored him; a so-called "patient representative" met with him the next morning and said: "Let's not get involved in what happened yesterday. Let's talk about today. Perhaps we can make a deal." Finally, an assembled conference of doctors admitted that Brenda had suffered brain damage during the time her breathing had stopped, and that she would soon die, although they could probably keep her "alive" for a while. Schucking said no and insisted they turn the respirator off, remove any restraints, and allow him to be with her when she died. The doctors reluctantly agreed.[4]

Professor Schucking originally told his story in New York's *Village Voice* on June 11, 1985; the medico-legal journal *Law, Medicine & Health Care* picked it up and asked the hospital and others to comment on it. The response by Anne Alexis Coté, associate director of New York Hospital and director of the hospital's patient representative program is worth quoting at length:

> Within ninety minutes of her admission [Brenda Hewitt] suffered what appeared to be a respiratory arrest. Full-code cardiopulmonary resuscitation was initiated, and Ms. Hewitt was intubated and put on a respirator. During the course of her resuscitation, a man entered the ICU and told the medical staff they should cease all resuscitation efforts. He produced several documents, which, he said, stated her wishes and gave him the right to make decisions on her behalf. He was escorted out of the ICU and resuscitation efforts were continued. The attending physician in charge of the unit spoke with this man, reviewed the documents, and finally contacted the administrator-on-call, who advised him to continue all medical treatments he felt were appropriate until the contents of the documents could be clarified. The attending physician attempted to reach the patient's primary physician, who had made the arrangements for admission. Those attempts were futile that evening.[5]

The account goes on in this vein, detailing the many steps that were taken before anyone met with Professor Schucking, since it now seemed there was a "situation" involving a living will and a durable power of attorney. Nowhere in two pages of cold prose is there the slightest indication that Brenda Hewitt was a person in pain, a human being with feelings and intelligence who did not want to be a guinea pig on whom interns could practice.

This may sound harsh, but while it is true that the best medical care can be secured at teaching hospitals, it is also true that medical students do need to practice before they are licensed to go out into the world. Unfortunately, this often produces an attitude that is, to say the least, insensitive to the human needs of the patient. When my younger son was only two years old, he had major surgery to remove a diseased kidney, and as we later learned from the surgeon, it had been touch-and-go for a while. He received excellent care from both the resident staff and the nurses at a suburban New York medical center. One day, however, as the interns were making rounds one of them looked at Robert's chart and said, "Oh, he's getting better. We can't learn anything from him." They walked on without even checking Robert's bandages. One can only hope that at some point that young man learned that patients are people, not test animals.

Ms. Coté does, however, go on to make a valid point, namely, how could the hospital be sure the documents were indeed valid, that the man presenting them was who he claimed to be, namely the holder of the durable power of attorney.[6] Medical science can delay death, she notes, but cannot restore life; it is therefore better to keep the patient alive until all these "details" can be resolved. But, she makes clear, this is not a primary concern of the hospital, which will rely not on the patient or on someone claiming to act for the patient. "If today a patient presented [himself] to the hospital and in a short time after admission his condition deteriorated or he suffered a cardiopulmonary arrest, *without information from the patient's attending physician to the contrary*, the patient would be resuscitated until such time as the facts could be determined."[7] *(Italics added.)*

Among the others asked by the journal to comment were medical ethicist George J. Annas of Boston University and Margaret A. Somerville, a member of the law and medical faculties at McGill University in Montreal, both of whom noted that unfortunately the procedures described by Professor Schucking, and in effect confirmed by Ms. Coté, were all too common, that few hospitals had regular procedures to deal with patient directives, and that in fact hospital needs, including training of interns, usually took precedence over patient intent.[8]

Dr. Ronald Cranford, a neurologist at the Hennepin Medical Center in Minneapolis, defended the medical treatment. Brenda Hewitt had been admitted to the hospital "not to die, presumably, but to receive antibiotics and other treatment." The staff did not know her, so they had to test her and evaluate her condition, and during that time, she suffered cardiac arrest. "The decision to resuscitate her at that point in time, therefore, was medically appropriate and morally justifiable." From Ms. Hewitt's standpoint, Dr. Cranford admits, "this decision was neither what she would have wanted nor in her best interests." But in an acute

situation, the physicians "had no choice" but to resuscitate. He
goes on to note that when faced by a staff unreceptive to his pleas,
Professor Schucking's "next thought was not to try to reach the
personal physician nor to ask the medical staff to contact him,
but to threaten to contact a lawyer and sue."[9]

A man designated in a legal instrument to make medical decisions for a woman now incompetent, a person armed with duly
executed documents authorizing him to make those decisions, is
ignored by the medical staff and the hospital administrator. Dr.
Cranford, who has no word of condemnation for a hospital staff
that he admits acted in a manner inconsistent with a patient's
wishes and even her best interests, can only regret that Dr.
Schucking threatened to sue. That threat, and only that threat,
finally got the medical staff to pay some attention.

It should be clear that while personal autonomy is highly valued
by the law, and in fact the whole notion of a right to die is
grounded in personal autonomy, the finality of death makes
nearly everyone involved extremely cautious. Many of the cases
we have looked at have not been litigated in the traditional way,
with two parties having completely opposing views contesting
against each other. Rather, one party, usually the patient or his
or her representatives, wants to end life support. The other, usually the hospital, the doctor, or sometimes the state, is not necessarily opposed, but wants a court decision to ensure that all of
the proper procedures have been followed and that no legal liability will result.

There is, however, a growing consensus that what might be
called a first stage in right-to-die litigation is nearing its end, that
we now have enough precedents to determine basic policies. In
the future, cases will arise less out of a need to clarify the procedures than out of new and unexpected situations that do not fit
current categories.

First, it is now well established that both the common law and
the Constitution support a right to die, that is, a right to terminate
medical treatment, including the cessation of nutrition and hydration. The common law grounds its approach in the doctrine
of personal autonomy. There is some confusion over whether

the constitutional ground is privacy, liberty interest, or personal autonomy. In addition, many states have erected either statutory or constitutional provisions. Whatever the doctrinal grounds, the cases since *Quinlan* have all recognized and acknowledged that such a right exists.

Second, the decision of a competent individual carries all else before it. If a patient, such as Helen Reynolds, says "No more," a doctor is obligated to make sure that the patient is competent and that the decision has been reached voluntarily; most hospitals now have some procedures in place to make these determinations. Once it is determined that everything is in order, then the doctor and the hospital must stop treatment.

Third, if the patient is now incompetent, for example, an automobile-accident victim in a coma, the law recognizes the right of a surrogate to make the necessary decisions. If there is a proper advance directive, the evidence is as compelling as if the patient were awake and able to act on his or her own. If the person is a minor, the courts will, with certain exceptions, rarely question a parent's decision to stop treatment. Problems arise, however, when the patient is not competent, has not made an advance directive, and there is no designated surrogate. Moreover, under our federal system, states may set different standards of proof to establish what the patient would have wanted were he or she conscious and competent. It is unlikely that this type of problem will disappear in the future.

What we have seen occurring in the last quarter century is the creation of a *procedural* framework in which individuals can express their personal wishes and in which the various health providers can express their medical, social, and legal considerations. Let us go through these, and in doing so bring together many of the strands we have explored earlier.

The first consideration is whether the patient is competent to make the necessary decisions regarding his or her health care. The simplest scenario is one in which the patient is conscious and competent and there is no need for resort to the courts. Established hospital review procedures are usually sufficient to allow doctors to stop treatment without fear of future liability.

If, however, the patient is not competent, either because mentally incapacitated or comatose, then the next step is to determine if there is an advance directive and if a surrogate has been named. If these documents exist, or if the patient is a minor and a parent claims authority to make the necessary decision, internal hospital procedures to validate these arrangements are normally sufficient. While a few states still require at least a nominal court order to authorize a surrogate, the trend is to keep the courts out of the process if the intent is clear and the documents are in order.

If nothing else, time may be an important factor. If the doctors have to wait until a judge validates a surrogacy, they may have to start procedures to keep the patient alive in the meantime, procedures that violate the patient's wishes and that may complicate future decision making by family or surrogate.

In addition, while judges are expected to resolve questions of law, they have neither special competence nor an obligation to decide the other issues that arise in right-to-die cases. "Courts are not the proper place," wrote Judge Marie Garibaldi of New Jersey, "to resolve the agonizing personal problems that underlie these cases. Our legal system cannot replace the more intimate struggle that must be borne by the patient, those caring for the patient, and those who care about the patient."[10]

It appears that most patients, their families, and their doctors are satisfied that the proper decision has been made without the necessity of going to court to validate that decision. Every day thousands of people die in hospitals, many because a decision has been made not to provide further treatment. Very few of these cases go to court or even require minimal judicial intervention, proof that the system is working relatively well in allowing doctors, families, and patients to make the necessary decisions. Nonetheless, even though courts may want to see the main issues resolved by the family, doctor, and hospital, there are situations that make the courts more appropriate forums in which to determine what should be done—or not done—for the patient.

First, health care providers will always look to the courts if they believe the law is not clear or if they might incur some legal liability if they rely on in-house clinical procedures. In our society, the courts are the proper mechanisms for determining *legal* issues, and given the complex nature of the problem, it is desirable that such questions be answered before a patient is disconnected from a respirator.

Second, no matter what procedures are followed, society wants to protect the patient against abuse. Not all decisions to terminate treatment may be in the best interest of a patient, even one who is seriously ill. The role of the state as *parens patriae*, or the impartiality of a court-appointed guardian, may be necessary to ensure that whatever decision is reached will be right for the patient. In some situations, protection may best be secured by utilizing the courts.

Few courts, it should be noted, still adhere to the view of the Massachusetts Supreme Judicial Court that questions of life and death "require the process of detached but passionate investigation and decision that forms the ideal on which the judicial branch of government was created."[11] Today most courts will examine only the procedural safeguards that are in place to determine whether they meet the state's legal requirements to protect the patient. If the procedure is satisfactory, the courts prefer not to get involved in the actual decision making.

What are these safeguards? Assuming the patient has not left an advance directive, the courts will want to know the following:

- Does the hospital have a method of determining if the medical decision (whether to treat or not) is appropriate?
- Has the decision been made on the basis of reliable evidence? For example, has evidence been presented as to what the patient would have wanted?
- Is a mechanism available to review the decision making?
- Is this mechanism able to detect improper motives?

But is this enough? Do we as a society value life so highly that we wish to place more protections about it, or do we merely wish to let the elderly and sick die as quickly, as painlessly, and as cheaply as possible? Certainly the argument can be made that resort to the courts will normally ensure a higher level of protection, while reliance on in-house clinical policies may tend toward acceptance of death more easily. But are these the right questions? Is the matter of who decides only procedural or is the real question one of individual autonomy? Who should make this most personal and most irrevocable of decisions—the patient or a surrogate to whom the patient has entrusted that power? Or does the state, through its courts, have any real business intervening at all?

The answer, even by one who values autonomy as the highest of rights, is that the state does have an interest,[12] and that to avoid abuse, it is better in some circumstances to be more careful, to take that extra step to ensure that the proper decision has been made, to review all the evidence just one more time. The type of abuse we worry about primarily is that in the desire to reach a decision quickly, the wrong choice might be made, the protective procedures bypassed, either in the name of efficiency or humanity. Even in the case of a terminally ill person who has no hope of recovery, all the steps in the process must be taken. Some critics worry that hospitals and doctors, once they grow confident that they will not be subject to liability, will speed up the process of withdrawing life support or medical care. Better, they argue, to keep the patient alive a little bit longer and be sure that the right decision is made.

While this appears to be a reasonable suggestion, delay deprives the patient of his or her rights. Going to court is time-consuming under the best of circumstances, and as the New Jersey court noted, "no matter how expedited, judicial intervention in this complex and sensitive area may take too long. Thus, it could infringe the very rights that we want to protect."[13] In fact, when the issue has been taken to court for one reason or another, the patient has often died before the question could be adjudicated.[14] This pleases critics, who argue that it is always best to let nature take its course, that it is better that the person died of natural causes a few days or a few weeks or even a few months later than to have in essence killed the patient earlier. Such arguments ignore the right of individual autonomy or the added pain and suffering the patient and the family must endure.

*   *   *

If resort to the courts is time-consuming—and also expensive, especially if litigation ensues—why take the judicial route at all? One answer, as we have seen, is that the legal issues are not always clear; often there is no advance directive or, if one exists, there are questions as to its meaning or legitimacy; and doctors and hospitals want to avoid any legal liability. Another reason to go to court is that conflicts may sometimes exist that cannot be settled at the patient's bedside, and if agreement cannot be reached, appeal to the law may be the best solution.

These conflicts may be among family members who differ over the proper treatment of an incompetent patient, or there may be conflict among the medical staff as to proper treatment. There may also be a wide gulf between what the doctors believe to be the appropriate procedure and what the family members want. We have, for the most part, been discussing cases in which the individual patient or his or her family has wanted to discontinue treatment. But what if the family wants the doctors and the hospital to do all that is possible, no matter the cost, and this decision totally disregards the prognosis of the disease or the pain and suffering inflicted on the patient? In terms of "who decides," how much weight should be accorded to the doctors, and how should the law evaluate that role? Take the case of Baby Rena.

The picture might be that of any bright-eyed child having a birthday, a party hat askew on her head, a small cake with a single candle. But there were few bright spots in the little girl's life. Her mother, a thirty-three-year-old drug user with AIDS and a history of mental illness, had no idea of the father's identity. She had given over custody of three previous children to public welfare agencies and had already signed a similar document before delivering Rena at George Washington University Hospital on October 10, 1989. Soon afterward the mother left the hospital and dropped out of sight.

Doctors quickly confirmed that the underweight infant was infected with HIV, but nurses in the pediatric ward soon made the little girl their favorite. She gained weight, she smiled, she played with anyone who would pick her up. Dr. Emily von

Scheven recalled that "there was something about this kid that was just incredibly lively. She had a really bright face. She had bright eyes." But Washington is a city with far too many unwanted children, so District of Columbia officials did not move very quickly to find her foster care.

Then, about four months after Rena's birth, an employee[15] from another part of the hospital came by the ward and spotted the animated infant. He stopped, and with the encouragement of the nurses, sat and held her for a while. The man, in his early thirties, had only recently been married, and he and his wife were evangelical Christians. Although the nurses told them about the baby's infection and the fact that she would probably die of AIDS, they decided they would care for her. "We believe that God told us to take the child," the man later said. They would raise her as proof of God's mercy and His ability to heal the sick.

Before the couple could apply for or take custody of the baby, Rena developed a breathing problem, and was transferred to Children's Hospital. Doctors there diagnosed the problem as a severe form of pneumonia, a leading complication of AIDS, and in order for her to breathe, they placed her on a ventilator. The couple continued to visit the child, and even brought their pastor along once. They met with Dr. Tamara Rakusan, who pulled no punches. Rena had excessive spinal fluid in her brain that might cause paralysis from the neck down. She also had eye problems and kidney abnormalities that already required continuous medication. In essence, the couple said, Dr. Rakusan was telling them they did not have to go ahead; there were other, healthier children available who also needed foster care.

But they stuck with Rena, and gradually the child rebounded, and, at the age of nine months, a fat and healthy little baby with "a gorgeous smile and dimples" went home with two people who loved her. The staff at Children's Hospital considered it a medical success; her foster parents believed that it was God's will. Three months later, Rena celebrated her first birthday and shortly after that the year ended on a happy note with a festive Christmas celebration.

About a month later, on January 30, 1991, something went

wrong. Rena did not respond as her foster mother attempted to wake her from a nap; her breathing was husky and labored, and when the two of them went to Children's Hospital, doctors immediately put Rena back on a respirator. They later determined that the one-year-old had suffered a cardiac failure that triggered the respiratory problem. This time no medical miracle occurred.

The child needed painkillers constantly, but as she came to tolerate them, required ever larger doses to control her thrashing. Her blood pressure skyrocketed. On February 15, Dr. Murray Pollak, supervisor of the intensive-care unit, took over the case. He tried a variety of treatments and slowly came to the conclusion that Rena would never recover. In his thirteen years at the hospital Pollak had come to believe that offering patients or their families futile therapies and false hopes was a cruel hoax. For patients or their parents to make truly autonomous decisions, they had to know the truth.

For Pollak, there seemed to be one course open—take Rena off the respirator and allow her to die. "We could have sedated her," he explained, "and kept her alive for a period until she got an infection or complication and died. But that would not have been giving her the respect that she deserved, that any human deserves." Pollak was not engaging in some cold cost-benefit analysis; rather, he was worried over the fact that Rena was not in a coma. She was suffering, and there was nothing the hospital could do to cure her. It could not even alleviate her suffering. But when he raised the issue with the foster parents, they either did not or would not understand what he was trying to tell them. They wanted him to continue an aggressive approach, trying one or thing or another, anything, that would help the baby. In late February Pollak decided it was time to contact city officials and meet with the parents to try to get them to agree to remove the respirator. He called Sanford Leikin, the head of the hospital's ethics committee and asked him to be present at the meeting.

Leikin, an oncologist, had been aware of the growth in the last few years of the number of futile cases coming into the hospital, patients for whom the staff could do nothing. He and some other doctors had been exploring whether ethically they should be expending significant resources keeping these children alive for a few days or even weeks, or letting them die as quickly and painlessly as possible.

A few years earlier, Leikin had written about how parents often made unreasonable demands on hospital staffs, especially in futile cases. "Children do not belong to their parents. In health care matters involving the imperiled young, especially newborns who neither have a history nor have expressed any desire about their future life, parents are not in a better position than the physician to know what is in the child's best interest."[16] Gordon Avery, chairman of the medical staff at the hospital, wrote in a 1990 article that doctors are doing "something offensive, something contrary to respect for the child's personhood, something *unethical*," if they allow parents to dictate useless treatment. Should doctors and nurses be "*compelled* to do a thing that they consider immoral?" he asked. "If physicians are to be held responsible for their acts, they must have some freedom of choice, some authority over their own actions."[17]

Pollak, who had been trained in the 1970s, could be considered one of the new breed of physicians who rejected the old paternalistic model of "doctor knows best and don't ask any questions." He believed in autonomy, and in his tenure at Children's Hospital he had done a great deal to get parents more involved in medical decision making for their children. At the same time, he believed that in truly futile cases, useless therapies did not help patients and only offered false hope to their families. The problem was where to draw the line.

In 1988 he had wound up in court trying to avoid what he considered futile treatment. A mother of a two-year-old boy had demanded that the hospital provide life support for her severely brain-damaged son and would not listen to Pollak or anyone else as they tried to explain that it would do no good; the boy would never recover. Finally, Pollak went to court and asked the judge to appoint a guardian in place of the mother to make medical decisions. The infant had no hope of recovery, Pollak told the judge. "The person that he was is no longer. We should acknowledge that fact and allow him to die." Instead, the judge ordered the hospital to abide by the mother's wishes. As of this writing, the boy is still alive and in a coma, supported by a respirator at a long-term care facility with no hope of ever regaining consciousness.

That episode, plus the increasing number of AIDS babies coming into Children's and other hospitals, led Pollak to ask the ethics committee, on which he sat, to consider a policy change that would give physicians greater autonomy in deciding whether to stop treatment. In a nine-page memorandum discussing that proposal, the hospital's resident ethicist, Jacqueline Glover, listed the pros and cons of such a policy. It is, she concluded, "a controversial proposal that should neither be eagerly embraced nor automatically shunned." She also pointed out that even if the hospital adopted the policy, no one could foretell how the courts would respond.

Pollak, Leikin, and several other staff members taking care of Rena met with her foster parents on February 21, 1991. He slowly and carefully detailed her prognosis and the futility of the treatment. She will die soon, he concluded, and all they were doing was prolonging her pain and suffering. The parents listened, and then the father said that he had heard the medical facts, but there was another side, and he began to talk about his belief in God. As one of the attending physicians noted, it was a clash of cultures, and neither side understood the other.

Searching for some consensus, Pollak suggested that they taper off Rena's treatment, then try to remove her from the respirator to see if she could breathe on her own. The parents approved, but only on condition that she be put back on if any trouble occurred. A frustrated Pollak said he would seek permission from the city authorities to stop the treatment.

In fact, a day earlier one of the hospital's attorneys, Tobey Lawson, had made contact with Sylvia Anderson, a lawyer at the District of Columbia's Department of Human Services. She summarized Rena's case, as well as the doctors' prognosis that further treatment would only prolong the pain and suffering. Would the city, as the child's legal guardian, give its permission to remove the respirator? Anderson contacted her superiors and a few days later called Lawson. The answer was no; if the hospital wanted to terminate treatment, it would have to go to court.

Stymied by the city, Pollak asked the hospital's ethics committee to help him find a way out of the quandary, to help put an end to Rena's suffering. Again there was a meeting of the doctors, Rena's foster parents, and a representative of the city, with another hospital attorney, Melinda Murray, also sitting in. Pollak explained the problem as clearly and as starkly as he could. The respirator could keep Rena alive, perhaps for months, but she would never recover from AIDS. Attempts to wean her from the respirator had failed; she could not breathe without it. The only way to alleviate her pain was to keep her so heavily sedated "that there's not much purpose in living."[18]

The social worker representing the city, Betty Bass, asked the foster parents what they wanted to do. "As the people who love Rena most, what is it that you want for Rena?"

"To have Rena back home with us," said her foster mother.

"And if that's not possible?"

At this point Rena's foster father stood up and asked the doctors' patience. He then went to the blackboard, drew some diagrams, and began explaining that while the hospital had been taking wonderful care of Rena's medical needs, they had ignored her spiritual side. Until the hospital addressed her spiritual needs, however, the doctors would not be able to defeat the AIDS virus; only with the help of God would they be able to cure Rena.

This sort of talk made the assembled physicians very uncomfortable, and finally Pollak tried to get the parents to face what he considered the central medical choice. They could try to improve Rena's condition and wean her from the respirator; they could leave her on the respirator indefinitely; or, if it was clear that further treatment was futile, then the doctors could unilaterally decide to stop treatment.

Melinda Murray, the hospital attorney, quickly spoke up. "From a legal point of view, I don't think a doctor can say that."

The meeting ended with no resolution of Rena's fate. Murray began preparing to challenge the city in court, but Pollak did not think that route would be particularly useful. From his own experience he knew that courts rarely went against the parents' wishes, especially if they wanted to keep their child alive.

The intensive care staff did all it could to build up Rena's strength and, on March 10, disconnected her from the respirator. To everyone's amazement, she did well. Murray wondered what to do next. How could she tell a judge that Rena was dying when the youngster seemed to be recovering? Pollak knew Rena was still dying, only more slowly, and then on the fifth day she had a relapse. From then on it was a roller coaster with Rena going from one crisis to the next and the ICU staff, including Pollak, doing all they could to save her. On March 25, when it appeared that Rena was close to death, Pollak called the foster parents to the hospital once again. The child was in great pain from all the medication and the shocks to her system and would soon die. Why not let her go in peace? The parents were unmoved. Until God took their child, she was alive.

An angry Pollak later said he had decided that he would withdraw the life support even without the parents' permission and without going to the ethics committee. "I would have done it. No harm could have come to me. It would have been a very safe decision. It was very clear the child was dying and it was a matter of hours. Everyone would have had this big sigh of relief. The city probably would have liked the kind of precedent it set, to get the decision out of their hands."

He did not have to make that decision. Later in the afternoon Rena died.

In Baby Rena's tragic case one can see all of the elements in the problem of who decides. The child herself is incompetent, and so the decision must be made for her. The foster parents, with their strong faith in God, are unwilling to abandon hope and therefore unwilling to stop treatment. The state, in this case the city's human services agency, with its interest in preserving life, refuses to approve termination of life support. A hospital, its facilities strained to the limit, wants to use those resources on cases where recovery is possible. And the doctors, attempting to alleviate suffering for a child doomed to die, want to stop what they consider futile treatment and let their patient depart in peace.

In the background is the law, the court to which the hospital would have turned in its efforts to secure approval of what the medical staff considered the appropriate course of action. It is also to the courts that the parents and the city could have turned for endorsement of their views.

Given the cases we have looked at, we can assume that the court would not have granted the hospital unilateral authority to turn off the respirator, not in the case of an incompetent infant, a person who had never been able to express her wishes on what she might have wanted.[19] In a Georgia case a few months later, Judge Leah Sears-Collins ordered a hospital not to terminate treatment for a thirteen-year-old girl in near-comatose condition. The hospital argued that continued treatment would be "abusive and inhumane," but the girl's parents declared they were waiting for a miracle. "This court finds," the judge wrote, "that if either parent, in the exercise of his or her rights with regard to the welfare of [the child], makes the decision to continue life, that decision must be respected."[20]

Why should the courts be involved at all? What business is it of judges to determine life and death in hospitals? Why are men and women with no medical training qualified to pass judgment on what doctors believe to be in the best interest of patients? What standing should the law have when confronted by a spiritual faith that recognizes only the will of God?

The answer is that in Baby Rena's case there is no clearly "correct" position. The foster parents believed strongly that only God can give life and only God can take it. People must do all they can to protect life, even if in human eyes the effort appears hopeless. "God has not given man the authority to serve as God," the foster father said. The medical staff, grounded in the scientific facts of human physiology and the daily crises of hospital life, had little appreciation of this view. To many people, however, it is a valid way to look at the world.

City officials feared that if they gave the hospital authority to determine unilaterally which AIDS children lived or died, they would not only abandon their own responsibility, but start down a dark and slippery path of determining which lives are "worth" saving, and which are not.

The hospital and the doctors did all they could for Rena and when they concluded that they could do no more, that their efforts only prolonged her dying and intensified her pain and suffering, they wanted to stop, to let her die quickly and escape her torment. Rena was not a "case" in the coldly analytical sense of the term. Doctors, nurses, and other staff worked heroically to help her and were bewildered at why her parents or the city would want to prolong the child's suffering.

It is in cases like this, where there is no clear answer, that Americans have always turned to the law, and judges have always tried to do their best to make sense out of complex situations. That is the function of the common law, and it has served us well throughout our history. To those who say that judges should not make policy, the answer is they always have, and that we as a people have then been able to determine whether we accept that policy or override it through our legislatures.

The law creates guidelines not just for individuals but for society as well. It reflects our values and our priorities, and if at times the law appears confusing on some issues, it is usually because we as a society are confused. The first right-to-die case, that of Karen Ann Quinlan, occurred less than two decades ago, and in that time medical technology has progressed at a breathtaking pace. We can hardly begin to deal with one set of ethical questions before new advances trigger other problems.

Yet in the past twenty years we have begun to carve out a fairly clear legal view of individual rights in these matters, and like all good law, it is evolutionary. The right to refuse treatment is not new, but an axiom of the common law. If we add to it the constitutional notions of privacy and personal autonomy, one can clearly see how a right to die—in the sense that a person may elect to refuse treatment—is firmly grounded in our legal traditions. While some hospitals and health care providers may resent the notion that patients may select death over life, at least in the case of competent adults that notion seems to be firmly planted in contemporary society, protected by both statute and judicial precedent.

But it is not a self-executing right. One has to make provision for it, so that if the situation arises where an individual cannot make the decision, advance directives and properly nominated surrogates will carry out the person's wishes. In the best of all worlds, decisions will be made by the individual, and respected by family, friends, and the medical community.

But there will always be hard cases, like those of Baby Rena and Nancy Cruzan, where the interests of the society and the family and the individual are not necessarily in harmony, where competing values may well lead to differing conclusions as to the "right" choice to make. And we will, in the future as in the past, turn to the courts, asking judges to make Solomon-like decisions on matters of life and death because, in a society based on the rule of law, where else would we turn?

Theresa Ann

Even as I wrote these previous pages, explaining why we, as a society, turn to our courts as guides through the jungles created by modern medical technology, newspapers carried a story that pointed out, even more starkly, how difficult such questions can be.

In her eighth month of pregnancy, Lauren Campo learned that the baby girl she was carrying did not have a fully formed brain, and would die within a week or two after birth. She and her husband, Justin Pearson, decided that the infant should be delivered by Cesarean section so the baby's organs would not be harmed. These organs could then be used for transplants to other babies that they might live.

A similar decision had been made by Karen Schouten and her husband in 1987 when they learned, also in her eighth month of pregnancy, that their child was anencephalic. They started talking to hospitals, but no one wanted to get involved except Loma Linda University Hospital in southern California, which has pioneered in infant transplants.

Mrs. Schouten's daughter, Gabriel, died after two days, and the hospital immediately transplanted her heart into a baby boy. "It was done beautifully," Mrs. Schouten said, "and with respect for my husband and me, for our baby, for her life." She said that she was "probably one of the proudest people around—to know another little human being is alive when you've lost your own child. It's like smiling through tears."

Ms. Campo delivered her child, named Theresa Ann, on March

21, 1992. The infant had no skull; her brain stem had developed sufficiently, however, to enable her to breathe, but she had no higher brain, and no higher brain activity. She could not feel pain or any other sensation, and functions such as breathing, heartbeat, and even the opening and closing of her tiny hands were all reflexive.

The parents sought a declaration that the child, even though still breathing, was brain-dead, and therefore her organs could be removed and used to save others. Doctors told the court that the child would die within a few days, but in that case the organs would probably be damaged to the point where they could not be used for transplantation.

Judge Estella Moriarty of the Fort Lauderdale Circuit Court ruled on March 26 that state law forbade a declaration of brain-death because a small portion of the brain still functioned. "I can't authorize someone to take your baby's life, however short, however unsatisfactory, to save another child," she declared. "Death is a fact, not an opinion." She did rule, however, that doctors could remove any organs not vital to Theresa Ann's life, such as one kidney.

Lawyers for the parents appealed Judge Moriarty's decision to a higher state court, which rejected the appeal, as did the Florida Supreme Court. No doubt the high court did not want to rule on so controversial an issue, and they were saved from doing so when Theresa Ann died on March 30. But the infant's parents declared that they would continue the legal battle, hoping to set a precedent to help other parents of anencephalic infants in the future.

The issue here is not keeping a child such as Theresa Ann alive, but deciding at what point she is dead. The judge's decision followed the accepted definition of death, which in all states where brain death is the accepted legal definition of death, requires "irreversible cessation of all functions of the entire brain, including the brain stem." Some scholars and doctors have suggested that the brain-death definition be amended to including "brain absent" conditions, but that is a policy decision that legislatures and not judges must make.

The story of Theresa Ann triggered an extensive discussion.

For some, the idea of "harvesting" organs opens a potentially dangerous scenario in which hospitals might rush to declare gravely ill patients dead so that organs could be removed, and indeed, in some parts of the world it appears that poor people are selling organs. The benefit to a small number of people who could be helped by taking organs from anencephalic infants like Theresa Ann is not worth the ethical difficulties raised by the practice. Even a child born without a brain, so long as she breathes, is alive, according to one editorial, and "if we deny Theresa Ann Campo Pearson her humanity, then we have also denied our own."[1]

Others, however, saw the opportunity to serve life, and applauded the parents' efforts to help others, knowing that Theresa Ann could not live. Philosophy professor Carl Cohen of the University of Michigan Medical School said that "cases like this oblige us to rethink our understanding, medical and legal, of when human life comes to an end."

It is interesting that Professor Cohen linked the medical and legal aspects, because here, as in so many other areas, it is the law that we resort to for guidance. Theresa Ann's parents went to court to secure a determination of death, a ruling that one would normally expect to come from a doctor, not a judge. While ethicists, doctors, editorialists, and others applauded or denounced the idea of taking the infant's organs, no one questioned that an appeal to the courts had been perfectly appropriate, the right procedure to follow.

Whether the case will force both doctors and lawyers to rethink the definition of death, as Professor Cohen suggests, here once again modern technology does not allow us the time to sit and frame rational, well-developed philosophies to meet unexpected emergencies. The first organ transplants took place only a short time ago; now, in many instances, they are routine. Infant transplants are an even newer procedure, but also appear well on their way to becoming medically routine. The latest news is about surgery performed on the fetus to correct potential birth defects. The possibilities of intrauterine procedures in infants with irreversible problems, such as anencephaly, raise a whole host of medical, moral and, of course, legal issues.

If we maintain, as I have throughout this book, that individual autonomy ought to be the guiding rule in legal decisions regarding life and death, and that when a person is incompetent to make decisions a parent, spouse, or child should have the authority, what limits, if any, can we or should we put on cases like Theresa Ann's?

There are people who claim that the courts are an inappropriate forum in which to debate these issues. Perhaps. But until another and better one is found, it is to the law that Americans will look for answers.

Notes

PRELUDE

1. Rocco Musolino's story is based on an extensive feature by Susan Okie in the *Washington Post*, 16 June 1991.

2. *New York Times*, 10 January 1991; *Time*, 21 January 1991, 67.

3. *In re the Conservatorship of Wanglie*, No. PX-91-283, Minnesota Dist. Ct., Probate Div. (July 1991).

CHAPTER 1

1. The Quinlans' ordeal is recounted by them in Joseph and Julia Quinlan, with Phyllis Battelle, *Karen Ann: The Quinlans Tell Their Story* (Garden City, N.Y.: Doubleday, 1977).

2. *In re Karen Quinlan*, 70 N.J. 10, 18 (1976).

3. *Id.* at 18–19.

4. *In re Karen Quinlan*, 137 N.J. Super. 227 (1975).

5. *In re Karen Quinlan*, 70 N.J. 10 (1976).

6. Father Andrew M. Greeley, pointing out that the Church did not oppose letting moribund patients die, angrily commented, "Some nuns were always holier than the church." Quoted in James Rachel, "Euthanasia," in Tom Regan, ed., *Matters of Life and Death* (Philadelphia: Temple University Press, 1980), 54.

7. *Cruzan* v. *Director*, 110 S.Ct. 2841 (1990), see Chapter 2.

8. Solomon B. Freehof, *Modern Reform Responsa* (Cincinnati: Hebrew Union College Press, 1971), 189.

9. See the committee report, "A Definition of Irreversible Coma," 205 *Journal of the American Medical Association* 337 (1968); see also 22A Am. Jur. 2d §549 (1988).

10. Alan Meisel, *The Right to Die* (New York: John Wiley & Sons, 1989), 135.

11. Gerald A. Larue, *Euthanasia and Religion* (Los Angeles: The Hemlock

Society, 1985), 26. Larue's book is a compact survey of the attitudes of many religions toward the right to die.

12. Seneca, *De ira*, quoted in Rachels, "Euthanasia," 33.

13. Samson, King Saul and his armor bearer, and Ahitophel, King David's counselor. One might also count King Zimri, who died in a fire he had himself ignited during a time of desperation. I Kings 16:15–20.

14. "Suicide," 5 *Encyclopedia Judaica* 489 (1972).

15. Immanuel Jakobovits, *Jewish Medical Ethics* (New York: Bloch, 1975 rev. ed.), 52–53, and Fred Rosner, *Modern Medicine and Jewish Ethics* (New York: Yeshiva University Press, 1986), ch. 17.

16. Shabbath 15lb.

17. Rosner, *Modern Medicine and Jewish Ethics*, 198–99.

18. *Ibid.*, 199. His contemporary, Rabbi Jacob ben Samuel, went so far as to claim that "it is forbidden to hinder the departure of the soul by the use of medicines," but nearly all other authorities disagree with this view.

19. See Levi Meier, "Code and No-Code: A Psychological Analysis and the Viewpoint of Jewish Law," in Levi Meier, ed., *Jewish Values in Bioethics* (New York: Human Sciences Press, 1986), 42–44.

20. Jakobovits, *Jewish Medical Ethics*, 120–21.

21. Freehof, *Modern Reform Responsa*, 193. Note again the words of Ecclesiastes, "There is a time to live and a time to die."

22. *Ibid.*, 200.

23. *Ibid.*, 203.

24. Fred Rosner, "Rabbi Moshe Feinstein on the Treatment of the Terminally Ill," *Judaism* 37 (Spring 1988): 195.

25. Larue, *Euthanasia and Religion*, 24–25.

26. *Ibid.*, 25.

27. Henry E. Sigerist, *Civilization and Disease* (College Park, Md.: McGrath Publishing Co., 1970), 69–70.

28. Augustine, *The City of God*, quoted in Beth Spring and Ed Larson, *Euthanasia: Spiritual, Medical & Legal Issues in Terminal Health Care* (Portland, Oreg.: Multnomah Press, 1988), 109. Augustine and the other Church fathers relied heavily on scriptures for this view; see Romans 5:1–5, Hebrews 12:7–11, and 2 Corinthians 4:16–17.

29. A good survey of the various attitudes in the 1970s, and the problems faced by Catholic physicians, is a work by two Dominican friars, Benedict M. Ashley and Kevin D. O'Rourke, *Health Care Ethics: A Theological Analysis* (St. Louis: The Catholic Hospital Association, 1978). One can assume the book accurately represents Catholic thinking at the time because it carries the Church's imprimatur. Their views on passive as against active euthanasia would be confirmed in the Vatican statement.

30. J. P. Kenny, "Euthanasia," 5 *New Catholic Encyclopedia* 639–40 (1967).

31. Daniel Maguire, *Death by Choice* (Garden City, N.Y.: Doubleday, 1974), 112. See also Charles E. Curran, *Medicine and Morals* (Washington: Corpus Books, 1970), and John F. Dedek, *Contemporary Medical Ethics* (New York: Sheed & Ward, 1975).

32. Russell L. McIntyre, "Euthanasia: A Soft Paradigm for Medical Ethics," *The Linacre Quarterly* 45 (Feb. 1978): 41–54.

33. A full copy of the "Declaration on Euthanasia" is reprinted in Larue, *Euthanasia and Religion*, 35–43.

34. John J. Paris and Richard McCormick, "The Catholic Tradition on the Use of Nutrition and Fluids," *America* 156 (2 May 1987): 356–61.

35. *In re Jobes*, 100 N.J. 394 (1987).

36. *New York Times*, 3 April 1992.

37. Quoted in Larue, *Euthanasia and Religion*, 58.

38. General Association of General Baptists, *Social Principles Booklet*, quoted in Larue, *Euthanasia and Religion*, 120.

39. Modern Lutherans still believe this. See Martin E. Marty, *Health and Medicine in the Lutheran Tradition* (New York: Crossroad Publishing, 1983), esp. ch. 3.

40. Quoted in Spring and Larson, *Euthanasia*, 115.

41. *Ibid.*, 115, 116.

42. Larue, *Euthanasia and Religion*, 61.

43. Paul D. Simmons, "Death with Dignity: Christians Confront Euthanasia," *Perspectives in Religious Studies* 4 (Summer 1977):141, 156.

44. (Richmond) *Times-Dispatch*, 3 July 1991.

45. Margaret Pabst Battin, *Ethical Issues in Suicide* (Englewood Cliffs, N.J.: Prentice-Hall, 1982), 28.

46. Derek Humphrey and Ann Wickett, *The Right to Die: Understanding Euthanasia* (New York: Harper & Row, 1986), 2.

47. Isma'il R. Al Faruqi, "Islamic Ethics," in S. Cromwell Crawford, ed., *World Religions and Global Ethics* (New York: Paragon House, 1989), 234–35.

48. Robert M. Veatch, *A Theory of Medical Ethics* (New York: Basic Books, 1981), 58–62.

49. A. Venkoba Rao, "India," in Lee A. Headley, ed., *Suicide in Asia and the Near East* (Berkeley: University of California Press, 1983), 210–13.

50. Katherine K. Young, "Euthanasia: Traditional Hindu Views and the Contemporary Debate," in Harold G. Coward, Julius J. Lipner, and Katherine K. Young, *Hindu Ethics: Purity, Abortion, and Euthanasia* (Albany: State University of New York Press, 1989), 71–121.

CHAPTER 2

1. *Pratt v. Davis*, 37 *Chicago Legal News* 213 (1905), cited in *Mohr v. Williams*, 104 N.W. 12 (Minn. 1905). The earliest reported case taking this view is the English case of *Slater v. Baker & Stapleton*, 95 Eng. Rep. 860 (K.B. 1767).

2. *Mohr v. Williams*, 104 N.W. 12, 16 (Minn. 1905).

3. *Schloendorf v. Society of New York Hospital*, 211 N.Y. 125, 129 (1914).

4. For the complex relationship between physician and patient, see Jay Katz, *The Silent World of Doctor and Patient* (New York: Free Press, 1984).

5. *Restatement (Second) of Torts*, §892A and comment b (1977); see also *Restatement (Second) of Contracts*, §15 and comment b (1982).

6. *Estate of Leach v. Shapiro*, 469 N.E.2d 1047, 1052 (Ohio App. 1984).

7. See, however, *Canterbury* v. *Spence*, 464 F.2d 772, 779 (D.C. Cir. 1972), in which Circuit Judge Spottswood W. Robinson III warned that the scope of the privilege had to be carefully circumscribed.

8. Meisel, *Right to Die*, 39.

9. Some ethicists and legal scholars question whether the distinction between "active" and "passive" euthanasia is valid. For the argument that there is a substantive difference, see Alex Capron, "The Right to Die: Progress and Peril," 2 *Euthanasia Review* 41 (1987), and a critique of that argument in Charles H. Baron, "The Fictional Distinction between Active and Passive Euthanasia and the Danger It Poses to the Civil Liberties of Patients," paper prepared for Substantive Plenary I at the American Civil Liberties Union Biennial Conference (June 1991).

10. Joseph and Julia Quinlan, with Phyllis Battelle, *Karen Ann: The Quinlans Tell Their Story* (Garden City, N.Y.: Doubleday, 1977), 256–58.

11. *In re Colyer*, 660 P.2d 738, 751 (Wash. 1983).

12. *Barber* v. *Superior Court*, 147 Cal. App.3d 1006, 195 Cal. Rptr. 484 (1983).

13. Humphrey and Wickett, *Right to Die*, 252.

14. *In re Spring*, 405 N.E.2d 115, 121 (Mass. 1980).

15. *John F. Kennedy Memorial Hospital* v. *Bludworth*, 452 So.2d 921, 926 (Fla. 1984).

16. *In re Hamlin*, 102 Wash.2d 810 (1984).

17. *In re Quinlan*, 355 A.2d 647, 664 (N.J. 1976).

18. 381 U.S. 479 (1965).

19. 410 U.S. 113 (1973).

20. 355 A.2d at 663.

21. Some state constitutions, however, do include an explicit right of privacy, and in those jurisdictions courts may ground right-to-die decisions on a state constitutional basis. See, for example, *Bartling* v. *Superior Court*, 163 Cal. App.3d 186 (1984); *Rasmussen* v. *Fleming*, 154 Ariz. 207 (1987); and more recently, *In re Browning*, 543 So.2d 258 (Fla. Dist. Ct. App. 1989).

22. As a New York court noted, it did not have to deal with this controversy, because the right to refuse medical treatment "is adequately supported by common-law principles." *Eichner* v. *Dillon*, 438 N.Y.S.2d 266, 273 (1981).

23. See Chapter 7, "Advance Directives."

24. *Superintendent of Belchertown State Hospital* v. *Saikewicz*, 373 Mass. 728 (1977).

25. See the discussion of the courts as decision makers in Norman L. Cantor, *Legal Frontiers of Death and Dying* (Bloomington: Indiana University Press, 1987), 113–17.

26. *In re Dinnerstein*, 6 Mass. App. Ct. 466 (1978).

27. *Eichner* v. *Dillon*, 426 N.Y.S.2d (1980). The case is discussed by C. Dickerman Williams, "Brother Fox and John Storar . . .," in A. Edward Doudera and J. Douglas Peters, eds., *Legal and Ethical Aspects of Treating Critically and Terminally Ill Patients* (Ann Arbor, Mich.: Health Administration Press, 1982), 164–72.

28. *In re Storar*, 52 N.Y.2d 363 (1981).

29. *Satz* v. *Perlmutter*, 362 So.2d 160 (Fla. Dist. Ct. App. 1978). One year later, the Florida Supreme Court in a unanimous ruling adopted the lower court's reasoning. Comparing disconnection of the respirator to the passive act of refusing surgery, the court held that only intentional death warrants the state's interest in preventing suicide. 379 So.2d 359 (Fla. 1980).

30. For a discussion of some of these cases, see Humphrey and Wickett, *Right to Die*, ch. 16, and Irving J. Sloan, *The Right to Die: Legal and Ethical Problems* (New York: Oceana, 1988), ch. 2.

31. Some special situations, such as severely retarded infants, are discussed in later chapters.

32. See Richard P. Byrne, "Deciding for the Legally Incompetent: A View from the Bench," in Doudera and Peters, *Legal and Ethical Aspects*, ch. 4. There is a debate over whether courts are the proper vehicles for deciding moral questions; in fact, courts do bring moral values to bear, especially when adjudicating highly emotional and sensitive questions for the first time.

33. For a perceptive discussion of these issues, see Cantor, *Frontiers of Death and Dying*, chs. 3–5.

34. 405 N.E.2d at 118.

35. George J. Annas, "Quality of Life in the Courts: Earle Spring in Fantasyland," *Hastings Center Report* (Aug. 1980), 10.

36. "Whose Right to Die?" *Time* (11 December 1989), 80.

37. *New York Times*, 14 January 1990.

38. *Cruzan* v. *Harmon*, 760 S.W.2d 408 (Mo 1988).

39. *Cruzan* v. *Director*, 110 S.Ct. 2841, 2851 (1990). The "prior decisions" included *Jacobson* v. *Massachusetts*, 197 U.S. 11 (1905), in which the Court upheld a state's interest in preventing disease over the individual's liberty interest in refusing a smallpox vaccination; reference to various Fourth Amendment cases involving seizure and body searches; *Washington* v. *Harper*, 110 S.Ct. 1028 (1990), administering antipsychotic medication to a prisoner; and *Parham* v. *J.R.*, 442 U.S. 584 (1979), involuntary confinement of a child for medical treatment.

40. *Cruzan* v. *Director*, 110 S.Ct. 2876, 2873, 2869.

41. See the discussion of how the decision may influence health care professionals in Larry Gostin and Robert F. Weir, "Life and Death Choices after *Cruzan*: Case Law and Standard of Professional Conduct," 69 *Milbank Quarterly* 143 (1991).

42. *Washington Post*, 16 October 1990.

43. *New York Times*, 16 December 1990.

44. *New York Times*, 22 December 1990.

45. See stories in *New York Times* and *Washington Post* in the two weeks following Judge Teel's ruling.

CHAPTER 3

1. The incident and my friend's response are recounted in Jerome Eckstein, *Metaphysical Drift: Love and Judaism* (New York: Peter Lang, 1991),

205–209. I am indebted to Professor Eckstein for sharing his work with me while it was still in manuscript form.

2. *Anthony and Cleopatra*, act 4, sc. 15, lines 80–82.

3. Glanville Williams, *The Sanctity of Life and the Criminal Law* (New York: Knopf, 1957), 251–54.

4. Augustine, *The City of God* (New York: Everyman's Library, 1945), bk I, ch. 19.

5. Joseph Fletcher, "In Defense of Suicide," in Samuel E. Wallace and Albin Eser, eds., *Suicide and Euthanasia: The Rights of Personhood* (Knoxville: University of Tennessee Press, 1981), 42.

6. Williams, *Sanctity of Life*, 259–60.

7. Quoted in *Commonwealth v. Mink*, 123 Mass. 422, 426 (1877).

8. 40 Am Jur 2d §583 (1988). For an account of English and American practice, as well as changing popular attitudes, see Howard J. Kushner, *Self-Destruction in the Promised Land: A Psychocultural Biology of American Suicide* (New Brunswick, N.J.: Rutgers University Press, 1989).

9. See, for example, *State v. Willis*, 255 N.C. 473 (1961), holding that an attempt to commit suicide is an indictable misdemeanor under North Carolina law; and *State v. LaFayette*, 15 N.J. Misc. 115 (1937), holding that an attempt at suicide is an indictable offense even though suicide itself is not punishable.

10. *Hales v. Petit*, 75 E.R. 398 (1562). The case rose out of the supposed suicide by drowning of Justice Hales, and, incidentally, is considered to have inspired the gravedigger's colloquy in *Hamlet*.

11. Blackstone, 4 *Commentaries on the Laws of England* 189 (1771).

12. *Regina v. Doody*, 23 L.T.O.S., 6 Cox 463 (1854).

13. *Williams, Sanctity of Life*, 276.

14. The notion of a "death wish" as evidence of mental incompetence has appeared in a few judicial opinions; see, for example, *People v. Stanworth*, 71 Cal.2d 820 (1969). The Supreme Court, however, has refused to make this connection. "The empirical relationship between mental illness and . . . a suicide attempt need not always signal an in inability to perceive reality accurately." *Drope v. Missouri*, 420 U.S. 162, 181 n.16 (1975).

15. Tom L. Beauchamp and James F. Childress, *Principles of Biomedical Ethics* (New York: Oxford University Press, 1979), 87–89.

16. Quoted in Eike-Henner W. Kluge, *The Ethics of Deliberate Death* (Port Washington, N.Y.: Kennikat Press, 1981), 82.

17. See the discussion of suicide from a humanist point of view in Joseph Fletcher, *Humanhood: Essays in Biomedical Ethics* (Buffalo, N.Y.: Prometheus Books, 1979), ch. 14.

18. Beauchamp and Childress, *Biomedical Ethics*, 89.

19. Meisel, *Right to Die*, §3.4.

20. Beauchamp and Childress, *Biomedical Ethics*, 87.

21. *In re President of Georgetown College*, 331 F.2d 1000, 1015 (D.C. Cir. 1964) (Burger, J., dissenting), quoting *Olmstead v. United States*, 277 U.S. 438, 478 (1928) (Brandeis, J., dissenting);

22. Some scholars have argued that only autonomy need be considered,

because it is the individual who must make the decision. See Thomas S. Szasz, "The Ethics of Suicide," 31 *Antioch Review* 7 (1971).

23. Beauchamp and Childress, *Biomedical Ethics*, 89. Although there are no cases in which a court has specifically approved a person's request to commit suicide, there are some in which we can see a form of this calculus applied in refusal-of-treatment cases. Several cases have followed the rule that where minor children are dependent upon the individual, the obligation to them precludes a right to refuse treatment, even on religious grounds. See, e.g., *Holmes* v. *Silver Cross Hospital*, 340 F. Supp. 125 (N.D. Ill. 1972). In *Raleigh Fitkin-Paul Morgan Memorial Hospital* v. *Anderson*, 42 N.J. 421 (1964), the court ordered a transfusion for a pregnant woman to preserve the life of her unborn child.

24. See, for example, Thomas J. Marzen *et al.*, "Suicide: A Constitutional Right?" 24 *Duquesne Law Review* 1 (1985).

25. *Washington Post*, 20 December 1990.

26. Kevorkian had tried in vain to secure rooms at either a motel or a funeral home, but when he had explained what he wanted to do he had been turned away. So the only place he had was an old 1968 Volkswagen van.

27. *New York Times*, 14 December 1990. The Michigan legislature finally acted in November 1992. It temporarily made assisting suicide a criminal act, but set up a special commission to recommend permanent legislation within fifteen months.

28. Transcript of NPR "Morning Edition," 11 January 1991, 35.

29. *New York Times*, 6 February 1991.

30. *Ibid.*

31. *New York Times*, 9 January 1991.

32. *Commonwealth* v. *Bowen*, 13 Mass. 356 (1816); *State* v. *Webb*, 216 Mo. 378 (1909); see also annotation at 13 ALR 1259.

33. See 40 Am. Jur. 2d §586.

34. *New York Times*, 6 February 1991.

35. *Time*, 4 November 1991.

36. *USA Today*, 24 October 1991. Opinion on the morality of Kevorkian's action was sharply divided, but many agreed that unless some rules were adopted and enforced, similar death machines could easily be invented and abused. *New York Times*, 25 October 1991.

37. *New York Times*, 9 December 1990.

38. *New York Times*, 9 June 1990. A recent survey conducted by a medical journal found that 10.7 percent of the physicians polled said they would write a prescription for a fatal drug overdose for an AIDS patient who asked, and 9.4 percent admitted to having taken some action to cause the death of a patient at some point in their careers. *Physician's Management* (July 1991).

39. See, for example, *In re Gardner*, 534 A.2d 947, 955 (Me. 1987); *In re Lydia E. Hall Hospital*, 455 N.Y.S.2d 706, 711 (Sup. Ct. 1982); and *In re Quinlan*, 70 N.J. 10 (1976). Courts have also ruled, in states that have natural-death acts, that "acts in accordance with a directive are not deemed suicide . . . and the cause of death shall be that which placed the patient in a terminal condition." *In re Colyer*, 660 P.2d 738, 751 (Wash. 1983).

40. *Satz* v. *Perlmutter*, 362 So.2d 160, 162–63 (Fla. Dist. Ct. App. 1978); see also *Bouvia* v. *Superior Court*, 255 Cal. Rptr. 297, 305–306 (Cal. App. 1986), and *McKay* v. *Bergstedt*, 801 P.2d 617, 625 (Nev. 1990).

41. How wrenching this issue can be for doctors is explored in Richard Selzer, "A Question of Mercy," *New York Times Magazine*, 22 September 1991.

42. The following account is based on Timothy E. Quill, "Death and Dignity: A Case of Individualized Decision Making," 324 *New England Journal of Medicine* 691 (March 1991), and transcript of NPR's "All Things Considered," 7 March 1991, 14–17.

43. *New York Times*, 27 July 1991.

44. *USA Today*, 12 March 1991.

45. *New York Times*, 11 May 1991.

46. "All Things Considered" transcript, 16.

47. *Washington Post*, 3 November 1991.

48. *New York Times*, 7 November 1991. The following year a similar ballot initiative in California, No. 161, went down to defeat by an identical margin. *New York Times*, 5 November 1992.

49. *New York Times*, 9 June 1990.

50. Complaint for Declaratory Relief, *Rodas* v. *Erkenbrack*, quoted in James Bopp, Jr., "Is Assisted Suicide Constitutionally Protected?" 3 *Issues in Law & Medicine* 113 (1987).

51. *Bouvia* v. *Superior Court (Glenchur)*, 179 Cal. App.3d 1127, 1147 (1986).

52. See George C. Garbesi, "The Law of Assisted Suicide," 3 *Issues in Law & Medicine* 93 (1987), for the legal arguments about why such penalties should ensue.

CHAPTER 4

1. *New York Times*, 29 and 30 December 1987.

2. *Ibid.*, 13 May 1988.

3. *Franz* v. *State*, 296 Ark. 181 (1988).

4. *Whitmore, as Next Friend of Simmons* v. *State*, 298 Ark. 255 (1989).

5. *Whitmore, as Next Friend . . .* v. *Arkansas*, 110 S.Ct. 1717 (1990); Justice Brennan and Marshall dissented, as they always did in capital punishment cases, because they believed the death penalty *per se* was unconstitutional.

6. *New York Times*, 26 June 1990.

7. *Furman* v. *Georgia*, 408 U.S. 238 (1972).

8. *Gregg* v. *Georgia*, 428 U.S. 153 (1976).

9. To take just one recent example, see Joseph H. Sharlitt, *Fatal Error: The Miscarriage of Justice That Sealed the Rosenbergs' Fate* (New York: Scribner's, 1989).

10. See, for example, Hugo A. Bedau, *The Courts, the Constitution, and Capital Punishment* (Lexington, Mass.: Lexington Books, 1977), 121–25.

11. *Gilmore* v. *Utah*, 429 U.S. 1012, 1013 n.1 (1976) (Burger, C.J., concurring in vacating stay of execution).

12. See Norman Mailer, *The Executioner's Song* (Boston: Little, Brown, 1979).

13. *Ibid.*, 521.

14. Several cases are examined in detail in Melvin I. Urofsky, "A Right to Die: Termination of Appeal for Condemned Prisoners," 75 *Journal of Criminal Law & Criminology* 553 (1984).

15. *Bishop* v. *State*, 95 Nev. 511, 597 P.2d 273 (1979).

16. *Lenhard ex rel. Bishop* v. *Wolff*, 603 F.2d 91 (9th Cir. 1979); stay of execution denied, 444 U.S. 807 (1979).

17. *Coppola* v. *Commonwealth*, 220 Va. 243, 257 S.E. 797 (1979), cert. denied, 444 U.S. 1103 (1980).

18. *Mitchell* v. *Lawrence*, 458 U.S. 1123 (1982); for criticism and defense of the Court's action, see *Los Angeles Daily Journal*, 3 September 1982.

19. "An Eye for an Eye," *Time*, 24 January 1983, 32.

20. Robert Lee Massie, "Death by Degrees," *Esquire*, April 1971, 179.

21. Clinton T. Duffy, *88 Men and 2 Women* (Garden City, N. Y.: Doubleday, 1962), 254.

22. Note, "Mental Suffering under Sentence of Death: A Cruel and Unusual Punishment," 57 *Iowa Law Review* 814, 815 n.5 (1972). In some prisons (and not just on death row) conditions were so bad that various state and federal courts ordered immediate remediation; see Comment, "Federal Intervention in State Prisons: The Modern Prison-Conditions Case," 19 *Houston Law Review* 931 (1982).

23. See, for example, Stephen M. Gettinger, *Sentenced to Die: The People, the Crimes, and the Controversy* (New York: Macmillian, 1979); Bruce Jackson and Diane Christian, *Death Row* (Boston: Beacon Press, 1980); Robert Johnson, *Condemned to Die: Life under Sentence of Death* (New York: Elsevier, 1981); and Harvey Bluestone and Carl L. McGahee, "Reaction to Stress: Impending Death by Execution," 119 *American Journal of Psychiatry* 393 (1962).

24. Johnson, *Condemned to Die*, 47, 48.

25. Gettinger, *Sentenced to Die*, 96.

26. Jacques Barzun, "In Favor of Capital Punishment," 31 *American Scholar* 188, 188–89 (1962).

27. Quoted in Mailer, *Executioner's Song*, 706.

28. *In re Kemmler*, 136 U.S. 436, 447 (1890).

29. *Trop* v. *Dulles*, 356 U.S. 86, 102 (1958); the Court held it unconstitutional to punish a person by denaturalization.

30. This argument is well made in Kathleen L. Johnson, "The Death Row Right to Die: Suicide or Intimate Decision," 54 *Southern California Law Review* 575 (1981).

31. See *Rees* v. *Peyton*, 384 U.S. 312 (1966).

32. *Culombe* v. *Connecticut*, 367 U.S. 568, 602 (1961).

33. *Rumbaugh* v. *Estelle*, 558 F. Supp 651, 653, (N.D. Tex. 1983).

34. See, for example, *People* v. *Stanworth*, 71 Cal.2d 820 (1969), and *Massie* v. *Summer*, 624 F.2d 72 (9th Cir. 1980).

35. Bedau, *Courts, Constitution and Capital Punishment,* 122; see also Justice Marshall's dissent in *Lenhard ex rel. Bishop* v. *Wolff,* 444 U.S. 807, 815 (1979).

36. Bedau, *Courts, Constitution and Capital Punishment,* 121–25.

37. Burton H. Wolfe, *Pileup on Death Row* (Garden City, N.Y.: Doubleday, 1973), 29–30.

38. One need not go as far as Thomas Szasz, a proponent of the death penalty, who claimed that Gilmore was trying to force Utah to live up to its "contract" with him. Szasz, "The Right to Die," *New Republic,* 11 December 1976, 8.

39. Martin Gardner, "Execution and Indignities: An Eighth Amendment Assessment of Methods of Inflicting Capital Punishment," 39 *Ohio State Law Journal* 96, 110–11 (1978).

40. See, for example, Ramona Ripston's discussion of this in the *Daily News,* 20 April 1992; Ms. Ripston is executive director of the ACLU of Southern California.

41. Fitzgerald, "The Loss of a Client," *The Advocate,* October 1982, 1. See the related discussion of whether prisoners should in essence be allowed to commit suicide in Steven C. Sunshine, "Should a Hunger-Striking Prisoner Be Allowed to Die?" 25 *Boston College Law Review* 423 (1984).

42. Johnson, *Condemned to Die,* 110–12; see also Jackson and Christian, *Death Row,* 264–65.

43. Glanville Williams, "Euthanasia," 41 *Medico-Legal Journal* 27 (1973).

44. Gettinger, *Sentenced to Die,* 70.

45. See Charles L. Black, *Capital Punishment: The Inevitability of Caprice and Mistake* (New York: Norton, 2d ed. 1981).

46. *Potts* v. *Austin,* 429 F. Supp. 326 (N.D. Ga. 1980); see also *Atlanta Constitution,* 14 January 1983, D1.

47. *Lenhard ex rel. Bishop* v. *Wolff,* 603 F.2d 91, 94 (9th Cir. 1979).

CHAPTER 5

1. For a moving story of how medical miracles kept one severely disabled child alive, and the enormous emotional damage it wreaked on his parents, see Robert and Peggy Stinson, *The Long Dying of Baby Andrew* (Boston: Little, Brown, 1983).

2. See, for example, Paul and Marlys Bridge, "The Brief Life and Death of Christopher Bridge," 11 *Hastings Center Report* 17 (December 1981), and the anonymous "The Parents Doe," *Nation,* 25 February 1984, 213.

3. *Science,* 25 November 1983, 908.

4. *Newsweek,* 14 November 1983, 84.

5. *Weber* v. *Stony Brook Hospital,* 467 N.Y.S.2d 685 (1983).

6. *Weber* v. *Stony Brook Hospital,* 469 N.Y.S.2d 63 (1983), *cert. denied,* 464 U.S. 1026 (1983). In its opinion the court chastized "the unusual, and sometimes offensive, activities and proceedings of those who have sought at various stages . . . to displace parental authority."

7. *Parham* v. *J.R.,* 442 U.S. 584, 602 (1979).

8. See *Parham* v. *J.R.*, 442 U.S. 584 (1979); *In re Philip B.*, 92 Cal.App.3d 796 (1979); and *In re Hofbauer*, 47 N.Y.2d 684 (1979), in which the court noted that "every parent has a fundamental right to rear its child."

9. *New York Times*, July 2 and 4, 1990. See Annotations, "Power of Public Authorities to Order Medical Care for a Child over Objection of Parent or Guardian," 30 A.L.R.2d 1138 (1953), and "Power of Court or Other Agency to Order Medical Treatment over Parental Religious Objections for Child Whose Life Is Not Immediately Endangered," 52 A.L.R.3d 1118 (1973). The Supreme Court has upheld the right of lower courts to declare children wards of the court and then order blood transfusions over the religious objections of the parents. *Jehovah's Witnesses* v. *King County Hospital*, 278 F.Supp. 488 (W.D. Wash. 1967), *aff'd* 390 U.S. 598 (1968).

10. *Custody of a Minor*, 358 Mass. 697 (1982).

11. *In re Barry*, 445 So.2d 365 (Fla. Dist. Ct. App. 1984).

12. Helga Kuhse and Peter Singer, *Should the Baby Live? The Problem of Handicapped Infants* (New York: Oxford University Press, 1985). The authors report that ethnographic studies of 393 societies indicated that 302 had practiced infanticide "at least occasionally." See p. 108.

13. Anthony Shaw, "Dilemmas of 'Informed Consent' in Children," 289 *New England Journal of Medicine* 885 (1973), and Raymond Duff and A. G. M. Campbell, "Moral and Ethical Dilemmas in the Special Care Nursery," *ibid.* at 890.

14. Mary Tedeschi, "Infanticide and Its Apologists," *Commentary*, November 1984, 34; see also the sensible and sensitive discussion of the Oklahoma experiment by Charles Krauthammer, "What to Do About 'Baby Doe,' " *New Republic*, 2 September 1985, 18–21.

15. Paul Ramsey, *Ethics at the Edges of Life* (New Haven: Yale University Press, 1978), 203.

16. Meisel, *Right to Die*, 432.

17. The issue is discussed at length in President's Commission for the Study of Ethical Problems in Medicine and Biomedical and Behavioral Research, *Deciding to Forgo Life-Sustaining Treatment* (Washington: Government Printing Office, 1983), 209 ff.

18. *In re Cicero*, 421 N.Y.S 2d 965 (Sup. Ct. 1979).

19. *Newsweek*, 6 July 1981, 24.

20. *Newsweek*, 22 June 1981, 40; *New York Times*, 16 May 1982, A-49; John A. Robertson, "Dilemma in Danville," 11 *Hastings Center Report* 5 (October 1981).

21. Senate Report 98–246, "Child Abuse Amendments," 98th Cong., 2d Sess. (Washington: Government Printing Office, 1984), 10.

22. *Ibid.*, 45–46.

23. Quoted in Tedeschi, "Infanticide and Its Apologists," 31.

24. *State ex rel. Doe* v. *Baker*, No. 482 S 140 (Ind. Sup. Ct. May 27, 1982), *cert. denied*, 464 U.S. 961 (1983).

25. Quoted in George J. Annas, "Disconnecting the Baby Doe Hotline," 13 *Hastings Center Report* 14 (June 1983).

26. In the first four weeks the hotline was connected, the agency received about 600 calls, most of which were either comments or requests for the

poster. Twenty percent were wrong numbers. Only sixteen callers made specific allegations, and of these only five were deemed worthy of initial investigation, and none of them proved to warrant further examination. As George Annas concluded, "Either there are no instances of withholding care inappropriately or the hotline is an ineffective means of identifying them." Six months later, the total number of calls had increased to 1600; the government had investigated 43 incidents without uncovering any wrongdoing.

27. 48 Fed. Reg. 9630, 9631 (7 March 1983).

28. *American Academy of Pediatrics et al.* v. *Heckler*, 561 F.Supp. 395 (D.D.C. 1983).

29. See, for example, Annas, "Disconnecting the Baby Doe Hotline," 15–16.

30. 49 Fed. Reg. 1622 (12 January 1984).

31. *Newsweek*, 28 November 1983, 45.

32. *United States* v. *University Hospital*, 575 F.Supp. 607, 614 (E.D.N.Y. 1983).

33. *Deciding to Forgo . . . Treatment*, 6.

34. *Christianity Today*, 16 December 1983, 48.

35. *Ibid.*

36. *United States* v. *University Hospital*, 729 F.2d 144 (2d Cir. 1984); the appeals court also rejected the government's request that it rehear the case *en banc*, that is with all of the judges on the court rather than the three-judge panel.

37. *Id.* at 161.

38. Robert F. Drinan, "The Supreme Court and Baby Doe," *America*, 8 March 1986, 182. Justice Rehnquist did not take part in the case because his son-in-law's law firm did work for the American Hospital Association.

39. *Bowen* v. *American Hospital Association*, 476 U.S. 610 (1986). In the Baby Jane Doe case, the Court of Appeals effectively negated the new rules before they went into effect. In a follow-up case, the district court actually invalidated the rules; *American Hospital Association* v. *Heckler*, 585 F.Supp. 541 (S.D.N.Y. 1984). It was that case, renamed when Ms. Heckler was replaced at HHS by Otis R. Bowen, that the Supreme Court took, but it involved the same issue as in the original Baby Jane Doe litigation.

40. 476 U.S. at 630. In other parts of the opinion the Court criticized the administration for impermissibly intruding on state authority, by its forcing state agencies to enforce compliance by other recipients of federal aid. "State child protective services agencies are not field offices of HHS bureaucracy, and they may not be conscripted against their will as the foot soldiers in a federal crusade."

41. The civil-rights advocate Nat Hentoff was a strong supporter of the legislation, and unlike many of his liberal colleagues, vigorously opposed allowing parents or doctors to decide that handicapped babies should die. In addition to his regular columns in the *Village Voice*, see "The Awful Privacy of Baby Doe," *Atlantic Monthly*, January 1985, 54–58, 61–62.

42. *Christianity Today*, 13 July 1984, 44. In fact, the AMA did oppose any governmental interference in medical decision making, holding that only

parents in consultation with their doctors should decide on what is best for the infant.

43. See the discussion of abortion and infanticide in Fletcher, *Humanhood*, chs. 10 and 11.

44. *Science News*, 14 July 1984, 25. As recently as 1989, the AMA's Council on Ethical and Judicial Affairs reaffirmed the organization's position that "in the making of decisions for the treatment of seriously deformed newborns . . . quality of life is a factor to be considered in determining what is best for the individual."

45. *Science*, 25 November 1983, 908; see also Arthur Caplan, "Is It a Life?" *Nation*, 21 January 1984, 37.

46. For a detailed examination of the regulations, see Dixie Snow Huefner, "Severely Handicapped Infants with Life-Threatening Conditions: Federal Intrusions Into the Decision Not to Treat," 12 *American Journal of Law and Medicine* 171 (1986).

47. In Louisiana, where state law anticipated the federal regulations, hospitals and doctors already report that their discretion and that of parents has been drastically restricted. See Michael Vitiello, "On Letting Seriously Ill Minors Die: A Review of Louisiana's Natural Death Act," 31 *Loyola Law Review* 67 (1985).

48. Meisel, *Right to Die*, §14.25.

49. Quoted in Andrew C. Varga, "The Ethics of Infant Euthanasia," 57 *Thought* 438, 439 (1982).

50. See the debate on this question between Ernest Van Den Haag and Lacey Washington in *National Review*, 10 February 1984, 36–38.

51. The lack of case law on this issue should not obscure the intense ethical debate that is currently going on. See, among many others, B. D. Cohen, *Hard Choices* (New York: Putnam, 1986); Richard McMillan and others, *Euthanasia and the Newborn* (Boston: Reidel, 1987); Jeff Lyon, *Playing God in the Nursery* (New York: Norton, 1985); and Earl E. Shelp, *Born to Die? Deciding the Fate of Critically Ill Newborns* (New York: Free Press, 1986).

CHAPTER 6

1. *New York Times*, 11 May 1991.

2. The major treatise on the subject emphasizes that so-called "mercy killing" does not come under the legal rubric of "right to die." Meisel, *Right to Die*, §1.8.

3. *People Weekly* 23, 27 May 1985, 100.

4. Gilbert later gave an interview to *People Weekly* reporter Linda Marx, in which he talked about his life with Emily, and her slow, painful deterioration. *People Weekly*, 27, 12 January 1987, 30–32.

5. *Time*, 27 May 1985, 66–67.

6. The lead attorney for Gilbert was the flamboyant Joe Varon, who believed he could make the debate over euthanasia work in his client's behalf. Varon, who had once defended mobster Meyer Lansky, accepted as his fee

the television and publishing rights to Gilbert's story, which he later sold for $50,000.

7. *New York Times*, 9, 23, and 27 August 1985.

8. Model Penal Code, Section 210.1 (1). The Model Penal; Code, drafted in 1962 by the American Law Institute, attempts to establish base norms for criminal statutes.

9. Model Penal Code, Section 210.2(1) (b).

10. Many states distinguish between murder and capital murder, killings committed under specified circumstances that may be punished by the death penalty.

11. Model Penal Code, Section 210.3(1) (b).

12. Different standards apply to grand juries as opposed to petit juries. For a grand jury to hand down an indictment, guilt does not have to be proven, only that there is reasonable cause to believe that the defendant has done what the prosecutor alleges. The accused may often be unaware of allegations against him or her, and the grand jury only hears witnesses the prosecutor calls. Before a petit jury, however, the state has the burden of proving convincingly that the defendant committed the alleged crime; the defense may call witnesses on its behalf, and it does not have to "prove" innocence, but merely raise a sufficient doubt as to the prosecution's case.

13. "I Helped Her on Her Way," *Newsweek* 7 November 1988, 101; "A Civil Lawyer's First Criminal Case," *Trial* 25, August 1989, 22–24.

14. "Newsletter," Society for the Right to Die, [n.d. 1991].

15. As noted in Chapter 3, assisting suicide is a crime in some states but not in others. The Model Penal Code proposes that aiding a suicide be considered a criminal act. "A person who purposely aids or solicits another to commit suicide is guilty of a felony of the second degree if his conduct causes such suicide or an attempted suicide, and otherwise of a misdemeanor." Sec. 210.5(2).

16. A number of people believe that society ignores many mercy killings that take place in the home. It is one thing to walk into a hospital and shoot a patient; it is another to withhold medication at home, or perhaps to take positive steps to put a loved one out of misery. Few doctors will order an autopsy on an elderly person unless there is clear evidence of foul play.

CHAPTER 7

1. In order to impose some order on the rash of cases that arose following *Quinlan*, the New Jersey Supreme Court set out three tests: 1) Is there evidence that the patient, when competent, would have refused the particular treatment involved; 2) If the patient would have refused, do the benefits of sustaining life (any physical pleasure, emotional enjoyment, or intellectual satisfaction) outweigh the pain and suffering involved; or 3) Is the patient in such terrible physical or mental condition and suffering from so much pain that prolonging life would be inhumane. *In re Conroy*, 98 N.J. 321 (1985).

2. *In re Farrell*, 108 N.J. 335 (1987). Kathleen Farrell had developed Lou Gehrig's disease, and after experimental treatment had failed, became paralyzed and dependent on a respirator. Conscious and capable of talking, she declared her wishes to be disconnected. Her husband sought court appointment as guardian in order to carry out his wife's wishes, and the trial court granted his application, but stayed its order pending appellate review. While the hearings were taking place, Kathleen Farrell died, but the court decided to pass on the merits because of the importance of the issue, and the fact that similar requests would be forthcoming.

3. *In re Peter*, 108 N.J. 365, 373 (1987).

4. Judge Alan B. Handler, in his concurring opinion, wrote that "Ms. Peter's granting of a durable power of attorney to Mr. Johanning, combined with the fact that he was a close friend of Ms. Peter, is sufficient evidence that the treatment decision made for Ms. Peter now that she is incompetent is one with which she would have been content." 108 N.J. at 386.

5. Although the terms "advance directive" and "living will" are often used interchangeably, they are not the same. A living will is one form of advance directive, although it is popularly used in reference to all kinds. The 1983 President's Commission for the Study of Ethical Problems in Medicine chose the phrase "advance directive" in an effort to be more precise. It appears, unlikely, however, that popular use of "living will" as a catchall phrase will fade away.

6. Over the centuries, of course, parents and spouses have given instructions to their families on what they wished, should they become incapacitated.

7. Luis Kutner, "Due Process of Euthanasia: The Living Will, a Proposal," 44 *Indiana Law Journal* 539 (1969).

8. *Estate of Leach* v. *Shapiro*, 469 N.E.2d 1047, 1053 (Ohio App. 1984).

9. In a New York case, the court agreed with the hospital that a patient's comments that she would never want to lose her dignity, that nature should be permitted to take its course, and that it was "monstrous" to use life-support machinery did not preclude the use of artificial nutrition and hydration. *In re O'Connor*, 72 N.Y.2d 517 (1988).

10. *Cruzan* v. *Director, Missouri Dept. of Health*, 110 S.Ct. 2841 (1990); see discussion in Chapter 2.

11. *John F. Kennedy Memorial Hospital* v. *Bludworth*, 432 So.2d 611, 614 (1983), the initial appellate hearing in Florida's Fourth Circuit of the Landy case, which is discussed next.

12. *John F. Kennedy Memorial Hospital* v. *Bludworth*, 452 So.2d 921, 923, 925 (Fla. 1984).

13. *Id.* at 926.

14. *In re Conroy*, 98 N.J. 321 (1985).

15. *In re Peter*, 108 N.J. 365 (1987).

16. *Saunders* v. *State*, 492 N.Y.S.2d 510 (1985). However, the court went on to give practical effect to the document by treating it as a variety of informed-medical-consent statement. See analysis by Sharon M. Paulus in 1 *Issues in Law & Medicine* 409 (1986).

17. 98 N.J. at 362. Newly discovered oral evidence also permitted the Cruzan family to prove that Nancy would not have wanted to live in a persistent vegetative state; see Chapter 2.

18. *Choice in Dying News* (Summer 1992):4. For recent evaluations of state law, see Christopher J. Condie, "Comparison of the Living Will Statutes of the Fifty States," 14 *Journal of Contemporary Law* 105 (1988), and Shari Lobe, "The Will to Die: Survey of State Living Will Legislation and Case Law," 9 *Probate Law Journal* 47 (1989).

19. See, for example, Code of Virginia, 1984 Cum. Supp. §54–325.8:1, codifying the Virginia Natural Death Act of 1983.

20. Society for the Right to Die, "Legislation Backgrounder," July 1990.

21. Nancy Cruzan's condition, for example, would not fit most state's definition of terminal condition or terminal illness. According to Leslie Pickering Francis, a law professor at the University of Utah, people with debilitating strokes or Alzheimer's disease or those in permanent comas are not included under most natural-death statutes. (*New York Times*, 19 March 1990.) For problems with terminology, see Susan J. Nanovic, "The Living Will: Preservation of the Right-to-Die Demands Clarity and Consistency," 95 *Dickinson Law Review* 209, 216–19 (1990).

22. The Florida Supreme Court later reversed this ruling, and interpreted the statute more broadly to give guardians greater authority in carrying out the intent of advance directives. By then, however, Mrs. Browning had died. *In re Browning*, 543 So.2d 258 (Fla. Dist. Ct. App. 1989), aff'd 568 So.2d 4 (Fla. 1990). For a similar problem, see *Delio* v. *Westchester County Medical Center*, 516 N.Y.S.2d 677 (App. Div. 2d Dept. 1987). See the discussion of such cases in Nanovic, "Living Will," 219–24.

23. Uniform Rights of the Terminally Ill Act (1989 draft), §1.

24. S. Van McCrary and Jeffrey R. Botkin, "Hospital Policy on Advance Directives," 262 *Journal of the American Medical Association* (3 November 1989) 2411.

25. The measure passed as part of the Omnibus Budget Reconciliation Act of 1990, Public Law 101–508, codified as 42 U.S.C. §§1395cc(f) (1) and 1396a(a).

26. According to one study, only one in ten mentally competent adults have signed a living will, and a far smaller number have designated someone else to make the decisions should they become incompetent. (*New York Times*, 8 December 1990.) Approximately half of the population has a regular will disposing of their property.

27. *New York Times*, 23 July 1990.

28. *Ibid.*

29. Joel M. Zinberg, "Decisions for the Dying: An Empirical Study of Physicians' Responses to Advance Directives," 13 *Vermont Law Review* 445, 458 (1989). See also Chapter 8.

30. *New York Times*, 11 June 1991.

31. In rare instances, if the woman was in the late stage of pregnancy, emergency surgery might save the fetus if it had reached a point of viability.

32. One might also note a rather limited study in which the researcher reports that courts are far less likely to give weight to a woman's wishes

regarding termination of life support than to a man's. In a study of twenty-two right-to-die decisions from appeals courts in fourteen states, Dr. Steven Miles found that women were consistently portrayed as less capable of rational decision making than men. (*New York Times*, 23 July 1990.)

33. 410 U.S. 113 (1973).

34. *Webster* v. *Reproductive Health Services*, 109 S.Ct. 3040 (1989); *Planned Parenthood of Southeastern Pennsylvania* v. *Casey*, 1992 U.S. Lexis 4751.

35. See Elizabeth Carlin Benton, "Note: The Constitutionality of Pregnancy Clauses in Living Will Statutes," 43 *Vanderbilt Law Review* 1821, 1828–29 (1990).

36. *In re T. W.*, 551 So.2d 1186 (Fla. 1989).

37. *Committee to Defend Reproductive Rights* v. *Myers*, 29 Cal.3d 252 (1981); see also *American Academy of Pediatrics* v. *Van de Kamp*, 214 Cal.App.3d 831 (Ct. App. 1989).

38. *University Health Services* v. *Piazzi*, No. CV86-RCCV-464 (Ga. Super. Ct., 1986). There are also some cases in which courts have ordered women to accept certain types of medical treatment, such as blood transfusions, in order to preserve fetal life. See, for example, *Raleigh Fitkin-Paul Morgan Memorial Hospital* v. *Anderson*, 42 N.J. 421, cert. denied, 377 U.S. 985 (1964), and *Jefferson* v. *Griffin Spalding County Hospital*, 247 Ga. 86 (1981). In both cases, the women objected to blood transfusions on religious grounds. In *Taft* v. *Taft*, 388 Mass. 331 (1983), the Massachusetts Supreme Judicial Court refused to order a pregnant woman to undergo surgery necessary to save the fetus, on the grounds that it would have violated her rights of privacy. In New York, however, a court found that the state's interest in protecting life was strong enough to override the woman's rights. *In re Jamaica Hospital*, 491 N.Y.S.2d 898 (1985).

CHAPTER 8

1. See David Rothman's fascinating exploration of the changes that have taken place in *Strangers at the Bedside* (New York: Basic Books, 1991).

2. Meg Greenfield, "The Land of the Hospital," *Newsweek*, 30 June 1986, 74.

3. Quoted in "Last Rights," *Newsweek*, 26 August 1991, 40.

4. Engelbert L. Schucking, "Death at a New York Hospital," *Law, Medicine & Health Care* (December 1985), 261–68.

5. Anne Alexis Coté, "The Hospital Perspective," *ibid.* at 269–70.

6. Dr. Schucking responded to this point as follows: "It's a pertinent question. However, in those critical hours the administrator-on-call, though alerted, did not see me to find out. The chart was there, I had the originals of the relevant documents and all necessary ID. Three doctors, independently—one of them the attending physician—studied the documents and disregarded the patient's wishes as conveyed by me."

7. Coté, "The Hospital Perspective," 270.

8. George J. Annas, "Into the Hands of Strangers," *Law, Medicine &*

Health Care (December 1985), 271–73; Margaret A. Somerville, ". . . Searching for the Governing Values, Policies, and Attitudes," *ibid.* at 274–77.

9. Ronald Cranford, "A Physician's Perspective," *ibid.* at 279–81.

10. *In re Jobes*, 529 A.2d 434, 451 (N.J. 1987).

11. *Superintendent of Belchertown State School* v. *Saikewicz* 373 Mass. 728, 370 N.E.2d 417, 434 (1977).

12. The state, as the Georgia high court noted, "has an interest in the prolongation of life," but not in "the prolongation of dying." Once that distinction has been made, then, the court held, the moral and ethical decisions about further treatment should be left to the patient or to the surrogate. *In re L.H.R.*, 253 Ga. 439, 321 S.E.2d 716, 723 (1984).

13. *In re Jobes*, 529 A.2d at 449.

14. Meisel, *Right to Die*, 155.

15. The story of Baby Rena is told in a lengthy two-part article by Benjamin Weiser in the *Washington Post*, 14 and 15 July 1991; all of the names are accurate with the exception of those of the foster parents, who remained anonymous.

16. Sanford Leikin. "Children's Hospital and Ethics Committees: A First Look," 141 *American Journal of Disabled Children* (September 1987): 954–58.

17. Quoted in *Washington Post*, 15 July 1991.

18. Pollak's choice of words shocked the hospital attorney, Melinda Murray, who wondered what gave a doctor any special credentials to make a quality-of-life determination.

19. As the law currently exists, it is doubtful if any court in the country would give a doctor or a hospital the right to terminate treatment for a patient, adult or infant, against the wishes of the family. Moreover, religious beliefs do play a strong role in determining whether to terminate treatment, either for a baby or a ninety-year-old person. While the medical staff may not have shared Rena's foster-parents' belief in divine intervention, there are cases in which people who were in a coma suddenly awoke, or where a deadly disease suddenly went into remission. Doctors cannot explain these things, and although such occurrences are extremely rare, family members with strong religious convictions may cling to the hope that they will happen. So long as the family feels that way, the courts will not interfere.

20. *New York Times*, 18 October 1991.

CODA

1. *New York Times*, 31 March 1992.

Index

A., Mr. and Mrs.; *see* Baby Jane
  Doe
Abolitionists, and condemned
  prisoners, 78*ff.*
Abortion, and right to die, 145–47
Adkins, Janet, suicide of, 63–64
Advance directives, 130–50;
  rationale behind, 133; legal basis
  for, 135–36; and families, 144;
  and doctors, 144; and abortion,
  145–47; model form, 148–50
AIDS, doctor-assisted suicide of
  patients, 68; 185 n.38
Alabama, death row in, 85–86, 93
Alderman, James E., 138
*American Academy of Pediatrics
  v. Heckler* (1983), 109–110
American Civil Liberties Union,
  and death penalty, 92
American Life Lobby, 110
Annas, George J., and *Cruzan* case,
  49–50, 54; on Quill case, 71; on
  Hewitt case, 159
Armstrong, Paul, 37–38
Artificial feeding and hydration,
  and *Cruzan* case, 49
Augustine, 22; and suicide, 56
Autonomy, and suicide, 60–62;
  and condemned prisoners,
  93–94, 96
Avery, Gordon, 168
Ayurveda, 28–29

Baby Doe, 107–108
Baby Jane Doe, 97–99, 102, 103,
  110–13, 115
Baby Lance case, 116
Baby Rena, 165–72
Baker, John G., 107
Ballot initiatives on doctor-assisted
  suicide, 72–73, 186 n.48
Baptists, and euthanasia, 25–26
Barber, Neil, 38–39
Barber v. Superior Court (1983),
  38–39
Barzun, Jacques, on death penalty,
  86–87
Battin, Margaret Pabst, 27
Beauchamp, Tom, criteria for
  suicide, 60–61, 93–95
Beccaria, on suicide, 59
Bedau, Hugo, and death penalty,
  90–92
Belois, Patricia, 8
Belt, Vera, 72
Belzer, Michael B., 7
Bernero, Virginia, testifies on
  Kevorkian, 65
Biathanatos (1644), 60
Bishop, Jesse Walter, 81–82, 96
Bishop v. State (1979), 82
Blackmun, Harry, 52, 77, 81
Blackstone, William, on suicide,
  57, 58; on assisted suicide, 66
Bouvia, Elizabeth, 74

Bowen v. American Hospital Association (1986), 112–13
Bowling, Alexander, 93
Brain death, 14–15
Brain-absent condition; *see* Theresa Ann Campo
Brennan, William J., 81, 83; opinion in *Cruzan* case, 52, 53
Browning, Estelle, 140–41, 146
Browning, In re (1989), 140–41
Burger, Warren E., 62, 80, 81, 83
Butzner, John D., 83

Callahan, Daniel, and *Cruzan* case, 49
Calvin, John, on suffering, 26
Campo, Theresa Ann, 175–77
Canon law, and suicide, 56–57
Caplan, Arthur, on Kevorkian, 64; on Quill case, 71; on Wanglie case, 7
Capron, Alexander, on Child Abuse Amendments, 114–15
Cardozo, Benjamin, 33
Catholicism, and views of illness, 22–23; and suicide, 23; and euthanasia, 22–25
Charaka Samhita, 29
Child Abuse Amendments (1984), 113–15
Childress, James, criteria for suicide, 60–61, 93–95
Christian Science, and failure to treat sick infants, 100–101
Church of England, and suicides, 57
Clark, William, 91
Clough, Arthur, 27
Cohen, Carl, 177
Colby, William, 50
Collums, Woodrow Wilson, 122
Colyer, In re (1983), 38
Common law, and suicide, 57, 58–59; and assisted suicide, 65–66; and parental control of children, 100; and right to die, 32*ff.*; and advance directives, 136–37

Competency, definition, 17; and waiver of rights, 88; and right to die, 161–62
Compton, Lynn D., 74
Condemned prisoners, and autonomy, 79
Conference on Uniform State Laws, 141
Conroy, In re (1985), 138, 192 n.1
Coppola v. Commonwealth (1979), 82
Coppola, Frank J., 82–83, 88, 94
Coté, Anne Alexis, comment on Brenda Hewitt, 158–59
Council of Braga, 56
Council of Hereford, 57
Council of Orleans, 56
Courts, and policy-making, 32, 37–38; ordering treatment for children, 105; and reluctance to intervene, 162–65; reasons for resorting to, 173–74
Cranford, Ronald E., 54; on Hewitt case, 159–60
Cranston, Alan, 113
Crossroads burials of suicides, 57
Cruzan, Joe, 48
Cruzan, Joyce, 48
Cruzan, Nancy Beth, 14, 48–54, 102, 136, 174; death of, 54
Cruzan v. Director . . . (1990), 50–53
Cruzan v. Harmon (1988), 50
Culpepper, Otis, defends Bertram Harper, 119
Customary professional practice test, 35

D'Ambrosio, Jack, 131
d'Holbach, 60
Daniels, Albert and Jennifer, 105
Dante, suicides in *Inferno*, 57
DaSilva, Taveira, 5
Death, definitions of, 14–15; determination of in special cases, 176
"Death in the Nursery," 108–109

Death penalty, and Constitution, 78, 87–88; as form of torture, 85; and possibility of error, 95

Death Row, prisoners on and right to die, 76–96; conditions on, 83*ff.*

Decision, who makes, 151–74

Declaration on Euthanasia (1980), 24

Delman, Vincent; *see* Rosier, Peter

Denton, Jeremiah, 113

Dillon, Dennis, 44

Dinnerstein, Shirley, 43

Doctor-assisted suicide, in Netherlands, 71; ballot initiatives on, 72–73, 186 n.18; public opinion on, 73; claim for a right to, 73–74

Doctors, and duty to inform, 35; exceptions to, 35–37; assisting suicide, 63*ff.*; and advance directives, 144

Donne, John, on suicide, 60

Down's syndrome, 104, 107

"Dr. Death"; *see* Kevorkian, Jack

Duffy, Clinton, 84–85

Durable power of attorney, defined, 134; rationale for, 139–40

Eichner, Father Philip, 44

Eichner v. Dillon (1980), 43–45

Electroencephalogram (EEG), 12

Emergency care, 35

Enlightenment, changing attitudes on suicide, 59–60

Epstein, Steven A., 4

Estate of Leach v. Shapiro (1984), 133

Euthanasia, definition of, 15; active, 15; passive, 15–16

Evidence, as to intent of formerly competent person, 51

Family members, and advance directives, 144

Farrell, In re (1987), 193 n.2

Feinstein, Moshe, on withholding food and medicine, 21

Ferris, John G., 45

Fieger, Geoffrey, 65, 67

Final Exit, 67, 153; *see also* Humphrey, Derek

Fletcher, Joseph, on euthanasia, 26

Florian, Hans, 122

Foster, Doris Ann, 83–84

Fox, Brother Charles, 43–45

Franz, Joseph, 77

Freehof, Solomon B., and euthanasia, 20–21

Furman v. Georgia (1972), 78

Gardner, Martin, 92

Garibaldi, Marie, 162

Gaudium et Spes (1965), 24

Georgetown University Medical Center, and Musolino case, 2–6

Georgetown College, In re President of (1964), 62

Gesell, Gerhard, 109–110

Gilbert, Alice, issues injunction against Kevorkian, 65–66

Gilbert, Emily, death of, 120–21, 128

Gilbert, Roswell, and killing of wife, 120–22; granted clemency, 122; case made into television drama, 122

Gilmore, Bessie, 80

Gilmore, Gary Mark, 80–81, 87, 88, 91

Gilmore v. Utah (1976), 80–81

Glover, Jacqueline, 169

Good Samaritan, 22

Goren, Shlomo, and suicide, 19–20

Goses (terminally ill patient), 20

Greeks, and euthanasia, 18; and suicide, 56

Greeley, Andrew, 179 n.6

Greenfield, Meg, 152

Gregg v. Georgia (1976), 78

Griswold v. Connecticut (1965), 41, 48

Guardian *ad litem*, definition, 17

Hager, Richard, and salvation on Death Row, 95

Hales v. Petit (1562), 58
Hancock, Kelly, prosecutes
   Roswell Gilbert, 121
Harper, Bertram, and killing of
   wife, 118–19
Harper, Virginia, death of, 118–19,
   128
Harvard criterion (brain death),
   14–15
Hatch, Orrin, 113
Health and Human Services, Dept.
   of, guidelines on treating infants,
   109; attacked in courts,
   109–110; revised, 110; struck
   down by Supreme Court, 113
Health care professionals, and
   euthanasia, 16
Hemlock Society, and Initiative
   119, 72
Hennepin County Medical Center,
   and Wanglie case, 6–8
Herbert, Clarence, 38
Hersey, George B., 136
Hewitt, Brenda, death of, 155–60
Higher brain activity, 15
Hindu views on euthanasia, 28–30
Hippocrates, 18
Holmes, Oliver Wendell, Jr., 33
Holmes, Oliver Wendell, Sr., 151,
   152n.
Homicide, distinguished from
   assisting suicide, 119–20;
   definitions of, 122–24
Hospitals, and fear of lawsuits,
   8–9; change in functions,
   151–52
Hotline, for reporting
   maltreatment of infants, 109
Hughes, Richard J., 37–38, 41
Human worth, and condemned
   prisoners, 94
Hume, David, on suicide, 60
Humphrey, Derek, 28, 67, 153; *see
   also Final Exit*

Incompetence, 36
Incompetents, and right to die,
   40–41

Infanticide, 103
Infants, Reagan administration
   policy, 99*ff.*
Informed consent, 33–34
Initiative 119 (state of
   Washington), 72–73
Isavaya Upanishad, 29
Islam, and euthanasia, 28

Jackson, Randy, 8
Jennison, Harry, 110
Jobes, In re (1987), 163
Johanning, Eberhard, 130–32
*John F. Kennedy Hospital v.
   Bludworth* (1983, 1984), 136,
   137–38; *see also* Landy, Francis
Johnson, Robert, 87, 93
Judaism, and euthanasia, 19–22
Juries, discretion in mercy-killing
   cases, 125

Karo, Joseph, and euthanasia, 20
Katz, Nevin, 2–5
Kemmler, In re (1890), 87
Kennedy, Edward M., 113
Kenney, J. P., on suicide, 23
Kenney, Timothy, prosecutes
   Bertram Harper, 119
Kevorkian, Jack, 63–67, 118;
   compared to Quill, 71
Koop, C. Everett, 110; and
   treatment of seriously ill
   children, 106–107, 112
Korein, Julius, 12
Kutner, Luis, devises advance
   directive, 132

Lamm, Norman, and Quinlan case,
   21
Landy, Francis B., and "mercy
   will," 137–38
Lawrence, J. Gray, Jr., 82–83
Leikin, Sanford, and Baby Rena
   case, 167–69
Lenhard . . . v. Wolff (1979), 82
Liacos, Paul J., 43
Liberty interest, as basis for right
   to die, 51

Linares, Rudy, 127–28
Living will, 17; *see* advanced directive
Living will statutes, adopted by all states, 140; need for, 142
Luther, Martin, on suffering, 26

Macklin, Ruth, 153
Maddox, Lester, 91
Maguire, Daniel, and euthanasia, 23
Maimonides, and euthanasia, 20
Marshall, Thurgood, 52, 81, 82, 83, 112
Martin, John K., 25
Martinez, Bob, grants clemency to Roswell Gilbert, 122
Massie, Robert Lee, 84
McCanse, Thad C., 50, 54
McGee, Paul, 12
McGough, Peter, 73
McGrew, Shanda; *see* Harper, Bertram
McIntyre, Russell L., and Catholic views on euthanasia, 23–24
McNally, Gerald, 64
Medical neglect, and treatment of children, 115–16
Meese, Edwin, and Baby Jane Doe case, 110
Meisel, Alan, 36, 105
Mercy killings, 118–29
"Mercy machine"; *see* Kevorkian, Jack
Meyer, John P., 106
Miles, Steven, 144
Miller, Sherry, 117; testifies on Kevorkian, 65; commits suicide, 67
Missouri Rehabilitation Center, 49, 54
Mitchell v. Lawrence (1982), 83
Model Penal Code, definitions of homicide, 122–24
Modelsky, Michael, 64
Mohr v. Williams (1905), 33
Montesquieu, 60

Moran, Martha Gilbert; *see* Gilbert, Roswell
More, Thomas, on suicide, 60
Moriarty, Estelle, 176
Mueller, Robert and Pamela, accused of child abuse, 105–106
Muir, Robert, 13
Musolino, Edith, 2–6
Musolino, Rocco, 2–6
Musolino, Scott, 5
Myer, Cathy, 143–44

National Conference of Catholic Bishops, 25
National Right to Life Committee, and treatment of children, 113–14
Natural death act directive, defined, 134
Nedjl, Robert, 38–39
Neonatal euthanasia, 103–104
New England settlers, and suicide, 57–58
New Jersey Catholic Conference, and *Jobes* case, 25
Newton Memorial Hospital, 11
New York Civil Liberties Union, and HHS guidelines, 110
Ninth Amendment, and right to die, 74
Non-Western religions, and euthanasia, 27–30

Oaks, Howard, 98
O'Connor, Sandra Day, 83, 112; opinion in *Cruzan* case, 52, 53
Oklahoma Children's Hospital experiment, 104
Organs, harvesting of, 175–77
Orr, Sharon, on Nancy Cruzan, 54
Owen, John, on suffering, 26

Pain and suffering, Catholic view of, 18
Parens patriae, 40, 53, 101, 163
Parents, and autonomy over children, 99–100
Parham v. J. R. (1979), 100

Patient Self-Determination Act
    (1990), 143
Patterson, John S., 76
Perlmutter, Abe, 45–46, 69
Perman, Joseph, and Quinlan case,
    21
Personal autonomy, and right to
    die, 32*ff.*; as constitutional basis
    for right to die, 41–42
Persons under disability, 40
Peter, Hilda, death of, 130–32
Peter, In re (1987), 131–32, 138
Physician, liability for treatment, 39
Pickens, Robert L., 145
Pollak, Murray, and Baby Rena
    case, 167–71
Potts, Jack, 95
Pratt v. Davis (1905), 32–33
Pregnancy, and advance directives,
    145–47
President's Commission for the
    Study of Ethical Problems in
    Medicine and Biomedical and
    Behavioral Research, 32n.
Privacy, and abortion clause in
    advance directives, 146–47
"Process of dying" and "process of
    living," 23–24
Protestantism, and euthanasia,
    25–27

Quality of life, as a factor in
    decision-making, 47
Quill, Timothy E., and assisted
    suicide of "Diane," 69–71;
    distinguished from Kevorkian, 71
Quindlen, Anna, 67–68
Quinlan, In re (1975), 13
Quinlan, In re (1976), 13, 37–38;
    and Jewish reaction, 21–22
Quinlan, Joseph, 11; attempts to
    secure guardianship, 12
Quinlan, Julia, 11
Quinlan, Karen Ann, 11–13, 31,
    38, 40, 92, 139, 173

Rakusan, Tamara, 166
Ramsey, Paul, 104

Reagan administration, and
    severely ill infants, 99*ff.*
Reasonable person test, 35
Refusal of treatment, adults and
    children, 101–102
Regina v. Doody (1854), 58
Rehabilitation Act (1973), and
    treatment of infants, 108
Rehnquist, William H., 77;
    decision in *Cruzan* case, 50–51
Religious reasons for denial of
    treatment, 100–101
Restatement of Torts, 34
Reynolds, Helen, 154–55
Right to die, common law sources
    of, 31*ff.*; of incompetents, 40–41;
    constitutional sources, 41*ff.*; and
    right to privacy, 41–42; law as it
    stood in the 1980s, 46–47; based
    on liberty interest, 51; of
    condemned prisoners, 76–96;
    and abortion, 145–47; legal bases
    of, 160–61; procedural
    protections, 163
Right to privacy, and right to die,
    41–42
Roberts, David, 116
Rodas, Hector, and claim for right
    to doctor-assisted suicide, 73–74
Roe v. Wade (1973), 41, 48, 146
Romans, and euthanasia, 18; and
    suicide, 56
Rosenblatt, Stanley and Susan,
    defend Peter Rosier, 126–27
Rosier, Pat, death of, 125–26
Rosier, Peter, and death of wife,
    125–27
Rousseau, Jean-Jacques, 60
Rubin, Richard, 2
Rumbaugh, Charles, 89–90
Rumbaugh v. Estelle (1983), 89–90

Saikewicz, Joseph, 42–43
Satz v. Perlmutter (1978), 45–46
Scalia, Antonin, opinion in *Cruzan*
    case, 53
Schouten, Gabriel, 175
Schreiber, Sidney, 37

Schucking, Engelbert, 156–60
Schweiker, Richard, and policy of treating newborns, 108
Schweitzer, Albert, on suicide, 60
Scott, Edith, 2
Sears-Collins, Leah, 172
Self-murder; *see* suicide
Seneca, and euthanasia, 18
Severely ill infants, and right to die, 97–117
Shaw, Anthony, 104
Sherwood, Carleton, 108
Siegel, Seymour, and Quinlan case, 21
Simmons, Paul D., on suicide, 27
Simmons, R. Gene, 76–78
Smith, David A., 146
Sneed, Joseph T., 96
Snyder, James, 144
Somerville, Margaret A., on Hewitt case, 159
State, interest of in right to die, 164; *see also parens patriae*
State-abetted suicide, 79; abolitionists' view, 90
Sterbehilfe and *Sternnachhilfe*, 18
Stevens, John Paul, 52, 83, 113
Stoics, and euthanasia, 18
Storar, John, 44–45
Substituted judgment; *see* advance directives
Suicide, 55–75; definition, 16; and canon law, 56–57; and treatment of bodies, 57; and common law, 57–58; and New England, 57–58; as a felony, 58; as common law crime, 58–59; changing secular views on, 59–61; criteria for, 60–61; and autonomy, 60–62; doctor-assisted, 63*ff.*; distinguished from foregoing treatment, 68–69; 185 n.39
Suicide Act (1961), 59
Superintendent of Belchertown . . . v. Saikewicz (1977), 42–43
Surrogate decision-making, 40*ff.*
Synod of Nîmes, 57

Talbot, Nathan, 100–101
Talmud, and suicide, 19
Tannenbaum, Melvyn, 98, 99
Teel, Robert E., 50, 54
"Terminal condition," defined, 140, 141
Therapeutic privilege, 36
Trop v. Dulles (1958), 87
Turner, Dale, 72–73
Twitchell, David and Ginger, tried for manslaughter, 100–101
Twitchell, Robyn, death of, 100–101, 102

Uniform Rights of the Terminally Ill Act, 40, 141
U.S. Catholic Conference, 25
U.S. Supreme Court, and right to die, 47*ff.*; strikes down HHS guidelines in infant care, 113
U.S. v. University Hospital (1983), 110–11
U.S. v. University Hospital (1984), 111–12
University Hospital at Stony Brook; *see* Baby Jane Doe
Unwanted touching, 32–33
Utility, and condemned prisoners, 94–95
Utopia (1516), 60

Varon, Joe, and Gilbert case, 191 n.6
Vegetative state, defined, 13n.
Voltaire, 60
Voluntariness, 34; definition, 16–17; and waiver of rights, 88–89
von Scheven, Emily, 165–66

Wachtler, Sol, 44
Waiver of rights, 88–89
Wanglie, Helga, 6–8
Wanglie, Oliver, 6–8
Wantz, Marjorie, suicide of, 66–67
Warriner, D. Dortch, 83
Washburn, A. Lawrence, 98–99
Weber, William, 98

Weber v. Stony Brook Hospital
    (1983), 99
Webster, William L., and *Cruzan*
    case, 50, 53
Weiss, J. Woodrow, 155
Wexler, Leonard, rules in Baby Jane
    Doe case, 109–110

White, Byron, 81
Whitmore, Jonas, 77
Whitmore . . . v. Arkansas (1990),
    77–78
Whole brain death, 14–15
Williams, Glanville, on suicide, 59
Wright, Bob and Shirley, 107

RENNER LEARNING RESOURCE CENTER
ELGIN COMMUNITY COLLEGE
ELGIN, ILLINOIS 60123